Arts, Entertainment and Tourism

To Andy and Claire with love

Arts, Entertainment and Tourism

Howard Hughes BSc (Econ), MA, PhD

Professor of Tourism Management
Manchester Metropolitan University

OXFORD AUCKLAND BOSTON JOHANNESBURG MELBOURNE NEW DELHI

Butterworth-Heinemann
Linacre House, Jordan Hill, Oxford OX2 8DP
225 Wildwood Avenue, Woburn, MA 01801-2041
A division of Reed Educational and Professional Publishing Ltd

A member of the Reed Elsevier plc group

First published 2000

British Library Cataloguing in Publication Data
A catalogue record for this book is available from the British Library

ISBN 0 7506 4533 4

Composition by Genesis Typesetting, Laser Quay, Rochester, Kent
Printed and bound in Great Britain by Biddles Ltd, *www.biddles.co.uk*

FOR EVERY TITLE THAT WE PUBLISH, BUTTERWORTH-HEINEMANN
WILL PAY FOR BTCV TO PLANT AND CARE FOR A TREE.

Contents

Acknowledgements

Just before finishing this book I spent a weekend in London. This trip was to celebrate a 'special' birthday and, although seeing a show was not the reason for the trip, it seemed an obvious thing to do as part of the celebration. With no particular show in mind, a search for something suitable (and with tickets available!) resulted in our seeing Andrew Lloyd Webber's 'Starlight Express' at the Apollo Victoria. I confess to having enjoyed the experience! About a year earlier I had spent another weekend in London but this time with the sole purpose of seeing Wagner's opera 'Parsifal' at the Coliseum theatre. I was not surprised at having enjoyed that! On these two different occasions, a visit to the theatre has been a part of my time spent away from home as a tourist. It is this experience of seeing shows, plays and dance and listening to concerts and operas whilst away from home that is the subject of this book.

Most of my visits away from home have involved some experiences of concert halls, theatres or cabaret clubs. During my first visit to Spain in the 1960s a visit to a Spanish floor-show was an obligatory part of this new experience of having a foreign holiday. The performances were designed for the foreign visitor and, even then, I could guess they provided nothing that remotely resembled an authentic experience. More recently, I went to see a play in a theatre in Samarkand where I had no idea whatsoever what was going on. This was during a week-long advisory visit to the local university. Concerts, opera and plays play an important part in my life, though more usually here in my home town than in London, the Costa Brava or Uzbekistan, and I have nothing but admiration for all those wonderfully creative people in the performing arts who give me such enjoyment and fulfilment. I gladly acknowledge their contribution to my life and to this book.

The origins of this book lie in a study I undertook of the Buxton Arts Festival in the 1980s. To that organization, I owe an abiding debt as it stimulated a continuing interest in the arts–tourism relationship. I also acknowledge a debt to many theatre managers, producers, performers and musicians and others in the arts world who are too numerous to mention individually. They have, over many years, given their time and resources willingly and eagerly to assist with advice and material.

I owe particular thanks to Danielle Benn who was my research assistant for four years and who was an invaluable support in a number of projects relating especially to entertainment and seaside resorts. Her enthusiasm and abilities were boundless and were exceeded only by her cheerfulness and kindness. I know that my loss is a wonderful gain for Bill and Amber.

Subsequent research work was undertaken by Paul Leighton and by Lynda Nyland. Thanks are due to both, especially to Lynda who managed to find the essential missing pieces.

Kathryn Grant at Butterworth-Heinemann has been supportive throughout and without her positive view and encouragement I may never have started this book, let alone finished it. I am very grateful for her inspiration and guidance.

Finally, thanks to Kevin for just being himself and for being part of my life.

Abbreviations

ACE	Arts Council of England (since 1994)
ACGB	Arts Council of Great Britain (to 1994)
ATLAS	European Association for Tourism and Leisure Education
BTA	British Tourist Authority
DCMS	Department for Culture, Media and Sport
ETB	English Tourist Board (to 1999)
LTBCB	London Tourist Board and Convention Bureau
NEA	National Endowment for the Arts
OVS	Overseas Visitor Survey
PANYNJ	Port Authority of New York and New Jersey
PSI	Policy Studies Institute
RSC	Royal Shakespeare Company
RSGB	Research Surveys of Great Britain
SOLT	Society of London Theatre
SWET	Society of West End Theatre
TIA	Travel Industry Association of America

1

Introduction

- Oasis at Loch Lomond in Scotland
- Cliff Richard in the musical 'Heathcliff'
- Glastonbury Festival (Somerset)
- Madonna's Bra
- The Edinburgh International Festival
- 'Jazz and blues: that's what makes Chicago'
- 'Seaside Special' at Cromer (Norfolk)
- 'Greece: the longest running theatrical event'
- Wagner's Ring Cycle at Adelaide (Australia) in 1998
- The Righteous Brothers at Bally's casino, Atlantic City (New Jersey)
- Tina Turner's European tour in 2000
- 'Fiesta fun at Gloria's Ranch'

All of these have a tourism connection: the concert by Oasis attracted an audience of 80,000. A fan of Cliff Richard travelled from Perth in Australia to London to see him perform and 90,000 people attended Glastonbury (1997) to hear performances by the likes of Van Morrison and New Order. A new 450-seat theatre (1998) nicknamed Madonna's Bra will, it is hoped, revive Ilfracombe's tourist trade. Over 40 per cent of those attending the Edinburgh International Festival are from outside Scotland. The descriptions of Chicago and Greece are promotional slogans to encourage international visitors to the two places. 'Seaside Special' is a traditional end-of-pier variety show at an English seaside town and the Righteous Brothers appear in a US seaside town that now draws most of its visitors for gaming purposes. For the first performances of the Ring Cycle in Australia, over half of the persons attending were from outside the state of South Australia. Inclusive packages of transport, accommodation and show tickets are offered to attract people from the UK to travel to see Tina Turner perform in Paris or Cologne. The 'Fiesta fun' refers to a 'special night out' of dressage exhibitions by horses and a 'colourful flamenco show' provided for sun and beach holidaymakers in Spain.

These examples illustrate a relationship between the arts and entertainment on the one hand and tourism on the other. They illustrate, in particular, two aspects of the relationship (see Chapter 4 for further discussion):

- Some arts and entertainment have the ability to draw audiences from a great distance, distances so great that some stay away from home overnight. Audiences who are attracted to a place by the arts may be termed 'arts-core' (see Table 1.1).

Table 1.1   Initial definitions

- **Visitors:** non-local residents who are either day visitors or staying visitors (tourists)
- **Tourists:** people who travel and stay away from home overnight
- **Arts:** performing arts and entertainment (a more popular form of the performing arts) performed in theatres, concert halls, arenas, etc.
- **Arts-related tourism:** any tourism that includes a visit to the arts (regardless of initial interest, etc.)
- **Arts-core tourists:** who travel in order to see the arts
- **Arts-peripheral tourists:** who travel for some non-arts purpose but who also see the arts
- **Culture-core tourists:** who travel in order to visit cultural attractions
- **Culture-peripheral tourists:** who travel for some non-culture purpose but who also visit cultural attractions
- **Seaside resort:** a coastal town, the prime function of which is as a holiday destination. This is different from the US usage of the term 'resort' which refers to a purpose-built holiday complex similar to a large hotel rather than a town
- **Tourist board:** an organization, usually with government involvement, which has the role of promoting a town, region, state or country as a tourist destination. Also known as a visitor bureau, convention and visitor bureau, tourist authority, tourism commission, etc.

■ Arts and entertainment may not be an attraction in their own right but are seen and listened to by people who are away from home for other purposes. These will include people away on holiday at a beach destination or in a city or people on business or conference trips. These audiences may be termed 'arts-peripheral'.

Such members of the audience are 'tourists' (see Figure 1.1). Some of the audiences at performances will be local residents, others are non-local and will have had to travel some distance but have not stayed overnight and are 'day visitors'. The non-locals who have stayed overnight are conventionally termed 'tourists' (see Table 1.1 and see also Chapter 3 for further discussion

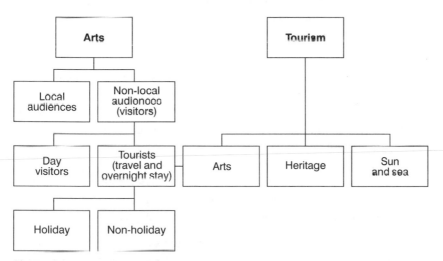

Figure 1.1 Tourism and the arts

of these terms). The distinguishing features of the tourist are travel and overnight stay. The word 'tourist' is often used interchangeably with 'visitor' but there are two types of visitor – those who stay overnight (the tourist) and those who do not (day-visitor or excursionist). The word 'visitor' is commonly used by many people and in this book it usually refers to the tourist. It is tourists, their activities and the organizations which seek to attract them that are the subject of this book.

Tourism usually refers to people on holiday but it also, confusingly, refers to travel and stay away from home for business reasons or to visit friends or in order to see a specific concert or play (without being on holiday) (see Figure 1.1). There is further discussion of this in Chapters 3 and 4.

The other focus of this book, apart from tourism, is of course the arts and, in particular, live performances of the performing arts. It is concerned with performances before an audience of music, plays, opera, dance and the like in places such as theatres, concert halls, arts centres and arenas. What is meant by 'the arts' and by 'entertainment' is discussed further in Chapter 2.

There is a great deal of current discussion about attracting tourists, especially in the holiday sense, to arts audiences with a particular emphasis on foreign tourists. Associated with that, though to a lesser extent, is the issue of the arts and domestic tourists. These perspectives are probably of greatest significance to tourist boards (see Table 1.1) and the tourist industry in a strategy to determine new tourism opportunities. The range of attractions for tourists is considerable and the arts is but one of those (see Figure 1.1). The approach is to develop and encourage arts that are part of the tourist (usually holiday) experience or to develop promotional strategies that will appeal to that market.

In the arts world there may be little concern about whether audiences are tourists or holidaymakers. There may, though, be a desire to extend the catchment area for audiences. The tourist market may be only one of several they choose to explore and exploit in order to catch the more 'distant' market. The approach will be to develop and encourage arts that will appeal to a wide geographical area (perhaps by being distinctive) and to have promotional strategies that will reach such a wide audience. Some may, if considered appropriate, be more deliberately aimed to appeal to tourist and holiday audiences. There is further discussion of this in Chapter 6.

The perspective in this book is derived from cultural tourism rather than from the arts. Much of this book will focus on tourists and those who are on holiday. This reflects current discussion. It will, however, also assist in illuminating issues that arise for arts managers in attempting to widen their catchment area. There is consideration of the arts perspective throughout the book and especially in Chapters 6 and 9.

For those who manage arts organizations, such as theatres, events arenas or concert halls, there is a particular interest in examining this segment of the audience. It is often represented as being an additional market to target in order to increase audiences and revenue. It is widely considered to be a growing market as more people are apparently seeking an arts related tourist trip, and to be a worthwhile market to capture because of the potential spending power of such tourists. In these circumstances a study of this specific market segment is appropriate. It will draw the attention of arts managers to the opportunities and hazards involved in seeking to include tourists in the audiences and enable them to develop appropriate managerial strategies and policies.

Culture and tourism

It is possible to identify a widely defined set of tourists – 'cultural tourists' – who are relevant to this study. There has been a considerable interest in cultural tourism which has grown in recent years as seen in articles, papers and books such as those by Wiener (1980), Tighe (1985), Myerscough (1988), Bywater (1993), Richards (1996), Robinson, Evans and Callaghan (1996), Gilbert and Lizotte (1998) and Dodd and van Hemel (1999). The increased interest in this form of tourism is partly a reflection of an apparent rise in such tourism. It is also the outcome of the maturity of tourism studies which have moved towards a recognition of the diversity of tourism activity. These studies have been broad in that they have encompassed many aspects of culture. There are many uses of the term 'culture' (see Chapters 2 and 4 for further discussion of this) but usually cultural tourism has included heritage visits (to museums, cathedrals and churches, castles and historic houses) and visits to the visual arts (art galleries) and to the performing arts presented in theatres and concert halls whilst a tourist (see Figure 1.2). These performing arts include plays, musicals, opera, ballet and orchestral concerts and are often referred to simply as 'the arts'. Cultural tourism studies have tended to overlook some of the more popular forms of the performing arts that might be called 'entertainment' such as variety shows and cabaret including singers, comedians, magicians, ventriloquists, dancers, etc. as well as rock and pop concerts (also see Chapters 2 and 4 for further discussion). Such entertainment has been and remains of particular importance in tourism especially in seaside resorts (see Table 1.1) (see Chapter 5).

This book will consider entertainment as well as the performing arts, which have been considered more frequently (see Figure 1.2). Although the word 'arts' has often been used to distinguish certain activities from entertainment (see Chapter 2), when it is used in this book it usually covers both as an umbrella term (see Table 1.1). The distinction between arts and entertainment is nonetheless frequently made in the book when it is necessary or useful to identify and distinguish between the two types of activity or to use the words as used by others.

The all-embracing aspect of cultural tourism studies is not particularly satisfactory as dis-similar activities are grouped together and dealt with as 'one' (see Figures 1.2 and 1.3). The attraction of each element (such as a museum and a theatre) and the reasons for visiting may be very different. It

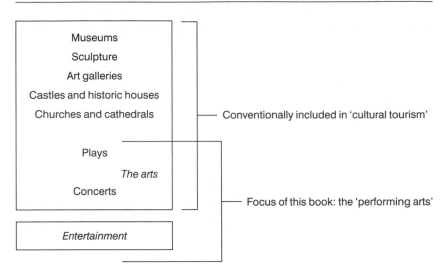

Figure 1.2   Culture and the focus of this book

may be that similar types of people will visit museums and go to the theatre but nonetheless the experiences are distinct and there are, of course, some people who will have an interest in only one or the other. Thus the nature of the link between the tourist and the museum or theatre visit may be obscured by considering all as an undifferentiated mass.

In addition there is a tendency to apply the term 'cultural tourism' to all visits by tourists to museums, theatres, etc. when in reality not all visits are the outcome of a deliberate decision to travel to visit the museum or theatre. The museum or theatre visit may be quite secondary and incidental to some other

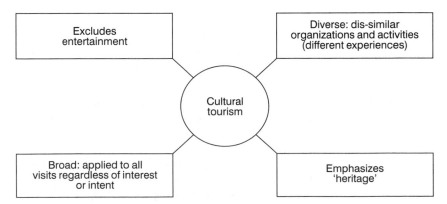

Figure 1.3   Difficulties with existing studies

more important reason for a visit to a city or seaside resort (see Chapter 4). Cultural tourism in the sense of tourist visits that are motivated primarily by culture ('culture-core' or 'arts-core') may be much less than the number of tourists who visit some aspect of culture during their visit to a destination ('culture-peripheral' or 'arts-peripheral'). Thus this book is entitled *Arts, Entertainment and Tourism* rather than *Arts and Entertainment-tourism*. The term 'arts-related tourism' is also used as it implies a less certain relationship between the arts and tourism than does the term 'arts tourism' (which is similar in implication to 'cultural tourism') (see Table 1.1).

The nature of this book

Because of these difficulties with existing cultural tourism studies (see Figure 1.3), this book focuses only on the performing arts element of culture and includes entertainment (see Figure 1.2). By isolating one aspect of culture, the nature of the relationship between it and tourism should be more evident. The particular choice of the performing arts reflects the fact that existing cultural tourism studies emphasize the heritage elements and there already exists a considerable body of work that examines the heritage–tourism relationship. The performing arts and entertainment aspects are relatively neglected. This is unfortunate if only because entertainment, in particular, appeals to, and is seen by, a large number of tourists. Despite the neglect, the issues that arise in the performing arts and entertainment can be as significant as those associated with heritage.

This book is a textbook aimed at undergraduates on both tourism management and arts management courses. It is appropriate for a typical ten to twelve week self-contained unit in the intermediate or final year of degree or higher diploma courses. A prior knowledge of marketing is assumed and also of the respective arts or tourism business 'environment' in each case. Given, however, that tourism students' knowledge of the arts is likely to be limited, the book includes an introduction to the arts (Chapter 2). The tourism chapter (Chapter 3) is similarly aimed at arts management students. These chapters on the arts and tourism contexts are necessarily limited. They identify the elements of each of the arts and tourism that are believed to have most significance in examining the arts and tourism relationship and which are necessary to understand the rationale and raison d'etre of those operating in and seeking to experience each sector.

This is primarily a student textbook and, as such, it draws on the work of many others. These sources are acknowledged in the text wherever possible and appropriate. Many students find this irritating but it would be bad practice (and unethical) to fail to indicate the source of material and acknowledge the work of others. Some parts of the book are unacknowledged, either because they are original to this book and are ideas and concepts not developed by others or because they are generally accepted and widely-circulating views unattributable to any single source. In addition one of the purposes of any textbook is to simplify and synthesize the work of others in order to make it accessible to students and in this sense also some of the content is original.

The book has a marketing perspective. It is concerned with audiences and their characteristics, motivations and experiences – audiences both actual and potential. By being aimed at students on management courses, one of the main purposes is to demonstrate the potential 'business' that lies within arts-related tourism for both arts and tourism managers. The book does however consider wider issues, such as the influence on creativity and artistic freedom, which have a bearing on and result from the relationship. These wider issues (discussed particularly in Chapter 8) can affect profitability but their inclusion in this book reflects a view that all management education programmes should be 'liberal'. They should consider issues that go beyond profit and which affect society and the economy beyond the organization being managed. Managers need to be aware of the 'dangers' of the activities that they manage even though they may never do anything about them; but in the hope that they will, this book is aimed at managers, future and current. It is issue- or topic-led, drawing on subject disciplines as and when appropriate to identify and examine particular issues.

The origins of the book lie in an undergraduate unit that initially was based on economic aspects of tourism and the book will undoubtedly reflect this origin. If it had been generated in an arts management course from a non-economic perspective then its content and structure would, more than likely, have been different.

It also has, perhaps inevitably, a British perspective though international cases are introduced where relevant and where the information exists. The book is written nonetheless in the belief that the issues and principles discussed here have universal relevance and application.

Apart from the cultural tourism studies briefly mentioned above there is a growing interest in the arts and tourism relationship from the respective industries. Some of the academic studies and many in the two industries are quite optimistic about the relationship, its effects and its growth potential. One of the purposes of this book is to examine the 'reality' of the relationship so that further consideration of it can be balanced and objective rather than clouded by unsubstantiated beliefs and deliberate propaganda. Any discussion of the relationship between the arts and tourism needs to be conducted with an awareness of any disadvantages of the relationship and also of the limitations of existing knowledge. It is important that students recognize the limits of knowledge about the area and appreciate that much that is intuition, commonsense or what may be desirable may not be borne out by 'the facts'. In this book the evidence is reviewed in order to determine the extent and nature of support and justification for many of the statements that are made and views that are held.

In particular the purposes of the book are to:

- identify the nature of the relationship between tourism and the arts and entertainment;
- determine the responses by firms and other bodies to the potential of the relationship;
- evaluate the effects of the relationship on both the arts and tourism;
- discuss the direction of future developments by arts and tourism organizations and the direction for future research.

The structure of this book

As a consequence the book is structured as follows. The two chapters following this one (Chapters 2 and 3) are, as previously indicated, introductions to and overviews of the arts and tourism respectively without a great deal of discussion of the relationship between the two. The structure of the industries is examined and the particular natures of the arts and tourism identified. Government agencies such as tourist boards and arts councils and boards play an important role in these two industries, especially the arts, and their role is discussed in these two chapters. They include an examination of the characteristics of art-goers and of tourists (especially holiday-makers). The motivations of people who attend performances and of people who go on holiday are also analysed.

Chapter 4 includes a brief discussion of the historical development of 'cultural tourism' in order to assist in determining what is meant by the term. The relationship between the arts and tourism is examined largely from a theoretical perspective. A number of possible dimensions to the relationship are proposed. These will be used as a framework or context within which to examine the 'evidence' in later chapters. It is difficult to make sense of the 'real world' without some context that can act as a reference point. It is not suggested that the framework discussed in Chapter 4 is 'the right one' but, at the least, it may provide some order to the chaos of reality and may ease the ability to comprehend the complexities of the relationship. The chapter includes a discussion to clarify terms used in studies of the tourism and culture relationship. The factors that might influence the development of the relationship between tourism and the arts in particular are also examined.

In Chapter 5 the discussion moves from consideration of the tourist (Chapter 4) to the 'product'. Once more the historical context is considered in order to determine what was offered to tourists in the past in the form of plays, concerts and other forms of entertainment. The chapter also includes an overview of the current provision and of factors that have influenced it. The problems faced by many seaside resorts (see Table 1.1) in the provision of entertainment are identified and discussed. Festivals are often regarded as a particularly successful form of arts-related tourism and their merits are analysed in the final part of this chapter.

Chapters 6 and 7 examine arts-related tourism from the standpoint of the arts and tourism respectively. In the first part of Chapter 6 there is an exploration of the possible motives that arts organizations might have for wishing to attract tourists into audiences – is there a special benefit or is it necessity? This will include consideration of the strategies they adopt to attract tourists. Much of the rest of the chapter focuses on audience surveys to determine two things: first, whether or not there actually are tourists in audiences and second, if there are, how important the play, for instance, was in deciding to visit the destination. Some of the difficulties associated with the audience survey approach are explored. This discussion facilitates an initial assessment of the importance of tourism to the arts, both perceived and actual importance.

The viewpoint shifts in Chapter 7 to that of tourism. As in Chapter 6, there is an overview of surveys that demonstrate some of the relevant issues. The surveys here are of tourists rather than of audiences. The tourist surveys are examined to determine the actual numbers who do 'participate' in the arts whilst tourists. They are used also to assess, as in the audience surveys, the importance of the play (for instance) in the decision to visit the destination. The respective merits of the audience survey and tourist survey approaches are analysed. The chapter also includes a brief discussion of the characteristics of those tourists who are arts and entertainment attenders in an attempt to evaluate their significance compared with other tourists. The material examined in this chapter is used, as in the previous chapter, to assess importance – though here it is the converse of that in Chapter 6 and is the importance of the arts to tourism.

Consideration of 'importance' in the arts and tourism relationship from a wider perspective is the subject matter of Chapter 8. First, some of the effects that each has upon the other are reviewed and, in particular, effects not examined in the two previous chapters including some of the less favourable outcomes. A particular relationship is considered that explains, in part, the convergence of interests of the arts and tourism and which may be responsible for some of these less favourable effects. Finally the phenomenon itself, arts-related tourism, is analysed from an economic impact perspective.

Chapter 9 summarizes the previous chapters and relates the contents of each to the others. In particular, it offers conclusions regarding the nature of the arts and tourism relationship. Drawing on these conclusions a number of suggestions are made for moving the relationship forward in the most beneficial ways. These recommendations refer especially to marketing strategies, appropriate product development and effective working relationships between the two sectors. Given that knowledge of arts-related tourism is still very limited, a number of recommendations for further research will be made in order to focus on issues that remain under-explored or unexplored.

The arts context

Introduction

This chapter provides an overview of the arts as a background for the examination of the arts–tourism relationship in later chapters. The overview will enable tourism managers and students to approach the arts with understanding. The point is often made that the arts and tourism don't fully comprehend or appreciate each other's particular methods of operation or objectives. The chapter therefore covers a wide range of issues especially those that have a bearing on the arts–tourism relationship.

The chapter includes a discussion of:

- what the arts and entertainment are and the distinction between them;
- how popular arts and entertainment are and who goes and doesn't go: participation and non-participation;
- who provides the arts and entertainment: the supply;
- the relationship between governments and the arts.

Culture, arts and entertainment

A distinction is commonly made between the arts and entertainment. Table 2.1 includes a number of terms that have been applied to each and which distinguish them. The word 'entertainment' is used to include a wide variety of activities such as watching television or playing computer games at home, listening to compact discs, cinema visits, watching sport and visits to theme parks and going to discos (see Figure 2.1). In addition it is applied to live performances of musicals, variety shows, band concerts, cabaret, street performers, pop concerts, rock, reggae, jazz, folk music, dancing, circus, comedy and magic, etc. It is the 'live performance' aspect of entertainment that is one of the concerns of this book (along with the arts).

Table 2.1 Some terms used in relation to the arts and entertainment

Arts	Entertainment
refinement	enjoyment
learned	frivolous
serious	passive
creative	self-indulgent
enlightenment	pleasure
expressive	fun
fundamental	excitement
purposeful	escapist
emotional	delight
inspirational	amusement
cultured	transitory

'The arts' usually refers to works and activities such as classical music, ballet, plays, opera as well as paintings and sculpture (see Figure 2.1). They are sometimes referred to as 'the high arts'. The arts are associated with 'refinement' and as being something more than the 'ordinary' man or woman could either produce or appreciate without training, education and effort (Tusa, 1999). They are regarded as the work of a few talented people and represent the highest levels of human creative ability. There is a view that they are created for their own sake as an expression of the creator's vision and are not created primarily with a view to making money. Similarly performers have chosen to enter this field because of some inner impulse and natural talent and not necessarily because of the prospect of financial reward. When reference is

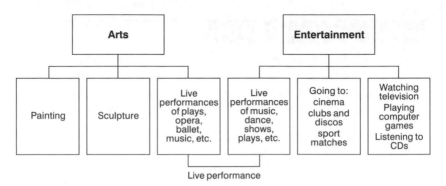

Figure 2.1 Entertainment and the arts

made to the 'culture' of a nation or society it often refers to these arts. The terms are, for some, interchangeable (Williams, 1988). People who understand and appreciate the arts are said to be 'cultured'.

Entertainment has overtones of being light, pleasurable and undemanding, requiring little effort to appreciate. Entertainment is considered to be, in some way, inferior to and less valuable and serious than the arts. At its most extreme, people who want entertainment and have no interest in the arts are said to be 'uncultured'. Entertainment and many other activities including football, shopping, watching television and visits to bars and clubs have been labelled 'popular culture' or 'mass culture' (Fiske, 1989; Storey, 1993). Most of this entertainment is provided by commercial enterprises and sold to consumers to make money rather than as an expression of human creativity. In the late twentieth and early twenty-first centuries the cultural experiences of the majority of the population of the industrialized world are received through television, video, compact discs and computers. They are industrially produced for mass consumption and consumers are persuaded to purchase through intensive marketing.

The reality may be that there is very little difference between the arts and entertainment and it is impossible to say what activity falls into which category. This entertainment–arts distinction is ultimately a matter of judgement and it has become exercised in a particular way to include, quite arbitrarily, some activities and not others as arts. The distinctions really are a matter of judgement: 'artistic value is an arbitrary aesthetic system. It is based upon and inscribed within social positions. It is not an "essence" that lurks within an artistic object' (Lewis, 1990: 11). The definition of what is or is not art has been made by people who have been educated and powerful and until recently this was a small body of people. Such a process enables them to differentiate themselves from others who are excluded from participation by the claim that the arts are something which are difficult to comprehend. An understanding and appreciation of the arts is limited to a few and is used as a distinguishing feature in society to distinguish those who are 'cultured' from those who are not. The terms 'arts' and 'culture' have become associated with each other in a common overtone of superiority and worthiness.

This view may however be much more difficult to sustain as populations become better educated, as the right to vote has become more widespread, standards of living have risen and as it becomes more readily recognized that what is or is not art is not easily decided. From a postmodern perspective, it is inappropriate to make such a distinction anyway (Featherstone, 1991). This view of the world, initially associated with architecture but now applied to many aspects of life including culture, regards clear distinctions such as those between arts and entertainment as unjustifiable. The (post) modern world is such that there are no certainties and everything has its own validity. There are no clear rules for interpreting the world and each individual can give and derive meaning from objects and activities as he or she wishes.

Participation

Going to the theatre or to a concert is a leisure activity that very many people do. Outside the home the most popular activities in Great Britain are going for a drink or meal, followed by visits to the cinema (a third of adults in the previous three months). Visits to historic buildings were made by 23% and to museums or art galleries by 19%. The same percentage (19%) went to the theatre but only 8% went to a pop or rock concert and 7% to a classical concert or opera. A quarter of all adults, however, had been to a nightclub or disco during the previous three-month period and just over 20% had been a spectator at a sports event (1993–94; Central Statistical Office, 1995). Participation figures obviously do not indicate frequency of attendance and the similarity, for instance, in museum and theatre participation disguises the fact that in the same period 90 million visits were made to museums and art galleries and only 23 million were made to the performing arts (Casey et al., 1996).

Surveys that focus solely on the arts indicate the relative importance of each of the art forms. In the USA about a quarter of the adult population attended a (musical) play and 16 per cent attended a non-musical play during 1997 (NEA, 1998a). Jazz and classical music, opera and ballet were less popular. Visits to 'art museums' and 'historic parks' were more popular than any of these and were undertaken by a third and nearly half of the population respectively. Total attendances at arts events grew from 441 million to 604 million between 1992 and 1997.

In Australia less than one in ten of the adult population attended a classical music concert in 1998–99, 16 per cent attended musicals or went to the theatre and 9 per cent went to a dance performance (Australian Bureau of Statistics, 1999a). As in Great Britain a far greater percentage of the population had been to the cinema (67 per cent).

During 1998–99 it is estimated that 22 per cent of the adult population in England attended plays and 12 per cent went to classical music concerts (Arts Council of England, 1999). Opera, ballet, contemporary dance and jazz are less popular but nonetheless are still seen and listened to in live performances by, literally, millions of people. Attendances at the performing arts in England have been steady over a long period of time.

Who goes to the arts?

The surveys discussed above show a very similar picture of the arts-goer. Participation rates are highest amongst people who are relatively well-off, well educated and in the older age categories. In the USA 'adults between 45 and 54 years of age had the highest attendance rates in seven out of the eleven activities covered in the 1997 Survey of Public Participation in the Arts' (NEA, 1999a: 3). These seven included classical music, opera, plays (musical) and ballet. In the case, however, of non-musical plays, jazz and other dance, the highest participation rates were in the 18–24 age group. The same survey shows 'a solid relationship between education and arts participation. Adults who attended graduate school had the highest attendance rates for every arts activity' (NEA, 1999a: 6). It is also clear that in terms of race and ethnicity the highest participation rates were amongst whites. African-Americans and Hispanics had lower participation rates in all categories except jazz and 'other dance'.

Participation rates were also highest amongst the highest income groups. For instance, 11.6 per cent of those with annual incomes of $10,000 or less went to musical plays whereas 51.3 per cent of the highest category (over $100,000) attended. For activities such as opera and ballet the differences were even more noticeable.

The result is that in any audience for the arts there is usually a distribution of people that does not match the general characteristics of the population. There are above-average numbers of people who are white, who have high incomes, who are well-educated and who have white-collar employment. In London West End theatres, for example, the average age of the audience is 42 and over half have completed further or higher education. Over half classify themselves as being middle or senior management (MORI, 1998).

What explains participation?

The motivations for attending the arts are wide-ranging, from engaging in a deep relationship with the art that heightens awareness through to escapism and boredom with other aspects of life (Cooper and Tower, 1992). The arts and entertainment provide the opportunity to expand the mind and senses but also to relax, to escape and fantasize, to be out in the company of others and an opportunity for display. Whilst these apply to all forms of the arts and entertainment, the motivations of relating to the arts at the highest levels of understanding and appreciation are often associated with the arts whereas factors such as escapism and relaxation are associated with entertainment.

Going to see a live performance may have particular attractions compared with home-based entertainment or any form of pre-recorded entertainment. The appeal is believed to lie in the opportunity to see, meet and be with others and, equally, to be seen by others (social interaction and display). It is considered to have a 'sense of occasion' that staying at home does not. The performance itself has a sense of excitement about it derived from the interaction of performers and audience and a directness that is unfiltered by television or compact disc.

Underlying the choice however are some deep influences. 'Educational attainment ... is the single most powerful determinant of (high) arts participation' (Heilbrun and Gray, 1993: 41). In Australia, four in ten of people with a higher degree went to the theatre compared with less than two in ten of people with a basic vocational qualification (Australian Bureau of Statistics, 1999a). Education will influence income and occupation, all of which have a positive connection with participation, but education seems to be the single most important influence (see Figure 2.2). Education may be necessary in order to understand the arts though it is obviously not a simple connection and in fact may be a myth cultivated by art-lovers. To understand art may require knowledge of the 'codes' which can make sense of it. This process of acquiring knowledge and understanding of the arts has been termed the accumulation of 'cultural capital' (Bourdieu, 1984). There is a common set of values that determines these codes and what constitutes arts and this is acquired through family, experience and education.

Going to see or listen to the arts is also influenced by childhood exposure to the arts. People who have grown up with little or no experience of the arts or theatre-going are less likely to go in adulthood. This means that some people are 'comfortable' with going to the theatre, they know what to expect and how to behave. People who were not familiarized in their early years will lack this 'comfort' factor.

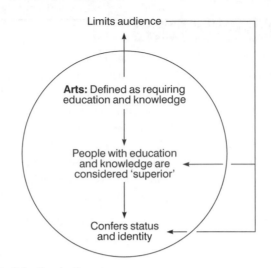

Figure 2.2 Participation in the arts

The arts have become associated with the more educated and wealthier sections of society. In those 'upper' sections of society, going to the arts is regarded as the usual thing and there is peer group pressure to attend. In others, peer group pressure is not to attend. This gives identity to sectors of the community (a middle class person is someone who goes to the theatre), it reinforces their sense of community (they have something in common which binds them together) and it acts as a means of excluding others (by not going to the theatre a person is not admitted to the circle of middle class) (Dimaggio and Useem, 1978). Leisure pursuits generally and arts participation may be explained therefore by the view that they are used to nurture relationships and consolidate identities (Roberts, 1981). There is an element of simplification and exaggeration here but nonetheless leisure does play a key role in the formation of social identity and class structure.

The association of the arts with the middle classes, in particular, means that people participate in order to raise their own status (Harland *et al.*, 1996). Going to the high arts boosts self-image by being with others who are regarded as being in the upper levels of society and also seeing or listening to something which is similarly regarded highly.

What explains non-participation?

Non-participation can be explained by practical factors such as cost, especially for low income groups (Moore, 1998), but also, more significantly, by the 'cultural' differences discussed above (see Figure 2.2). Certain dominant sectors of society have defined what was art and in the process have, in effect, excluded others from it. Theatre and the arts generally have been regarded as the pursuits of the middle classes rather than of working classes. This process probably started in the mid nineteenth century and by now is difficult to reverse. Many people do not go to the theatre as they do perceive it as something that is not for them. 'The main barriers to the enjoyment of the arts are psychological rather than practical . . . Perception of the arts as being exclusive, difficult to understand and expensive' (Mass Observation and Greater London Arts, 1990: 3).

People believe that they would not understand what was going on and it would be too heavy and incomprehensible; this is referred to as the 'talent' barrier (Harland *et al.*, 1996). Others believe that the arts are irrelevant to them and are only for others. For some, especially ethnic minorities and lower status people, theatres and concert halls are seen as unwelcoming, which is referred to as the 'lack of relevance and the comfortability' barrier. Non-participation may also occur because of 'image' barriers: 'involvement . . . does not sit comfortably with an individual's self-perception or results from an anticipation of external negative attitudes and the reactions of others' (Harland *et al.*, 1996: 55). Some people just do not see themselves as 'arty' people or believe that their esteem in the eyes of others would be reduced by participating. Among certain sectors of the population, theatre-going is not a usual pursuit and for any individual to do so would invite adverse reactions.

There are obvious attractions too in being entertained at home. There is a variety of activities offered by television, computer, music system and video. These do not require leaving the comfort of home and are accessible without having to be concerned about the correct way of behaving. Theatre-going and concert-going are constrained in terms of time whereas home entertainment is more controllable by the individual. It is also regarded as cheaper even though it may not be so in fact.

The supply

The supply has several dimensions including (see Figure 2.3):

- **people:** composers, playwrights, choreographers, the people who create the artistic works; performers such as musicians, actors and dancers; technical staff for lighting, sound, scenery, etc.;
- **venues:** the places where performances are held, which include theatres, concert halls, arts centres, arenas, bars and clubs.

19

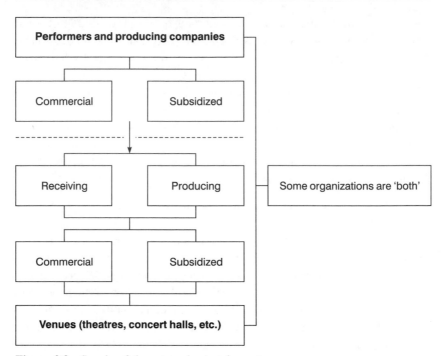

Figure 2.3 Supply of the arts and entertainment

Any individual performer may be self-employed or employed by a producing company such as an orchestra or dance ensemble. Performers and producing companies may receive income from sponsors or government grants. The arts, in particular, are dependent upon such non-box office income in order to survive. They are often referred to as 'the subsidized sector'. Entertainment, however, is characterized by performers and producing companies that operate commercially and which rely upon box office income to generate sufficient income to make a profit.

Similarly, theatres may operate on a commercial basis or may receive sponsorship and grants. One of the distinctive features of the arts is the high number and continuing existence of organizations that do not earn a profit and which frequently, by any commercial standards, make a loss. In the UK, most theatres outside the West End are either owned by or depend for finance on local government or are run by trusts and are non-profit making. Many theatres are run by non-profit making trusts though often the building itself is owned by local government (Audit Commission, 1991; Myerscough, 1988).

Despite the large number of subsidized people and companies in the arts there are a significant number of commercial theatre operators especially in the West

End and Broadway and in most major towns and cities. Although this is more likely to be in the entertainment rather than arts sphere, the subsidized arts are often performed in commercial theatres (if 'receiving' – see below). There are also some significant commercial producing companies. The Apollo Group owned over twenty theatres and arenas in the UK, most of which were outside London. Apollo was taken over in 1999 by the US group, SFX Entertainment. This enterprise owns a large number of theatres on Broadway and is the largest concert promoter in the USA. Ownership of London's West End theatres is dominated by a few commercial companies such as the Really Useful Group, which now owns 13 theatres after the purchase of the Stoll Moss theatres in 2000. This group is owned by the composer Andrew Lloyd Webber whose work includes 'Cats', 'Jesus Christ Superstar' and 'Phantom of the Opera'. The integration of activities (production and theatre ownership) and widening of ownership are part of a move towards reducing risks and sharing costs.

Some theatres, halls and arenas are 'receiving' organizations (see Figure 2.3). They do not produce their own events and productions but present those of others. A producing company may produce a play which is then performed in several different receiving theatres across the country. The company producing the play may be part of some large producing organization or may be a small band of performers in a form of worker's co-operative or anything in between, including individuals. The financial arrangements are varied and operate on differing shares of risk applying to the theatre and the producing company. A straight hire means that the producing company pays a fee for use of the theatre and bears the financial risk, taking the profits or accepting the loss. A guarantee is the opposite: the theatre pays a fee to the producing company and also bears the risks (profit or loss). The risk is shared where there is a form of box office split. Most receiving theatres operate on shorter runs of productions than those in the West End or Broadway, often a different production every one or two weeks. These are often productions that are on tour around several theatres nationwide.

Others are 'producing' theatres and mount their own in-house productions. They hire directors and performers, construct sets, etc. and may commission the writing of plays or music. The producing theatres may (or may not) have a 'repertory' company of performers who are linked with a particular theatre and perform in all or many of their productions. Such in-house productions may, of course, be toured and performed in receiving theatres elsewhere.

Government and the arts

Many arts organizations depend on non-box office sources of revenue, especially government grants and sponsorship, in order to survive. The English

National Opera, London, had an income of about £21 million in 1997–98, of which only £7 million was box office income. Arts Council funding was £12 million and nearly £2 million was from private and other sources (Eyre, 1998). Arts organizations receiving Arts Council (of England) and regional arts board funding received an average of less than half (45 per cent) of total income from the box office in 1998–99 (ACE, 1999). In the USA, not-for-profit (tax-exempt) theatre producing organizations outnumber the commercial organizations (NEA, 1998b). Theatres in Germany are even more heavily subsidised than in England: public theatres received 86 per cent of their income as a local government subsidy (Feist, 1998). Tax-exempt theatres in the USA received half of their income from admissions (1992) and nearly a quarter from private support (NEA 1998c). An international comparison of orchestras showed that in the USA, central and local government provided 6 per cent of total income whereas in England the figure was 30 per cent (Feist, 1998).

In the USA there has always been more reliance than in the UK on funding from charitable trusts and foundations and on sponsorship from individuals and corporations than on government. The US situation is a reflection of a philosophy about the role of government that differs from that in most of western Europe. The US, as one of the most successful free-enterprise economies, has always been more imbued with a sense of minimum government intervention and, at the same time, a sentiment that individuals have some obligation to distribute their wealth in a philanthropic way.

In large part, the justification for the continuation of the 'uneconomic' arts lies in the idea of 'market failure'. If the arts were to be supplied solely on a pure commercial basis, the market mechanism would underproduce and the output would be less than desirable at a 'socially optimal' level. Outside support, especially from government, is given in most industrialized countries to both artists and performers and to performance spaces (theatres and concert halls). Many governments have set up 'arms-length' bodies through which they finance the arts: the Arts Council of England (ACE) (founded as Arts Council of Great Britain in 1946), the Australia Council (1975), the Canada Council for the Arts (1957), Creative New Zealand (1994) and the US National Endowment for the Arts, the federal grant-making agency created by Congress (1965). They all operate on the similar principle of national and federal governments passing money to them but the decision about who should be financed lies with the arms-length body and not with the government. These bodies have similar objectives, which are to encourage 'excellence' in the arts, including encouragement of new performers and new art forms, and to encourage the widest access to or participation in the arts. The support is usually confined to the 'high' arts though there is an increasing desire to promote cultural diversity and in the case of Australia and New Zealand, for instance, to preserve and stimulate the arts of the original cultures of those countries: Aboriginal and Maori arts.

In the UK the Department for Culture, Media and Sport is the government department responsible for government policy on the arts, museums, tourism, and a number of other related matters. It, in turn, provides funding to the Arts Council of England, the British Tourist Authority and others. Seven 'national' companies such as the Royal Opera, the Royal National Theatre, the Royal Shakespeare Company and the Royal Ballet are funded directly by the ACE (£63 million, which was a third of all ACE grants in 1998–99). Others are funded indirectly through the network of Regional Arts Boards which, apart from the ACE funding (£58 million), also receive considerable funding from local governments.

In the UK, local government has been a particularly important supporter of the arts. There is no obligation on them to do this but they are the largest single funder and provide nearly half of all non-box office income for the funded performing arts (Casey et al., 1996). Their expenditure is comparable with that of the Arts Council. Their assistance takes many forms including providing and operating theatres and concert halls, funding arts organizations and artists, contributions to local arts boards and support for festivals. In seaside holiday towns their role has been critical. Local government provides and operates most of the theatres and concert halls outside London and about one-third of these are in seaside towns (Audit Commission, 1991; Myerscough, 1988).

The reasons for support by national and local governments are many and include (Casey et al., 1996; Audit Commission, 1991):

■ The arts are important and deserve to survive even if they cannot do so commercially. Their importance is considered to lie in their representation of the best of human achievement and the ability to enhance the quality of life of people who experience them. People in audiences can be raised to the highest intellectual and emotional experiences. 'The arts are an end in themselves: through participating and understanding the arts we grow, we learn about ourselves . . . They are not essential to our existence but they are central to it' (Eyre, 1998: 38). 'The arts matter because they embrace, express and define the soul of a civilisation' (Tusa, 1999: 22).
■ The arts find difficulty surviving because there is little scope for productivity improvement and, in the case of new works and minority interest works, there is a problem of generating enough revenue to survive. Support is therefore given to encourage new talent as well as to ensure that

existing artists survive. Innovative and experimental arts are important for the health of the arts and of society and are usually nurtured in the subsidized theatre. The subsidized sector provides opportunities not available elsewhere for new work which may, eventually, become mainstream.

■ A 'civilized' society is characterized by a diversity of artistic activity and by a continuing desire to create and be innovative. The enabling legislation for the USA's National Endowment for the Arts in its 'Declaration of Findings and Purposes' states that it is 'necessary and appropriate for the Federal Government to help create and sustain not only a climate encouraging freedom of thought, imagination and inquiry but also the material conditions facilitating the release of this creative talent'. The implication is that without such support the quality of life and a free-thinking democracy would be lessened and new artistic outputs would not emerge.

■ Support is also based on the view that the arts are so important that access of everyone to the arts should be encouraged. Therefore government support is justified in the form of enabling the arts to survive and also keeping prices down. In this way, the widest participation and attendance are encouraged. It does also reflect the view that the arts are superior to entertainment and that people would gain more benefit from the arts if they were exposed to them.

■ Arts are considered to be worthy of support because of their ability to attract tourists or create jobs or help the balance of payments. The cost involved in subsidizing the arts may be considered to be a good investment if a good financial return is received elsewhere. In a similar way, the arts may encourage people to live in a particular town and may encourage business-people to set up factories or offices there because it is a desirable place to live and work (see Chapter 8). This sort of argument for the arts is relatively recent and has been proposed since the 1980s in particular. The arts are not valued for their own sake but for what they can achieve for some other purpose. In the case of holiday areas and especially seaside towns, local governments have been willing to support the arts as 'an investment'. Theatre and entertainment have a role to play in attracting tourists and therefore it is important that they should be available. The argument is extended to make the point that the inflow of tourists generates income throughout the town and therefore the cost borne by local government as an investment is worthwhile.

These justifications for support for the arts reflect the views that they are somehow 'special' and worthy of support, more so than many other leisure activities including entertainment.

Despite this discussion highlighting the special issues surrounding the arts and how these might justify subsidy, there has been increasing pressure on the arts, in the last two decades of the twentieth century, to be 'more commercial' (Casey *et al.*, 1996). The particular nature of the arts, with artistic matters having priority over profit, has meant that many arts organizations have been run without a commercial edge to them and they may have been regarded as less than efficient in their operations. The encouragement to be more commercial may mean many things including adopting more of the management strategies of the business world. It also implies reducing dependence on subsidy and becoming more self-reliant. The activities of funding bodies such as the ACE and NEA have been curtailed. The NEA's budget, for instance, was cut from $162 million before 1996 to $98 million after and the number of full-time employees reduced by 43 per cent (NEA, 1999b).

Sponsorship and lotteries

In the UK there has been considerable encouragement for the arts to seek partnership with the private sector and raise funds from sponsorship. Government funds are increasingly diverted to schemes where the arts are encouraged to raise matching funds from the private sector and to schemes that do not support on-going expenditure but which are one-off payments to enterprises that will become self-supporting.

Sponsorship has, especially in the past, been a philanthropic activity. People and corporations have donated to the arts because they were public spirited, they believed it to be 'the right thing to do' and it gave them a sense of fulfilment. It was an act of unselfish concern for others. This continues but sponsorship is increasingly regarded as a mutually beneficial business arrangement. Sponsors are looking for a 'return' in the form of a raised corporate profile or the promotion of particular products as well as a favourable public relations image. The organization A&B (ex-ABSA) has operated since 1976 in the UK to encourage partnerships between the arts and the private sector.

One of the issues that arts organizations have to face when raising money from governments or sponsors is that not all art forms are equally popular with funders. There is limited sponsorship of novel, adventurous and controversial artistic activity and there can be threats to artistic independence as evidenced for instance by Mayor Giuliani of New York threatening (in 1999) to withdraw financial support from the Brooklyn Museum of Art. This was mounting 'Sensation', an exhibition of contemporary art from Britain, which had been uncontroversial in Britain. The focus for protests was a painting of the Madonna that included dung in the artist's materials. The UK Secretary of State for Education expressed the view in 1999 that taxes should not be used to finance some performances abroad of a controversial contemporary play 'Shopping and Fucking'.

National or state lotteries exist in most countries, though only since 1994 in Britain. The British lottery provides funds for the arts usually on a basis of partnership funding from other sources. Most of this funding was initially for capital projects – for buildings and equipment – rather than for revenue. Undoubtedly there has been a considerable number of new venues developed and re-furbishment of others, including the Royal Opera House, London (£78 million grant) and the reconstruction of Shakespeare's Globe theatre in London (£12 million). The theatre stock in the UK is largely 'old', many having been built in the early part of the twentieth century. This means that they are often lacking the facilities expected by modern audiences and also that they experience considerable maintenance and restoration costs.

There has been criticism of the approach nonetheless, as the main financial issue facing the arts has been that of survival and of paying for productions. There have been instances of theatre companies closing because of inability to meet running costs even though they had received substantial lottery capital grants. There has though been some recent modification by introducing funding designed to secure the existence of some companies and to encourage strategies to develop new audiences.

The allocation of National Lottery funds has been through the Arts Council. In 1998–99 the Arts Council of England's own grants were £188 million and the National Lottery arts grants amounted to £143 million with a total of over £1000 million having been distributed since 1995. The lottery is a major source of arts funding but there has been some concern that is displacing government funding and removing the 'obligation' of government to ensure the existence of the arts. Lottery funds are subject to fluctuation according to the popularity of the game and this introduces a degree of uncertainty that many would prefer to see replaced by firm government commitment to arts funding.

The lack of government financial support for the arts in the UK has led many, including the Theatre Trust, to be concerned about the future of theatre. The Theatre Trust is a statutory body (established 1976) with a remit to protect the theatre stock. It warned, in a 1999 report, that the new lottery funded performance spaces would stand empty for a lack of revenue. The reduction in the real value of funding to the ACE has been on-going for some time and despite a considerable increase in 1999 there is concern that the Labour government (since 1997) has been more interested in the popular arts and the cultural industries (including pop music and film) than in culture and the minority interest (high) arts have been neglected. Access has been promoted at the expense of excellence. The government's policy undoubtedly reflects a desire to move away from the past and the support for the interests of the few. In addition it has been a recognition of the economic worth of the popular creative industries compared with the high arts and, of course, the fact that they do not require subsidy, which is in line with current government thinking (Smith, 1998). The arts always understandably plead a case for special consideration but there is a genuine concern that financial constraints and preoccupation with business management methods will stifle creativity, inspiration and innovation and leave the new and less popular arts short of funds because they are seen as elitist and not popular enough (Tusa, 1999).

Chapter summary

The particular focus of this book is live performances of music, dance, plays and the like before audiences in places such as theatres, halls and arenas. These live performances are often categorized as being arts or entertainment. In its usual usage the term entertainment has overtones of being undemanding and light but enjoyable. In one form or another entertainment features in most people's lives as it is a term that covers a wide variety of activities including watching television and going to a nightclub as well as seeing a performance, for instance, of a musical in a theatre. The arts, however, have been considered to be more demanding and requiring effort to appreciate and, in some ways, to be more serious than entertainment. The arts are associated with the highest levels of human creativity and the work of relatively few gifted people whereas entertainment is something that can be created more easily and by more and less gifted people. The term 'arts' is applied to plays, music and dance but to performances that are, in some way, different from entertainment. It is obvious that it is very difficult to decide what is art and what is not and ultimately it is a matter of opinion but the distinction is commonly made nonetheless. What is considered art has probably been determined in the past by people with an interest in keeping it limited to themselves and in preserving a mystique about it in order to enhance their own status.

Whereas most people experience some form of entertainment frequently, relatively few go to see live performances of the arts or entertainment. The proportion of the population that goes to the theatre is low compared, for instance, with cinema-going. The people who do go tend to be unrepresentative of the population as they are usually older, wealthier and better educated than the rest of the population. This is partly a matter of cost but also the transformation of theatre into a pursuit of people in the professions, management and white-collar occupations. Theatre and the arts have become the preserve of the few in their desire to differentiate themselves and appear superior. As a consequence, many people have come to believe that theatre-going is not for them. People who have been accustomed to going to the theatre from an early age and who have been exposed to the arts in school are more likely to participate than are others. It may be that appreciation of the arts is something that is not easily acquired and it does require some education.

It is not too surprising in view of these perspectives on arts and entertainment that the supply of each differs. Both are the outcome of work by individuals who create or perform and which is performed in venues. The individuals and the venues may operate on a fully commercial basis and this is usually associated with entertainment. Many, however, operate on a non-commercial basis and creators, performers and venues such as theatres exist only because of financial support from government or private sponsors. This is largely associated with the arts.

The arts have been singled out for support by governments for many years whereas entertainment has been left to market forces to determine and for commercial providers to supply. This is largely accounted for by the view that the arts are 'special' and as being the embodiment of human achievement and they therefore deserve to be encouraged and to survive. Most governments have believed it necessary to support the best of the old and to stimulate new creativity. At the same time, given the belief that the arts are so important, governments have tried to encourage participation by a wider range of the population by opening up access through support that keeps prices relatively low. In some countries such as the USA there has been a greater reliance on private sponsorship than on government, but the same issue is a consideration – that of supporting a non-commercial enterprise.

It is evident therefore that the arts are quite different from many other activities. The people who are involved are often there for reasons that are non-monetary and they will often claim that the arts are worthy in their own right regardless of monetary value. In the early part of the twenty-first century, however, it is becoming more difficult for the arts to survive on this non-commercial basis. Governments in particular have been re-thinking their support for the arts and have been encouraging a reliance on other sources of finance.

3

The tourism context

Introduction

This chapter is similar to Chapter 2 in that it provides a background overview. It is gives an overview of tourism as a background for the examination of the arts–tourism relationship in later chapters. The overview will enable arts managers and students to approach tourism with understanding. The point is often made that the arts and tourism don't fully comprehend or appreciate each other's particular methods of operation or objectives. Like Chapter 2 it therefore covers a wide range of issues, especially those that have a bearing on the arts–tourism relationship.

The chapter includes a discussion of:

■ what tourism is and its complex composition;
■ where tourists go;
■ why people go on holiday;
■ who provides the tourism product: the supply;
■ the relationship between governments and tourism.

Tourism

The word 'tourism' is most often associated with people who are on holiday. This is a form of leisure activity that takes place away from home (and place of work). People can, however, be away from home for reasons other than being on holiday: on business or to attend a conference or to visit friends and relatives, for instance (see Figure 3.1). These too are classified as 'tourists' which may cause confusion on occasions. Out of a total of 122 million tourist trips made in the UK by UK residents in 1998, 14 million were for business reasons and 38 million were to visit friends and relatives (BTA, 1999a). Of 1100 million trips made in the USA (1996) 36 per cent were to visit friends and relatives and about 22 per cent were for business.

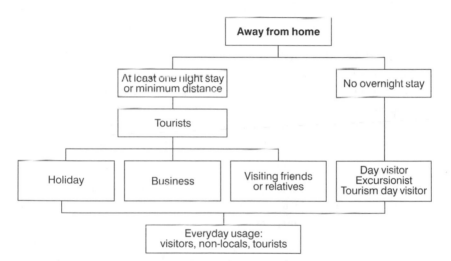

Figure 3.1   Classification of people who are away from home

There are, in fact, a confusing number of definitions of tourism and the tourist. Each country tends to adopt a slightly differing definition but there have been attempts by the United Nations and the World Tourism Organisation (WTO) to bring some uniformity into the usage of terms. In respect of international tourism, a distinction is made between the tourist who stays at least 24 hours in a country and the day visitor or excursionist whose stay is less than 24 hours (see Figure 3.1). Tourism is also domestic – within a country – but the same time distinction is not made by WTO. The domestic or national tourist organizations may make such a distinction however. The tourist boards of the UK define a tourist trip as being 'of at least one night

31

spent away from home . . . and has its end marked by the respondent's return home' (ETB *et al.*, 1998: 33).

In the USA, data is more usually collected about 'travel' with the criterion for inclusion being distance travelled rather than an overnight stay. National surveys compile information relating to a person travelling 100 miles (one way) or more away from home. In 1998, 87 per cent of these trips did entail at least one night away from home (TIA, 1999).

People who leave home for leisure purposes but return the same day without staying overnight are not usually included as tourists even though many of their activities are identical (see Figure 3.1). Again this causes confusion, as often there is no distinction in many people's minds between those who visit a museum as part of a day trip and those who do it whilst away from home on holiday. Day-trippers and tourists are often, in everyday usage, lumped together as 'visitors', 'non-locals' or 'tourists' (see Figure 3.1).

Whatever the official definitions, holiday tourism is a use of time (away from the usual environment) that encompasses many activities. A holiday is made up of numerous components: transport, accommodation and activities such as sun-bathing, eating out, entertainment and visiting museums and castles. The experience of a holiday is influenced by many factors as there are many components of any one person's holiday, including the weather.

Tourism may be considered an industry in as much as there are organizations whose purpose it is to supply transport, accommodation or souvenirs to tourists. Many of these such as shops or train services or museums will also be supplying services to locals and there may be some doubt as to whether they consider that they are in a tourism industry or not. Tourism may not be an industry from the consumer's point of view as he or she buys parts of the holiday from many different suppliers and may fail to regard them as comprising one industry. In addition many components of a holiday such as weather, landscape and scenery cannot be conceived of as being products of an industry.

The holiday is, though, a major part of most people's lives. It is probably one of the largest single items of expenditure in a year and one of the greatest sources of satisfaction and fulfilment, so that it is regarded by many as a necessity (Hughes, 1991). It is something the majority of the population takes. In Britain, the proportion of the adult population that takes a holiday (of four or more nights) has been about 60 per cent for many years (BTA, 1999b). The participation is not evenly spread amongst the population however. In the USA, 37 per cent of all trips in 1996 were taken by people in professional and managerial occupations whereas 'blue collar' workers accounted for only 12 per cent (Waters, 1998).

Overall pattern

Holiday tourism is something that is most frequently found in the richer industrialized countries of the world. The inhabitants of these countries are the people who travel most, both within their own countries and to other countries. Domestic tourism far exceeds international tourism in terms of numbers of trips taken but the statistics for it are often less reliable than are statistics for international movements. Despite the popularity of exotic and long-haul destinations such as Africa, the Far East and South America, most tourism movements still occur within western Europe and North America. In terms of international tourist expenditure, 60 per cent of the total was generated by only five countries in 1995: USA, Germany, Japan, UK and France (BTA, 1999b). Total international tourist arrivals, in 1997, were 612 million of which over half were in Europe and 19 per cent in the Americas (BTA, 1999b). The top five destinations accounted for over a third of all arrivals: France at 67 million, USA 49 million, Spain 43 million, Italy 34 million and UK 26 million (Waters, 1998). The USA and the UK are therefore amongst the most important tourist countries in the world. In western Europe the flow of tourists tends to be from the 'core' of the more northern built-up areas to the periphery of the south, to the beaches and warmer climate of the Mediterranean. The most popular destinations, in 1997, for holiday travellers from the UK were France (7.2 million visits) and Spain (7.5 million visits) (BTA, 1999b).

There has been hardly any growth in domestic holidays in Britain. Domestic holidays (four or more nights duration) have fluctuated in number but in 1997 were the same number (30 million) as they were in 1965. Holidays in foreign countries however have risen over the same period from 5 million to 27 million (BTA, 1999b). Domestic holidays remain the more important numerically but the numbers have not shown growth.

This dash for the sun has been the case in particular since the 1960s when many of the holiday destinations in countries such as Britain, the Netherlands, Germany and northern France experienced a decline in their business. Holiday-makers shifted from holidaying domestically in those countries to holidaying in resorts in Spain, southern France, Italy and Greece. The shift was associated very much with the introduction of the cheap package holiday (inclusive tour). The tourist flows are heavily seasonal with most occurring during the summer months.

There is a similar pattern in North America though the desire for the sun and fine beaches means that holiday-makers do not have to leave the country. The size of the USA means that a person living in the heavily populated north-eastern part of the country (including New York-New Jersey, Pennsylvania, and Virginia) can holiday in the sun in Florida or on the west coast in California. International tourism is, as a consequence, relatively less important for the USA than in it is in western Europe and domestic tourism is much more important. The climate in these sun spots is less variable than that in the European sun destinations and is therefore less seasonal.

In Australia and New Zealand the climate differences are not so marked and generally are favourable to tourism. Most of the tourism, as elsewhere, is focused on the coast such as the Sunshine or Gold Coasts, north and south of Brisbane in Australia. Further north, Australia lies within the tropics and the Queensland coast including the Great Barrier Reef is popular during the southern hemisphere's winter. As with many other countries, most of Australia's tourism is domestic. For international tourism it is a long-haul destination for most generating countries though there is a strategy to build up tourism from Japan (already an important market) and south-east Asian countries. Strong family links with other countries that have arisen from the relatively recent large inflows of immigrants to Australia (and New Zealand) account for a large 'friends and relatives' market (especially from the UK).

In all of these countries there has been a growth of additional holidays. More people are now taking more than one holiday a year (Smith, 1996). These additional holidays are often of shorter duration than main holidays and are more likely to be to city or rural destinations though the main holiday may still have a sun and sea focus.

Why go on holiday?

As with the arts there are a number of social factors, such as status, social identity and peer pressure, which explain participation. The penetration of tourism into most sectors of society does not detract from the fact that the participation rate does vary across social class, occupational group, income band and ethnic origin. As a leisure activity that requires both money and a significant amount of time, participation rates are greatest amongst higher income earners and professional and managerial workers. In addition these are the people who are most likely to have more than one holiday and to travel to locations that are more 'exclusive'. The fact of going on holiday, the multi-holiday pattern and the different destination combine to give status and social identity.

At an individual level, most explanations relate to the motivation of the tourist. The term is not applied in a consistent manner but broadly it refers to a drive or need which impels a person to act in pursuit of a particular goal. Many journeys have a purpose and are 'instrumental' and a means of achieving an identifiable objective (see Figure 3.2). A need or obligation to visit friends or relatives or a desire to attend a particular event may lie behind the journey. Some journeys – holidays – are non-instrumental in that they are ends in themselves and do not have such a purpose. The distinguishing characteristic is 'expectation of pleasure from novelty and change experienced' (Cohen, 1974: 533). This conceptual definition of a holiday does not

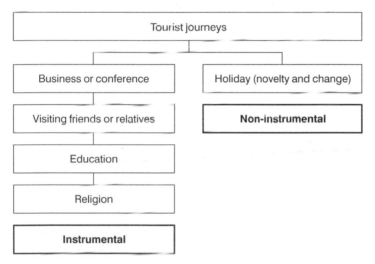

Figure 3.2 Instrumental and non-instrumental journeys

necessarily coincide with the meaning of the word as used by tourist boards. Holidays are to do with 'change' – that is, travel to and stay at a different place regardless of the things done or seen (see Figure 3.3). A desire to see and learn about other cultures or the opportunity to see famous buildings and sites may feature as reasons for going on holiday but this is still non-instrumental in that basically the driving force or need is 'novelty and change'. It is a desire to get away rather than the attraction of particular places that distinguishes most holidays. The 'push' is more important than the 'pull'.

A common theme in explaining this drive to 'get away' and the desire for change is 'recuperation' both physical and mental. The contrast with everyday life may simply be relaxation and rest. This in itself may be the necessary

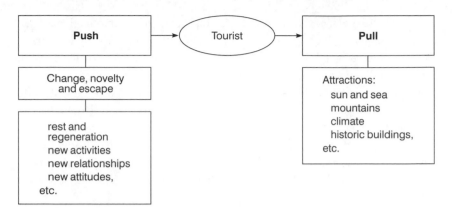

Figure 3.3 Push and pull factors in tourism

change that a person cannot achieve at home. Many holidays may, though, be far from relaxing or restful in this sense and may involve a great deal of activity such as sports or leisure pursuits or sight-seeing.

Change may be evident in a different dimension. Holidays may be one way of escaping the reality of everyday life. Such periodic 'escape' is necessary if identity is to be built and survival ensured. The holiday injects novelty or at least change from daily routine. It may be a very strong contrast with everyday life that can show itself as wholly different activities, behaviour and attitudes from those at home. It may give the opportunity to undertake activities for which there is no opportunity or time when at home.

A tourist may also adopt postures and play roles so that a new persona is adopted, at least temporarily. This may be a whole new identity adopted as a fantasy or, less dramatically, a role as a caring family person, as a lover or romantic, as a spendthrift, as a person of some superior social standing and so on. Some change is for tourists to integrate wholly with host populations. Tourists may also be able to be themselves. The holiday may, for instance, play an important role for gay men who may be reluctant to reveal their sexuality in the everyday environment (Hughes, 1997; 1998a). There is also a strong fantasy element in many holidays apart from different behaviour. There is often a hope that something 'better', 'exciting' or 'romantic' will happen whilst on holiday or as a result of the holiday. These may be rarely fulfilled but they are recurring hopes.

The holiday may provide an opportunity for self-evaluation and self-discovery. A new environment also enables new relationships to be established without any long-term commitment. It is regarded by many as an opportunity to relate more closely to family or friends.

The purpose served by going on holiday therefore goes beyond the obvious and immediate desires such as acquiring a sun-tan or viewing an historic building. For many holiday-makers the choice of holiday destination is largely immaterial. Many destinations could serve as a medium through which an individual's needs could be satisfied. This is evident in tour operators' brochures where the distinctive attributes of destinations are played down in favour of an emphasis on escape, change, excitement, building relationships and so on.

Supply

It has been seen above that tourism is not one product or an experience provided by one supplier (see Figure 3.4). The two specific characteristics of tourism, however, are travel and 'stay' and, as such, transport and accommodation are vital parts of the experience. Many tourist trips, especially domestic trips, are undertaken using the car. In the USA 80 per cent of trips

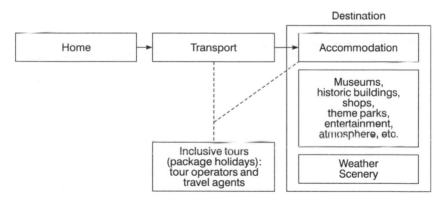

Figure 3.4 The holiday product

use a car or similar road vehicle (1998) (Waters, 1998). For domestic tourism in Britain the car was used for 74 per cent of long holidays (four nights or more) in 1997 but for holidays abroad (one night or more) the plane was the most popular method of transport (78 per cent of all trips out of UK by residents) (BTA, 1999b).

The plane is particularly important for longer distance tourist journeys and innovations in air transport have accounted for much of the growth of international tourism (Page, 1999). Air transport has become quicker, more comfortable and relatively cheap since the mid twentieth century. This has been associated, in particular, with the development of the jet engine. The use of the plane is also bound up with inclusive tours or package holidays. These have been particularly important in encouraging the flow of people to holidays in Mediterranean countries.

Many British holiday-makers when abroad use hotel or motel accommodation (50 per cent in 1997) and this too is associated with inclusive tours which originally were linked with 'serviced' accommodation of this sort. There has, however, been a growing importance of rented (non-serviced) accommodation such as rented villas and apartments which were used on only 3 per cent of holidays abroad in 1974 but 22 per cent in 1997. This informal sector is also widely used for domestic holidays. Hotels and motels were used on only 25 per cent of holidays in Britain in 1997 (35 per cent in 1971) and rented accommodation and caravans were used on 14 per cent and 23 per cent respectively.

In the USA, hotels or motels are used in nearly half of all trips and stays with friends and relatives accounted for 35 per cent. Direct comparison with the UK is difficult because of differences in coverage and definition but, nonetheless, the hotel and motel sector appears to be comparatively important. This is possibly due to the much greater number and network of motels, which do confer considerable flexibility.

Australian domestic tourists also showed a preference for staying with friends and relatives when on holiday (41 per cent of visitor nights) and staying in hotels, resorts and motels (23 per cent) in 1998 (Australian Bureau of Statistics, 1999b).

There are many well-known hotel chains such as Holiday Inn, Hilton, Sheraton, Marriott and Hyatt. Most originated in the USA though the first two are currently British-owned by Bass, originally a brewing concern, and by Ladbroke, most well known for gaming and betting in the UK. These chains own or manage hotels in most countries of the world and have succeeded by offering a high quality and consistent standard. The traveller going abroad could do so with confidence about the services and quality of accommodation to be expected. This in itself has undoubtedly stimulated international travel. Despite their high profile, there are obviously a great number of alternatives to these multi-national chains and to hotels generally. They and similar chains may dominate certain sectors of the market (usually up-market) but many holiday-makers choose to stay elsewhere. The hotel may be considered too formal and inflexible and contrary to the spirit of many people's holiday, which is associated with a desire for informality, freedom and flexibility.

In most countries, there are very many smaller non-chain hotels, boarding houses and guest houses which outnumber the chain hotels. Most of them are relatively small in size and are owner-managed, 'mom-and-pop' enterprises.

Inclusive tours and tour operators

The inclusive tour has been especially significant for holidays abroad by British residents. Since the 1970s they have accounted for around 60 per cent of holiday visits abroad (BTA, 1999b). Foreign visitors to the UK do not however show the same usage of inclusive tours. Of 1.9 million holiday visits by USA residents (1997) only 24 per cent were inclusive tours and the rest were independently organized (BTA, 1999b). Such pre-packaged holidays offer the convenience of being able to book flights and accommodation in one transaction (see Figure 3.4). These inclusive tours have offered the 'security' of destinations that are tourist-oriented and which are not too different from domestic resorts but with the added advantage of sun. The flights have usually been charters and as such are arranged solely for the convenience of the customer of the tour operator.

Inclusive tours are offered by tour operators. These companies are 'assemblers' in that they put together 'packages' of transport (usually air) and accommodation for sale to consumers. In the UK the market is dominated by a few companies. Thomsons, Airtours, Thomas Cook and First Choice between them sell 78 per cent of all inclusive tours (1998). Their domination of the market has increased but there is still a large number of operators who offer specialist products for niche markets (Laws, 1997). Whereas the larger operators tend to focus on the 'mass' family market for holidays to the sun (usually on the Mediterranean coast), smaller operators may specialize in different destinations (perhaps long-haul) or activity (such as golf or trekking) or city tourism.

The tours have usually been sold through travel agents though a small number are sold directly to consumers. The operators produce brochures which are available through travel agents, the retail outlets for the operator's product. The agents receive commission for holidays sold. There has been a domination here too by large chains of agents and many small and independent agencies have disappeared. The situation is such that now the largest agency chains are owned by the large tour operators. Thomson, the largest UK tour operator owns Lunn Poly and Airtours owns Going Places. Tour operators also own their own airlines. Thomson owns Britannia Airways, which is the second biggest airline after British Airways, and First Choice owns Air 2000. Some also own hotels.

Most domestic tourism however does not involve inclusive tours. Individual arrangements are easier to make and it is possible that more tourists will make their own arrangements for foreign travel in the future as they become more familiar with foreign travel. Visits into the UK are also usually individually arranged. There are, however a number of incoming tour operators and ground handling agents who organize transport, accommodation and visits to places of interest, chiefly aimed at the American market.

Attractions

The elements of supply that have been discussed so far are secondary to the main components of the holiday, which are the attractions. The factors that attract tourists to a destination in the first place are varied but it is significant that the actual product that holidaymakers are experiencing is a place. This can be a town, a city or a country. For many holidaymakers, sea and beach locations are important. A large number of holidays are still taken at the seaside. For instance, 37 per cent of holiday trips in England and 53 per cent of trips in Wales by the British were to the coast (BTA, 1999a). Most of these trips are to seaside towns (resorts) which have been established since the mid nineteenth century and which reached the peak of their popularity in the 1950s and 1960s. These towns have experienced a down-turn in their fortunes. The falling numbers of staying visitors has been explained by factors such as (Shaw and Williams, 1997):

- British holiday-makers have turned to foreign 'sun' destinations available in a relatively 'cheap' packaged form.
- Widespread car-ownership has lead to domestic holidays that are centred on several destinations rather than on one resort.
- Competition from leisure activity domestically including from theme parks.
- The seaside resort represented the mass consumption age of the early and mid twentieth century but, during the latter years of the century, holiday-makers have searched for new destinations and new, more individual, forms of holiday activity.
- Until it was recognized that there was a problem, a certain amount of decay set in. This, in turn, accelerated the shift to foreign destinations.

Even when all of this had been recognized, it has been obvious that revitalizing domestic holidays is a huge task requiring resources that have not been available on a scale large enough to provide swift remedies. The product is a place and that is not as easy to reformulate as other services or a manufactured good. It frequently means a re-structuring and re-development of towns that were fashioned from the mid nineteenth century onwards. For many of the resorts the main business now comes from short breaks and day-trippers.

Private enterprise is responsible for many of the facilities that tourists use when on holiday such as fairgrounds, theme parks, amusement arcades, golf courses and swimming pools. Some of these are attractions in their own right such as Alton Towers theme park in the UK and Disneyland Paris and will draw tourists from long distances. Others are part of an overall bundle of attractions that make a place worth visiting. More often than not these attractions are owned locally and are not part of a chain.

In addition to these private enterprise attractions there are attractions that are owned by other types of bodies whose interest is not to satisfy a consumer or to make a profit. Visits to museums, historic houses, castles, churches and cathedrals are significant in many tourist trips. The latter clearly have a function for worship and museums a function of preservation and study. Historic houses and castles may have been preserved as part of a place's heritage and have been taken into public ownership or into the care of a body such as the National Trust for that purpose. Some, including many historic country houses in England, are privately owned. These facilities have a prime function other than tourism and would probably exist even without it, though many now are alive to the potential of tourism and earn some revenue from that source. Historic and picturesque towns and cities attract tourists though clearly that was not the original intention and they have become tourist attractions by chance.

Even transport routes can be major tourist attractions. Sydney Harbour Bridge and San Francisco's Golden Gate Bridge have a primary transport purpose but they have great potency as symbols of their respective cities and attract many tourists just to gaze on them. Seats of government such as London's Houses of Parliament and the White House in Washington DC have similar incidental tourist roles. A cultural facility that has great symbolic importance for tourism is the Sydney Opera House.

Natural resources are also important elements of tourism. Mountains, rivers, forests and wildernesses provide the setting for rural and inland tourism. They are not provided by any human enterprise though they may be preserved through human initiative such as the National Parks of the USA and Britain. These natural resources are also modified by humans. In the case of the English countryside, wealthy landowners have in the past landscaped it for cosmetic reasons and farmers have transformed it for agricultural reasons.

Views, scenery and the weather are significant components of the holiday but are beyond human control.

The tourism experience does not come therefore from any one provider. It is the outcome of activities and facilities provided by many different individuals and organizations and some by none at all.

Government and tourism

The role of national governments in tourism has usually been much less than that in the arts. Unlike the arts, tourism has not usually been regarded as something that is worthy in its own right and something to which access for all should be granted. It has been regarded more as an economic activity in the same way as the arts are increasingly being regarded (Richards, 1995). If encouraged or supported at all it is likely to have been on the grounds of generating an inflow on the balance of payments, creating employment or regenerating run-down cities and the like.

In the UK, government responsibility for tourism was divided amongst a number of departments until the establishment of the Department of National Heritage in 1992, renamed the Department for Culture, Media and Sport (DCMS) in 1997. This body is also responsible for policy on the arts. Given the wide-ranging nature of tourism it is not surprising that different government departments have had an interest in and influence on tourism. Many matters that bear upon tourism, such as care of historic monuments and the maintenance of museums and support for the arts, have been brought together in the DCMS – but only so that some co-ordination might occur, not that tourism interests should dominate. Many other departments, including transport, continue to have an interest in and effect upon tourism.

In the same way as arms-length bodies exist for the arts, similar bodies exist for tourism. Tourist boards typically have functions such as:

■ marketing, especially promotion;
■ product development: by financing or encouraging new attractions, accommodation or basic infrastructure.

In most countries the first function is the prime one. Development functions are particularly important in countries where tourism is new or non-existent.

In the UK the initiative for establishing tourist boards came from a recognition of its potential for assisting the balance of payments. An inflow of foreign tourists would bring in much needed foreign currency. The

Development of Tourism Act 1969 set up statutory bodies for tourism that were funded by government. The British Tourist Authority has an overview of tourism policy and, in particular, it has the function of promoting the UK to foreign tourists. Separate national boards were also established, one each for England, Wales and Scotland. Initially they were to promote their own countries but only within the UK. These were followed by networks of tourist boards at a more local, regional level. A number of Regional Tourist Boards were established in England and Area Tourist Boards in Scotland. These have always received funding from their respective national boards, from local government and from private enterprise.

In addition to promotional activities the boards have had powers to influence development of the product. In the early years in the UK, this took the form of a scheme of grants and loans for financing the building of new hotels and re-furbishment of existing ones. After this short-lived but very successful scheme, the boards continued on a much reduced scale to give grants to a variety of tourism projects and not just hotels through the regional boards. This grant scheme was ended in England in 1989.

Similar bodies set up and funded by governments exist in many other countries. The Australian Tourist Commission is a statutory body that promotes Australia as a tourist destination. In order to do that it has offices in places such as London, Los Angeles and Tokyo. The United States Travel and Tourism Administration (USTTA) was set up as a Federal body in 1981 with similar functions. It was however closed down in 1996 and overseas offices were closed or were transferred to US embassies. Responsibility for marketing the USA as a tourist destination now lies very much with private industry especially through the trade fairs held by the private sector Travel Industry Association of America (TIA). Involvement in tourism by individual state and city governments has been much greater then the limited Federal contribution. Several states such as New York have had promotional budgets exceeding that of the USTTA (Pearce, 1992).

Governments have supported tourism for a number of reasons though, as noted above, it has usually been for its 'spill-over economic effects' rather than because of the intrinsic merits of tourism itself. There has not been the same view as there has been about the arts, which have been considered to be worthy in their own right (Pearce, 1992; Hughes, 1994a). Reasons for support have included:

■ Destination marketing probably would not occur without government support. It is an activity that potentially benefits all in a destination whether it be country, region, city or seaside resort. Because of this no private enterprise would be willing to finance destination marketing without a guarantee that everyone else would contribute. As this is unlikely it falls to government – national, state or local – to finance it out of general taxation.

- In order to ensure the existence and quality of natural resources such as landscape and scenery owned by private enterprise with different and non-tourist objectives, government intervention may be necessary.

Tourism has been regarded as a commercial activity rather than as a 'social-welfare' activity. It has not been seen as having the same beneficial attributes as the arts though it may well, in fact, have such attributes (Hughes, 1991; Smith and Hughes, 1999).

As with the arts there has been a movement towards reducing this reliance on government to promote the tourism product. 'The market place should normally develop its own solutions in response to changes in customers' preferences . . . The government's role is to support the tourism industry by taking action to address market failure' (DCMS, 1999: 14). The English Tourist Board has been re-structured as the English Tourism Council (1999) with a role of supporting the business of tourism but by focusing on a national strategic framework rather than on the provision of direct services (DCMS, 1999). The emphasis and funding is shifted to the regional level where the regional tourist boards, for instance, are encouraged to operate in partnerships with private enterprise.

Despite this, the holiday product has been much influenced by the activity of local government. Coastal holiday towns or seaside resorts were initially developed in the mid nineteenth and early twentieth century in many countries (see Chapter 5). This development owed much to local government: coast protection, promenades and boardwalks, public parks and gardens, swimming pools, bandstands, theatres, concert halls, piers, etc. Local government has therefore been, and usually still is, a supplier or funder of a significant part of the holiday tourism product. It also has, through its planning function, a wider influence on tourism developments. It has already been noted above that the 'product' that many holidaymakers are buying is, in a sense, a town or city and local government has a role to play in guiding re-development of the older destinations. In many cases local government is also responsible for the marketing of the resort as a tourist destination. Although of necessity some of the 'product development' of a town such as public spaces and gardens will remain with local government, other aspects, such as sports and leisure centres, are being given over to the private sector or to joint endeavours, such as leasing theatres to commercial operators. The marketing or promotional role has also been rethought. Local government may not have adequate marketing expertise nor operate with a commercial enterprise approach as their reason for being has been to operate non-commercial and welfare-oriented services. These factors combined with limited financial resources have caused many to enter into joint marketing bodies – bodies that are ventures between the public and private sectors. A well-funded and commercial approach is especially necessary in the face of the competition from the large tour operators who are seeking to encourage people to holiday abroad.

Impact of tourism

As a final comment on tourism it needs to be acknowledged that it has been the subject of a great deal of criticism (see Mathieson and Wall, 1982; Hunter and Green, 1995; Smith and Eadington, 1995). Despite its many positive aspects, including the pleasure it brings to a large number of people, the enrichment it brings to lives of the tourist and the economic benefits that are claimed for it, tourism has its downside. Criticisms in the industrialized world are most often directed at its impact on the physical environment. There have been concerns, for instance, about the effects of large numbers of tourists on the Great Barrier Reef. Tourism in rural areas may give rise to particular problems such as damage to farmers' crops and livestock, litter, erosion of sensitive land surfaces, noise and the feeling that the presence of tourists may destroy the peaceful and uncrowded atmosphere of the countryside or wilderness.

Similar comments about numbers of tourists are made in relation to tourism in cities and historic towns, especially with regard to the wear and tear on the old structures of historic houses, castles and cathedrals. Deliberate or unthinking vandalism may also occur. Other criticisms are directed at the behaviour of tourists in museums, historic houses and cathedrals which may not be undertaken with the respect that others believe is due. Crowding is another comment about tourism. The tourist areas of many towns and cities can become particularly busy and locals are crowded out. This applies to traffic flows and parking as well.

In the less industrialized parts of the world rather more serious criticisms have been made. Tourism has been blamed for turning many local customs and traditions into tourism spectacles and thus reducing their significance. Older ways of life have been undermined by tourism as it brings in new ideas and people with possessions and approaches to life that local residents in the host countries may wish to imitate.

Tourism has been considered to be a 'new imperialism'. Up until the mid twentieth century many countries in western Europe had colonies in Africa and Asia which supplied Europe with cheap supplies of raw materials and food. This has often been regarded as an exploitive relationship, with the European countries gaining far more than the colonies. Most of these are now independent countries but in a number of cases they may be as dependent upon the countries of western Europe and, now, the USA as ever. If they have a strong tourist industry it will usually be dependent upon tourism from the industrialized world. Often hotels and other services such as casinos, and airlines and tour operators will be based in the industrialized countries.

Chapter summary

Tourism is a term that covers many activities including holidays but it involves temporarily moving away from home for some purpose and usually staying away for at least one night. It includes business and conference trips and visiting friends and relatives as well as going on holiday. Most tourist trips are, however, for holiday purposes. When people go on holiday they are usually looking for 'change' and a break from their usual life pattern. This can refresh and regenerate a person as well as provide the opportunity to behave in ways that are different from patterns at home. The push to 'get away' is strong and, by now, going on holiday is an accepted and expected part of life for most people. It is a highlight of many people's lives.

A holiday is not, however, a single readily identifiable product. Many holidays are focused on sea and sun but there is also a demand for many other types including holidays focused on sport or on heritage or shopping. Any holiday also has many components that vary according to the individual tourist concerned. Some of the components are provided by commercial suppliers but others such as scenery and weather are natural. Some are provided by individuals and organizations that are not primarily concerned with tourism. There are however a large number of commercial suppliers of part of the product. Hotels, motels and guest houses are numerous and the supply of the upmarket hotels, at least, comes from some very large multinational companies. Most of the rest of accommodation however is owned by relatively small organizations. Transport is frequently provided by holiday-makers themselves as many holidays, especially domestic, are taken using the car. Longer distance and international holidays are reliant on air transport where there is, at least until recently, a domination by large airlines. Tour operators and travel agents are particularly concerned with international travel and in the UK there is a concentration of supply into a few large firms. The inclusive tour (or package holiday) provided by tour operators has been particularly significant in generating international travel.

Although the majority of the population of most industrialized countries does take a holiday every year this is only a recent phenomenon. 'Mass tourism' only emerged in the second half of the twentieth century. It coincided with a shift in many countries towards holidays that were sun-based as well as sea-based. In the case of northern countries it meant that domestic resorts lost holidaymakers to countries with Mediterranean coastlines. Towards the end of the twentieth century there has been a noticeable growth in second holidays, many of which have been less concerned with sun and sea and more with domestic destinations and with countryside and cities.

Apart from the obvious components of weather and scenery, tourism has always been a commercial activity. Tourism has not been identified as something special that deserves to survive regardless of whether it is profitable. It is therefore unlike the arts where unprofitable activities have been supported by government or private sponsorship finances. Governments have, nonetheless, intervened in tourism in most countries. The intervention has usually been limited to the financing of marketing bodies on the grounds that they will not be provided otherwise.

4

The arts-related tourist

Introduction

In previous chapters the nature of tourism and the arts and of the tourism and arts consumers were examined. Although comparisons were made between them, the two were considered separately and not as part of the same activity or 'product'. In this chapter the arts and tourism are brought together and examined in terms of their links. A structure is developed for analysing the relationship further in later chapters.

This chapter includes:

- an examination of the connection between the arts and tourism in the past;
- the current perspective on this form of tourism;
- a consideration of terms used in order to clarify analysis;
- the development of a framework for classifying the arts-related tourist;
- an examination of the influences on the development of arts-related tourism;
- a discussion of the relative roles of heritage and the arts in tourism.

Culture and tourism

Since the end of the Second World War (1939–45) there has been a tremendous growth in the number of people in North America and western Europe who have become tourists. This has sometimes been labelled the emergence of 'mass tourism'. Going on holiday is now the experience of many rather than of just a few people. This tourism is associated with the pursuit of pleasure and with time spent on beaches in fine sunny weather and not primarily with time spent in museums, art galleries, and the like with a view to self-improvement. In many ways the era of mass tourism, where the majority of the population now regularly has a holiday, stands in contrast with earlier times when tourism more often had a cultural or educational motive. This distinction is an over-simplification but undoubtedly some of the earliest reasons for tourism were associated with the desire to experience other societies and systems of government and to be exposed to great works of art, buildings and sculptures. This is seen most clearly in the European 'Grand Tour' (Feifer, 1985; Towner, 1996).

Before the mid twentieth century, most travel was for the purpose of trade, pilgrimage or education and not primarily for pleasurable holiday purposes. Some travel for pleasure purposes has, however, always been evident, including during the Roman Empire period. Even then it had a cultural tourism element in that some travellers ventured to Greece or Egypt in search of antiquities. From the sixteenth century through to the early nineteenth century a particular form of travel emerged which has served to give the view that 'early' tourism was associated with culture. Young British men (of some wealth) travelled through Europe in order to gain experiences of government and culture before returning to 'settle down' to the business of land-owning and governing. This, by the eighteenth century, had become common for men of wealth, accompanied by tutor and servants. The particular focus was usually Italy as the birthplace of the Renaissance and of the earlier Roman civilization though France was an important destination also. 'Pleasure' undoubtedly featured in this Grand Tour despite the high-minded intentions and there were many opportunities for pleasurable diversion such as plays, concerts, parties, socializing, sexual encounter, eating and drinking during the journey and at destinations. By the end of the eighteenth century the 'pleasure' attractions of Italy, its people, climate and way of life, were increasingly recognized as being the reason for travel (Withey, 1998).

At the same time there was a growing interest in the natural world and scenery became an object of the tourist gaze. This 'Romanticism' arose out of a belief that the simpler and unspoilt things in life were to be respected partly as a reaction to the increasing pace of industrialization. These views, which encompassed an opinion that 'simple' or 'peasant' ways of life were to be esteemed, were popularized by Rousseau in France and by Wordsworth and the Lake Poets in England. Travel therefore was still a semi-serious business of appreciation of the grandeur and picturesqueness of the natural landscape and waterscape and of the merits of pre-industrial communities.

Even though much early tourism may have had some fine sounding justification, it was associated with 'pleasure' and 'play'. Travel, for instance, to spas (inland and coastal) occurred ostensibly for health reasons but the related spa facilities for entertainment, eating, drinking, and gambling may have been more appealing to tourists than were the rigours of spa treatment itself. Ultimately, at least in Britain, the health motives (or excuses) disappeared and the more pleasurable motives dominated (see also Chapter 5). Mid and late twentieth century 'mass' tourism has been characterized by such 'pleasure' rather than cultural motives.

Regardless of this, there has been a confidence in recent years that tourist interest in culture has re-emerged and strengthened. 'Cultural tourism is one of the growth sectors of the West European tourism industry' (Bywater, 1993). 'In the twentieth century ever-increasing numbers of people are participating in arts and heritage based forms of cultural tourism' (Zeppel and Hall, 1992: 49). There is a view that the mass tourism market for sun, sea and sand may have matured and there is a search by tourists for new experiences. It may be, of course, that the interest has never gone away and it is just that the spectacular growth of beach-related holidays has overshadowed a continuing presence of cultural tourism. The conclusion of the recent pioneering European-wide study undertaken by the European Association for Tourism and Leisure Education (ATLAS) was that there was little new about the convergence of culture and tourism and it was likely that recent cultural tourism in Europe had grown no faster than tourism in general (Richards, 1996). The influence of culture on the appeal of tourist destinations may appear to have become greater if only because culture has been increasingly used as an important marketing tool (Zeppel and Hall, 1992).

Unfortunately 'very little is known about the cultural tourism market in Europe' (Richards, 1999: 18) and there is little evidence that demonstrates clearly whether cultural tourism has been growing. The way in which statistics on tourism are recorded does not enable patterns in cultural tourism to be determined. The undoubted popularity of short breaks and city breaks does though provide some indirect evidence for believing that culture is an increasing focus for tourism (Gratton and Taylor, 1992).

For some tourist destinations, such as the UK, the main form of leisure tourism (for in-coming visitors) is cultural, particularly in the heritage sense (see Chapter 7). The particular strength of Canada as a tourist destination has been its scenery but 'the Canadian Tourism Commission has identified cultural and heritage tourism as a critical area of development for Canada. If Canada is to remain competitive on the world tourism scene it must be able to meet the demand for cultural tourism' (Canadian Tourism Commission, 1997b: 1).

- **Greece** has promoted itself, within a wider campaign, as 'the longest running theatrical event' where 'musical shows, theatrical plays and other cultural events (are) featured each summer in the land that is the birthplace of the dramatic arts' (1998). Despite the importance of beach-based holidays to the Mediterranean countries, culture remains a vital component of tourism for some.
- **Poland**, during 1999, promoted itself as the birthplace of Chopin and emphasized that it had been voted 'best destination for culture' by the readers of an upmarket Sunday newspaper. Eastern European countries have endeavoured to find ways of appealing to tourists from the west after the fall of communist governments and the opening up of frontiers from 1989 onwards.
- **'Vienna** salutes the king': the Austrian capital has a particular reputation for heritage and culture and, during 1999, exploited the centenary of Johann Strauss, the 'waltz king' in a marketing campaign.
- **Amsterdam**: 'there are so many cultural pursuits to enjoy in Amsterdam this winter' (1999–2000). The city is well known for a liberal atmosphere and for alternative lifestyles but its marketing emphasizes its museums and 'a rich tradition of classical music and opera'.

Nonetheless, relatively little is known about what holiday-makers do whilst on holiday and therefore whether their holidays are 'cultural' or not. Data collected by UK tourist boards, for instance, classify the tourist primarily by 'purpose' – holiday, business, visiting friends and relatives, etc – and not, until recently, by activity or type of trip (see Chapter 7).

Definitions

There are difficulties in defining 'cultural tourism' (see also discussion of culture, art and entertainment in Chapter 2). 'The existing tourism literature has not yet settled upon a generally accepted single definition of the heritage and cultural tourism concepts' (Alzua *et al.*, 1998: 3). It therefore becomes difficult to discuss its size or growth or to explain why it occurs. The term 'cultural tourism' is used to cover several different (but related) activities:

1 **'Universal'** cultural tourism. The word 'culture' itself has different meanings. In the widest sense it is 'a complex of values, ideas, attitudes and other meaningful symbols' which binds people into groups and imparts group character so that a distinct way of life results – a different culture such as German, English or Mexican (Williams, 1988). Most international tourism is 'cultural' in this sense because it usually involves some exposure to aspects of other cultures. Even those tourists who do not deliberately seek to experience other cultures will be exposed, to some degree, to the culture of destinations. It would be misleading though to classify it as cultural tourism as it does not have a deliberate 'cultural' purpose.

2 **'Wide'** cultural tourism (see Figure 4.1). Some tourists will set out with the purpose of experiencing a different culture, in the widest possible sense, of a destination visited: the arts, crafts, work, religion, language, traditions, food and dress. Some of this takes the form of visits to societies that have not been affected by industrialization and western commercial values and which may represent a 'vanishing life-style'. Walle (1998) uses the term cultural tourism to refer solely to the culture of 'ethnic groups and hinterland peoples' living usually in small-scale societies that are relatively untouched by western values. Aspects of this have also been described as 'ethnic tourism' (Smith, 1989).

3 **'Narrow'** cultural tourism (see Figure 4.1). 'Cultural tourism' is most widely used however in a narrower sense of tourism which includes visits to experience the 'artistic and intellectual activities' of a society (Williams, 1988) rather than the whole different way of life of a society. Usually it refers only to those activities which are regarded as being in some sense 'superior' and are a reflection of the 'best' of worthy creativity (see discussion of culture, arts and entertainment in Chapter 2). It includes visits to:

   (a) historic buildings and sites (castles, churches, battle fields, etc.);
   (b) museums and art galleries;
   (c) theatre (to attend the performing arts).

This usage of the term cultural tourism is similar to that adopted in the ATLAS study.

A Canadian study defined cultural tourism to include the above and also visits to festivals and fairs, zoos and national parks and viewing wildlife or birds and attending aboriginal or native cultural events (McDougall, 1998). Aboriginal sites and cultural displays were also included in an Australian study (Foo and Rossetto, 1998).

4 **'Sectorized'** cultural tourism. The components of cultural tourism identified above in 3 may be distinguished individually so that visits under (a) and (b) may be classed as historical or heritage tourism and visits under (c) as arts tourism though this is arbitrary and there will be elements of 'history' in (c) and of the arts in (a) and, in particular, in (b). A large proportion of the stock of art galleries will be of 'old masters'.

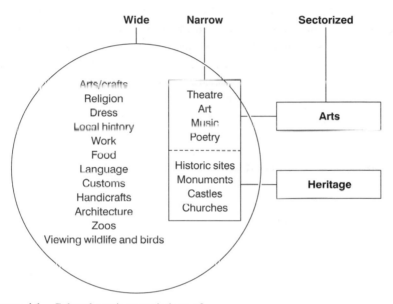

Figure 4.1 Cultural tourism: variations of

This book adopts a 'sectorized' approach to cultural tourism with a focus on the performing arts alone.

The term 'arts tourism' has been used, confusingly, by Myerscough (1988) to cover museums and art galleries and theatre (b and c above). The terms 'historical tourism' (Smith, 1989) and 'heritage tourism' have been used to include visits to view modern paintings or sculptures. Prentice (1993) also uses the term 'heritage tourism' to include natural history attractions (including zoos) and the performing arts. Heritage tourism is used by Zeppel and Hall (1992) to include local cultural traditions and they include in arts tourism, 'the visitor experience of paintings, sculpture . . . and all other creative forms of human expression and endeavour' (Zeppel and Hall, 1992: 48). Gratton and Taylor (1992) use a time dimension to distinguish arts tourism ('consumption of contemporary culture') from heritage tourism ('consumption of historical culture') though this also is too simplistic.

There is thus considerable confusion and no agreement about terms. Anyone reading material relating to cultural tourism or to its components has to be aware of what exactly is being discussed. In addition to the above confusions about inclusions, the terms are applied regardless of motivation or interest (see below).

The studies also tend to focus on the arts and ignore entertainment (see Chapter 2). The focus is culture and not popular culture. Regardless of the fact that entertainment is conventionally distinguished as some form of 'inferior' activity, it is undoubtedly part of 'popular culture' in the sense of being the pursuit of many people. It is surprising given this and the apparent importance of entertainment and 'popular pleasures' in holidays both past and present (Urry, 1990 and see Chapters 5 and 7) that entertainment has been neglected. There is some recognition, however, in the ATLAS study that the scope of cultural tourism is widening to include entertainment (Richards, 1996).

Motivation and interest

The term 'cultural tourism' (however defined) is applied to tourists regardless of motivation or interest in culture (see Table 4.1). The same applies to heritage or historic or arts tourism and all who visit the relevant site or building are frequently classified under that heading. Arts-tourists were widely defined in the Policy Studies Institute (PSI) study of the economic importance of the arts as any who attended or visited any of the arts (widely

Table 4.1   Classifications of cultural tourists: a summary of some related studies

- Myerscough: any who visit a cultural attraction
- McDougall: any who visit a cultural attraction
- Foo and Rossetto: any who visit a cultural attraction + specific cultural visitors with culture as primary motivation
- Alzua *et al.*: any who visit a cultural attraction + different types of cultural tourist according to benefits sought
- ATLAS: any who visit a cultural attraction + specific cultural tourists with a focused cultural intent
- Prentice: any who visit a cultural or heritage attraction + some with sole or primary holiday activity
- PANYNJ: 'arts-motivated' if arts as 'main reason' for visit
- Silberberg: greatly motivated + motivated in part + adjunct + accidental
- Bywater: culturally-motivated + culturally-inspired + culturally-attracted

(see Chapters 6 and 7 for estimates of relative size of some classifications)

defined), regardless of motivation (Myerscough, 1988). McDougall (1998) defined cultural tourism trips in Canada as any which included participation in any of the activities or visits to any of the sites specified. Similarly a cultural tourist to Australia was defined as 'an inbound visitor who attends at least one of the ... cultural attractions during his or her stay' (Foo and Rossetto, 1998: 1). Alzua *et al.* (1998) focused on cultural tourists outbound from the UK and they were also distinguished as those who had participated in at least one of the specified cultural activities. This particular study did, though, go on to identify categories of cultural tourist on the basis of motivations (see later).

As a first step in clarifying the discussions the reasons for tourists being in, for instance, a theatre audience can be classified into two (see Figure 4.2).

1 **arts-core**: they have chosen to travel in order to see a performance;
2 **arts-peripheral**: they will be away from home for other reasons such as business, visiting relatives or wanting to enjoy heritage or sun and sea. They are at a performance as part of the stay away from home for another reason.

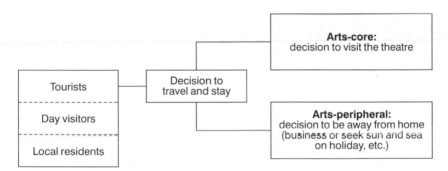

Figure 4.2 Segments of theatre audiences

In the first case (arts-core) the decision is equivalent to any decision to attend a performance but with an extra time and distance dimension included. Why would anyone do this?

- Although theatres and live performances are widespread, they are not found everywhere. Large towns and cities, in particular, usually have a high concentration of theatres and of the arts performed in them such as drama, comedy, plays, musicals, opera and ballet. These are resources that small towns and rural areas may not have and it will be necessary for the people who live there to travel.

55

- There will be people who do live in large towns and cities which are well-endowed with theatres and concert halls but certain productions or performers are not being presented in these. To see them, people will have to travel.
- Seeing productions away from home may occur because the standards are better or because the theatre itself is preferable or because there is an opportunity to do other things as well such as shopping and eating out. The decision here is less of a necessity than it is in the other two cases.

For the arts-peripheral audiences it is not the production that is the decisive factor in being away, it is other reasons such as wanting to enjoy sun and sea or business. The opportunity to see a performance in the theatre may be an important part of that time however, especially as part of a holiday experience. It will probably be secondary to the main 'purpose' of the trip but it would appear that many holiday-makers visit the theatre during their stay in the tourist destination (see Chapters 6 and 7).

There will obviously be a number of variations of these two simple cases (see next section).

A classification by interest and intent

The distinction between arts-core and arts-peripheral conceals a further distinction. Tourists may have varying degrees of interest and intent in the arts (see Figure 4.3). These will range from trips where the performing arts are the

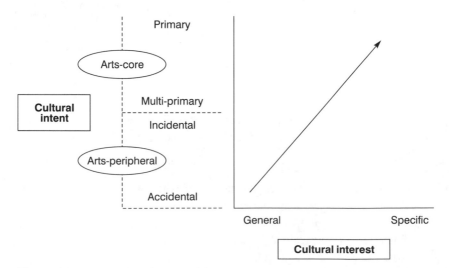

Figure 4.3 Arts tourism: intent and interest

prime motivation and main activity through to trips where they are an incidental motivation and a secondary activity and no more than an entertaining holiday diversion.

Arts-core tourists may be further classified as either:

- 'primary' arts-related tourists. Their main purpose in travelling to a destination is to see a performance and they will have made the decision to see it before arrival at the destination;
- 'multi-primary' where the arts are equally important with some other reason(s) for the visit.

Arts-peripheral tourists can be further classified as either:

- 'incidental' arts-related tourists will be people whose main reason for visiting a destination was something else and their theatre visit-decision was made before arrival at the destination. Interest in the show is a reason for the visit but is secondary to some other reason.
- 'accidental' arts-related tourists will have shown no interest in attending a theatre performance before arriving at the destination and the visit-decision is made after arrival. Theatre does not feature at all in the decision to visit the destination.

In addition to this differentiation by 'intent' tourists can be distinguished by 'interest'. In some cases they are content to 'see a show' without preference and interest is non-specific. Others will have a distinct desire to see a particular production or performer and the interest is very specific.

The extent of the arts in arts-related tourism will vary from little in the lower left-hand sector of Figure 4.3 through to high in the upper right-hand sector. The arts-tourist by a strict definition is limited to the upper levels even though there may be a combination of all other tourists in an audience. This form of categorization applies to all of the variations of cultural tourism including theatres, museums, art galleries and historic houses.

Motivation is, however, featured in a few studies (see Table 4.1). In the ATLAS research project any tourist who visited a museum, art gallery or heritage site was classified as a 'cultural tourist' regardless of motivation but the report did acknowledge a distinction between 'specific cultural tourists' (those with a focused cultural intent to tourism) and other visitors to cultural sites (Richards, 1996). Prentice (1993) also acknowledged two broad types of 'heritage tourists': any who made a visit to a heritage site and those who visited as 'their principal or sole holiday activity' (p.51). Like Richards, he concluded that those visitors with a specific interest were in a minority. Demand for cultural tourism was segmented by Bywater (1993) into three, though the dimensions of each was not estimated: culturally-motivated, culturally-inspired and culturally-attracted. The first of these were those who chose a holiday on the basis of the cultural opportunities and was likely to be a very small proportion of the market.

A study of the arts in New York-New Jersey identified some out-of-region visitors surveyed at theatres and museums as 'arts-motivated'. This was on the basis that they had indicated that the arts were the 'main reason' for the visit to the region (Port Authority of New York-New Jersey 1993) (see Chapter 6).

Alzua *et al.* (1998) classified tourists as 'cultural' on the basis of at least one visit to a cultural attraction. They did however further distinguish 'types' of cultural tourist and for two out of the five cultural tourist clusters identified, culture and educational benefits were particularly important when choosing a destination. It was concluded that cultural tourists were not a broad mass but a differentiated market with different needs and characteristics (see Chapter 7).

Silberberg (1995), in a study of museums, identified four categories of cultural tourist. The 'greatly motivated' were equivalent to the arts-core, primary tourist: they travel specifically to see a museum and were estimated at 15 per cent of out-of-province visitors (Ontario, Canada). There were also tourists whose cultural motives were as important as other reasons for visiting; these are motivated 'in part' and were 30 per cent of out-of-province visitors. Silberberg's 'adjunct' tourists are equivalent to those with incidental intent above (20 per cent of visitors) and the 'accidental' are identical with the use of the term above (20 per cent of out-of-province visitors).

In a study of foreign visitors to Australia, specific cultural visitors were identified as those 'whose primary motivation for travel to a cultural attraction is based on a specific desire to experience a particular aspect of Australian culture' (Foo and Rossetto, 1998: 55). For 'general cultural visitors' culture is a secondary motivation (see Chapter 7).

It may not be justifiable, therefore, to categorize many of those who visit cultural attractions as 'cultural-tourists'. It would appear that most visitors to cultural attractions are culture-peripheral and not culture-core. Nonetheless the blanket term 'cultural tourism' continues to be widely applied to less-specifically motivated visits and statistics require careful interpretation. It was noted in Chapter 1 that the term arts-related tourism would be used in this book. Arts-tourism is that which relates only to tourists with a primary intent and specific interests – the upper right-hand sectors of Figure 4.3

A final part of the framework for analysing tourists is to distinguish between those who are on holiday and those who are not (see Figure 4.4). It is evident from the previous discussion that this is a dimension that can be introduced to further classify people in audiences. Some arts-core persons could consider the trip to be a holiday and others would not. What is or is not a holiday is essentially a personal internal construct. In other, arts-peripheral cases, they could be holiday visits or business or visiting friends. 'Holiday' cuts across arts-core and arts-peripheral categories as the visit can be a holiday with a purpose of going to the theatre or a holiday with a main purpose of enjoying sun and sea.

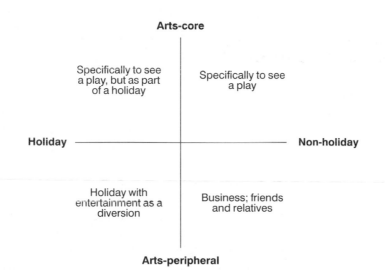

Figure 4.4 Arts-related tourists: a classification framework

It is important to remember that non-holiday does not necessarily mean that the trip is a business one or for the purpose of visiting friends and relatives. It was seen in Chapter 3 that a holiday can be conceptualized as a non-instrumental trip and a non-holiday trip is instrumental. An arts core, non-holiday trip can therefore be one with a purpose of visiting the theatre and which is not considered by the tourist to be a holiday. It is likely that the longer the trip, especially to foreign countries, that this becomes considered as a holiday. This distinction, as noted in Chapter 3, does not coincide with tourist board data relating to 'holidays'.

Tourists who attend or visit cultural events can therefore be categorized in a matrix of arts-core or arts-peripheral and holiday or non-holiday. The arts-core (primary intent) classification cuts across both holiday and non-holiday categories. Similarly there are arts-peripheral tourists in both holiday and non-holiday categories (see Figure 4.4).

Several non-local market segments can therefore be identified, in theory. In practice, there may be little justification for targeting each in a separate way. This would only be the case if the usual criteria for identifying and targeting market segments were present. Each segment would need to be large enough, stable enough and readily identifiable and reachable in a cost-effective way (see Chapters 5 and 6).

The characteristics of those who do participate in cultural activities as tourists is discussed in Chapters 6 and 7.

Special interest tourism?

The identification of the arts-tourist or cultural-tourist as a person with a specific intent is similar to the concept of the special interest tourist. These are tourists whose motivation and decision-making are primarily determined by a particular special interest (Hall and Weiler, 1992). Arts and heritage tourism are 'an important component in the special interest tourism market' (Zeppel and Hall, 1992: 62). In this particular form of tourism there is an implication that the visit is experiential. The tourist is in some way 'committed to' and involved with the object of the visit. It is this that makes it different from, for instance, mass tourism associated with sea and sun. The term is applied to a variety of tourist activities including sport-related and nature-based trips and visits to experience other societies and cultures. The involvement of the tourist will therefore take different forms. In the case of sport (e.g. yachting) the tourist may engage in the relevant physical activity but in the case of the arts this is less likely as he or she is a 'spectator' rather than a participant. The involvement lies in a stimulation of the senses, such as emotion and 'escape', rather than in physical participation. Activity and special interest holidays are more narrowly defined by Martin and Mason (1993) to include only trips that were carried out on an organized basis.

Special interest tourism is therefore defined, not so much by type of activity, but by interest, motivation and involvement. It is frequently observed that tourists are currently looking for rewarding, enriching, adventurous or learning experiences during their trip and 'culture' becomes a focus of some of their tourism (Craik, 1997). A 'learning' element is considered by Richards (1996) to be a distinguishing feature of cultural tourism. These apparent shifts in the requirements of a holiday are the outcome of many factors including broad changes in society.

Arts-related tourism: influences

The reasons for the apparent growth of culture-related tourism have been well-explored but usually relate to the culture-core rather than to culture-peripheral and to heritage rather than to the performing arts. Zeppel and Hall (1992), for instance, attribute the growth to 'an increasing awareness of heritage, greater affluence, more leisure time, greater mobility, increased access to the arts and higher levels of education' (p.50). Some factors such as increased incomes and leisure time are easily identified as explaining the growth but others are motivational and reflect wider cultural changes.

Some of the more obvious influences on the development of cultural and arts-related tourism include (see Figure 4.5):

■ **Income.** Participation in culture-related tourism has required relatively high levels of discretionary income as it is expensive compared with package holidays (associated with sun and sea). The equivalent of the cheap package holiday has not existed to the same extent and, until recently, the availability of package holidays to cities and culture-related holidays has been limited. Assuming an interest in culture-related tourism exists, then as levels of discretionary income have increased since the mid

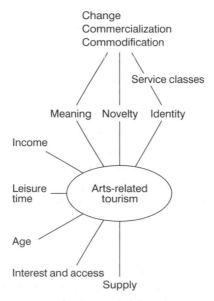

Figure 4.5 Influences on growth of arts-related tourism

twentieth century people have been 'enabled' to satisfy that interest and have contributed to the demand for such tourism.

- **Leisure time.** Increases in leisure time (including holidays with pay) have provided the opportunity, in particular, for more holidays and for shorter additional holiday breaks. There is some argument about whether or not there has been a significant increase in leisure time (Gratton, 1996) but even a decrease in leisure time may lead to an increased demand for short breaks as the time may not exist for a longer holiday (Richards, 1996). Pressure on leisure time may actually lead people to go on more meaningful and satisfying holidays.

   Main holidays may continue to be sun and sand oriented but on additional (often shorter) holidays, tourists may be looking for something different, which may, in turn, lie in more culture-related trips. Growth in the short break market may have particular relevance for culturally related tourism.

- **Age.** Another influencing factor associated with leisure time may be the large proportion of the population that is at post-retirement age and which, as well as having free time, has relatively high levels of discretionary income.

   People in all older age groups (pre- and post-retirement) have an increasing tendency to have holidays especially short breaks and holidays with 'added value'. They are less likely to have an interest in sun and sea holidays and more likely to have a greater interest in culture and heritage. People in the older age groups make more frequent visits to museums and theatres when at home than do younger people. The ATLAS study demonstrated that, in fact, the younger age groups accounted for a disproportionately large share of culture-related tourism.

- **Access and interest.** In the post-war period, there are far more people across the whole spectrum of society who have access to the arts and heritage. In part this has resulted from the introduction of compulsory education for all in many countries. In addition many governments have deliberately set out to encourage the widest possible access to the arts rather than allowing them to be the preserve of a limited sector of society. Awareness of and interest in culture has also been fostered by exposure through television programmes and magazines. Potentially therefore there could be considerable interest in arts-related and heritage tourism.

The opportunity therefore exists to take more holidays and to afford more expensive holidays and more people than ever before have been exposed to and understand the arts. In addition, however, there are a number of other underlying factors that explain the development of arts-related and heritage tourism.

Underlying influences

The interest in culture-related tourism is explained by the 'maturity' of tourism in the main tourist-generating countries (Richards, 1996). Tourism's great growth period was associated with relatively cheap package holidays to the sun and sea but, possibly, a saturation point in this has been reached so that other forms are becoming important. The demands of tourists are changing and differ from those evident in the 1960s and 1970s and the growth of mass package tourism is slowing down. This may be due to:

■ existing tourists tiring of the sea and sand holiday and looking for alternatives;
■ a 'new breed' of holiday-makers who are less interested in such holidays.

Whichever it is, the explanation lies in the desire for more fulfilling holidays and again, the explanations tend to relate to culture-core rather than to culture-peripheral tourism and to heritage more so than to the performing arts. New tourism is characterized by more flexibility and segmentation in contrast to the mass standardized market of the mid and late twentieth century (Jansen-Verbeke, 1996). In post-industrial society, manufacturing is less important and service employment more so. The corresponding decline in mass production and assembly line employment may have resulted in a desire for more independent holidays and fewer 'mass' holidays. The market is more fragmented with niche markets appearing. Nonetheless mass tourism is still important and has not been displaced completely by other forms such as cultural. It is not breaking up completely into a large number of segments. Any explanations of a demand for the arts on holiday should recognize that the demand arises within both mass and niche tourism. It arises, for instance, as arts-peripheral demand within mass tourism and as arts-core within niche tourism. The growth in cultural tourism may be arising more from this arts-peripheral segment than from the arts-core (Richards, 1999).

It is noticeable that the influences on the holiday choice of holiday-makers on activity and special interest trips differ from the influences of those on other types of holiday trip (Martin and Mason, 1993). The former are more likely to refer to influences such as 'being adventurous', 'expanding capabilities' or 'visiting new destinations' whereas other holiday-makers refer to 'security', 'resting' and 'relaxing'. Learning, enrichment and exploration are important in many holiday trips.

Behind this desire for 'fulfilment' on holiday and for holidays that are more than merely frivolous and hedonistic episodes in life lie many complex but related influences that go deeper than those identified above (see Figure 4.5). Since the mid twentieth century, people's identities and roles have been less clear-cut than they used to be. Change characterizes much of life and the pace of that change far exceeds anything previously experienced in human history. What a person is and to what class or socio-economic group he or she belongs is less certain and is a complex matter. The defining characteristics of each have become less clear and movement between the categories has become more possible and frequent. Individuals are less able to relate to a clearly identifiable reference group and with that has come uncertainty and a greater need to establish identity.

At the same time there has been an increasing emphasis on consumerism and pressure to continually purchase goods and services. Corporations continually seek to grow, keep ahead of competitors and encourage consumers to purchase a stream of 'new' products in order to remain in business (Harvey, 1990). According to this view, corporations have encouraged rapid shifts in fashion in order to maintain their profit flow. The outcome is a society where difference, change, spectacle and fashion are acclaimed and substance minimized.

There is also increasing commodification, i.e. the shift from 'free' activities to purchased activities (Britton, 1991). This has been the case in many instances including leisure. Whereas at one time people might have engaged in leisure activities that required little expenditure (at its simplest, conversation) they now increasingly purchase, from the 'culture and leisure industries', leisure activities such as television, membership of health and sport clubs, expensive gardening or DIY equipment, going to night-clubs, etc. Tourism has always involved the commodifying of places: towns and cities have become places to sell to visitors and to be marketed in ways similar to those associated with consumer products. Tourism may also have been partly responsible for the commodification of history itself by making history a product to be sold as an experience in heritage centres and inter-active and 'living' museums in the 'heritage industry' (Hewison, 1987). This industry may give a view of history that is distorted and sanitized but the outcome has been an increased number of 'attractions' available for tourist consumption.

Arising from these features of modern society – change, commercialization and commodification – people seek meaning, novelty and identity, all of which contribute to the development of cultural and arts-related tourism:

■ **Meaning.** The move towards cultural tourism can be explained by this increasing pace of change and the commercialization of societies. Many people may resent it and believe change to be un-nerving and commercialization to be false and superficial. They therefore search for stability and for 'true meaning' and 'authenticity' in some other way (Kneafsey, 1994). People go in search of more meaningful experiences which they may obtain from participation in or viewing of the arts. They also search for what has been lost and, in particular, the values and artifacts of earlier times which may be found through travelling away from home to museums or to experience different societies. A disillusionment with the present leads to a search for the reassurance of the past (Hewison, 1987). Consumers seek refuge from the complexities of the present in the comfort of the past.

■ **Novelty.** For others, the post-industrial and consumerist society is one in which they are totally absorbed and from which they obtain great satisfaction. The whole process of change and of purchasing new and different consumer goods and services is fulfilling and there is a continuing search for 'novelty' and for experiences that give rise to a heightened sense of stimulation and excitement. In an increasingly technological and sophisticated world people are continually seeking 'new out-of-the-ordinary experiences'. The seaside resort, at one time the only place for these, is no longer unique in that respect and such experiences are now characteristics of most places (Urry, 1990). This in itself may encourage people to move from the 'old' sun and sea holidays (at home or in foreign countries) to other types of holiday experience.

■ **Identity.** In addition to the search for meaning or for novelty, the process of commercialization etc. may contribute in another way to the interest in the arts and tourism. People can make statements about themselves through their purchases as they are symbols that give, confirm and enhance identity. The use of goods and services is in many ways less important than their image and symbolism and it is these 'signs' that are being purchased (Baudrillard, 1983). The display of consumed goods and services demonstrates standing to others. Social status is determined by what people buy. As goods and services become more widely available, however, and bought by a greater proportion of the population, there is a constant striving to consume goods and services that no one else has and which are distinctive. There is a continuous search for new and unusual symbols that confer distinction through their consumption. The consumption of services (including leisure services, arts, heritage and holidays) is increasingly replacing consumption of goods as a means of social differentiation (Britton, 1991).

The process of conferring identity through consumption of the arts and heritage has been especially important for people working in the services generally and the middle or service classes (especially teachers and lecturers), and for people in occupations that are culturally-linked. These 'cultural intermediaries' in the media, the arts, design, marketing and heritage may have an approach to life that is characterized by 'learning' and by a concern for identity, style and new experiences (Featherstone, 1991). There has been a considerable growth in the numbers in service and culture-related occupations. For many, the consumption of cultural tourism is a means of differentiating themselves. As noted earlier in Chapter 2, the consumption of culture itself may be particularly associated with these service classes, especially with those who are well-educated. The increased numbers of people with access to cultural capital enhances the likelihood of participation in cultural tourism.

This has occurred alongside the reduction in the significance of the 'working class'. The seaside holiday (especially at the British resorts) became a particular means of reinforcing their identity but with the blurring of social identities that has characterized the second half of the twentieth century there has been less need for the seaside holiday, at least in the same form.

Many of these factors may seem to have more relevance to tourism that is concerned with heritage or differing cultural life of destinations rather than with the performing arts. Listening to music and seeing plays can also, however, meet the needs for meaning, novelty and identity. In addition much of cultural tourism is heritage-led (see Chapter 7) but theatre and concert-going are associated with that. They are in joint demand. Short-break holiday-makers who are particularly interested in culture – museums, art galleries, historic houses – also place above average importance on evening entertainment in destination choice (MEW, 1994). Factors explaining cultural or heritage tourism will therefore also explain attendance at the arts.

Much of the explanation for cultural tourism lies in the search for 'something different' and specific to the destination visited, especially historic sites, museums and art galleries. The performing arts and entertainment, at least those seen by tourists, are often not unique to the destination nor different. Such visits should be, perhaps, regarded in a different way from visits to museums and historic sites, especially if they are not the main focus of the tourist visit. They may be more of a holiday diversion for people with other priorities such as a sun and beach holiday or a heritage-based holiday. In tourism, the interest in the arts may be more peripheral than is interest in heritage.

There are, nonetheless, tourist visits that are arts-led (arts-core) and there are tourist visits with no heritage content but which include a visit to the performing arts (see Chapters 6 and 7). There are a number of issues that will help explain attendance at the arts in particular.

Arts and tourism in combination

One of the defining characteristics of a holiday is 'change'. For some, who do not often go to the theatre when at home, the change may take the form of seeing live entertainment. A holiday with an arts component does seem improbable however as the factors that restrict attendance at the theatre when at home are still present when on holiday (see Figure 4.6). Nonetheless one of

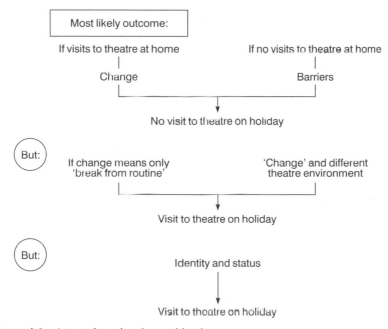

Figure 4.6   Arts and tourism in combination

the elements of change associated with holidays may be going to the theatre (see Chapter 7). The holiday may be regarded as an opportunity to get away from television, video and computer entertainment. It may be a case of experimenting or of seeing the theatre visit as part of the special atmosphere of being on holiday.

Similarly people who go to the theatre when at home may not do so when on holiday, because of the desire for change (see Figure 4.6). Some may consider the need for change to be so great that the main holiday should not include 'normal' activities such as going to the theatre or concert hall. It will be on the additional holidays, which have less significance, that tourists are more likely to consume the arts.

For families with children, main holidays may be occasions when individual members of a family have little opportunity to develop their own particular special interests. Second holidays may provide that opportunity. The size and composition of other households may, however, be such that arts-related holidays are extremely attractive, e.g. single-person households, no-children households with double-incomes or where all have similar artistic interests or a common view about the role of a holiday.

Change may be the significant factor for those who do have an interest in the arts but are unable to visit the theatre because of limited opportunity or restricted leisure hours. A holiday may be the only occasion when they can visit the theatre and indulge their interest.

The basic forces explaining an interest in both tourism and culture consumption are, however, similar. If change is interpreted only as a break from routine, though, then consuming the arts on holiday as well as at home is likely (see Figure 4.6). The kind of activities in which many people engage when on holiday are often not too different from leisure pursuits when at home. On holiday 'the mundane elements in the routine were discarded but the preferred discretionary elements ... were retained' (Crompton, 1979: 415).

Attending the performing arts whilst a tourist can be particularly fulfilling for some. The combination of culture and tourism in an arts-related holiday trip may be an effective way of demonstrating identity, differentiation and superiority (see Figure 4.6). Cultural capital differentiates classes and, as seen in Chapter 3, the act of going on holiday itself conveys certain meaning about the holiday-maker. Going on holiday is part of the identity-creation and identity-confirmation process. The form and type of holiday-taking reflects income and class and certain places and certain types of holiday have superior codings. The arts and tourism can be mutually supportive and reinforcing in that the needs satisfied by both in terms of fulfilment of identity creation, etc. may be similar. An arts-related tourist trip may therefore confer status and confirm belonging to a particular social group. Holidays where arts are a focus may give identity and status for those in non-service occupations. They may deliberately include 'culture' in their holidays in order 'to impress'. The service classes have differentiated themselves from others by drawing on their cultural capital and adopting a 'romantic' tourist gaze. This is a more solitary and sustained relationship with the object of the gaze than that which characterizes the more widespread 'collective' or 'spectatorial' tourist gazes (Urry, 1990) associated with sun and sand package holidays. There is a search for 'real' holidays.

Supply

In addition to the demand for culture-related tourism, there has been a considerable increase in the opportunities for such tourism as the number and range of cultural facilities has increased. The number of museums and heritage centres in Europe has risen greatly since the 1970s (Richards, 1996). The rise in museum and heritage centre numbers has been due partly to increased interest and demand but the 'cultural producers' (the managers and owners) have also been under some pressure to survive without government assistance (see Chapter 2) and find new audiences. There has been a shift in emphasis by museums, in particular, away from being regarded primarily as centres of learning or conservators of history towards being regarded as leisure facilities. It is not evident, however, that the number of theatres and concert halls has increased in a similar manner to that of museums and heritage centres.

Undoubtedly many cities have set out to attract tourists through the cultural assets they possess (Bianchini and Parkinson, 1993). Some 'cultural cities' have attracted tourists for many years but older industrial cities have also, more recently, attempted to do this. The regeneration of such cities is a complex matter but part of the strategy has been to encourage tourism. Given the obvious absence of sun and sea and absence of long-standing tourist markers such as the Eiffel Tower in Paris or the Coliseum in Rome they have utilized what heritage and arts facilities they do have – theatres, concert halls, event centres, museums, art galleries – as major elements of their tourism strategies. The development of policies towards cultural tourism have, in many ways, been supply-led with relatively little attention having been paid to the motivations of the tourist (Richards, 1999).

The interaction between demand and supply is always complex so that it is not simply a case of the increased supply having stimulated consumer interest or of the growth in demand having encouraged the development of events, festivals, theatres, museums and concert halls. The reality is that is has been an on-going interaction that has been the outcome of many influences.

Heritage versus the arts

It was suggested earlier that tourists' interest in the performing arts is more likely to be peripheral than is interest in heritage. Within cultural tourism, the arts are likely to be less popular than is heritage, both in terms of numbers of people who participate and in terms of the ability to attract tourists (see Chapters 6 and 7). This can be explained by a number of factors:

- Interest in the past and the search for meaning, novelty and identity.
- Heritage adds to understanding and appreciation of the country or town visited. Getting to know a place better, for many people, means knowing more about its history rather than its plays or music.
- Many older buildings and sites have become closely identified with the places they are located and are signifiers of those places. They become 'must-see sites': Westminster Abbey and the Houses of Parliament (London), Notre Dame and Versailles (Paris), the Coliseum and St Peter's (Rome), Rialto Bridge and Doge's Palace (Venice) the Statue of Liberty and Empire State Building (New York), etc. The performing arts are less tangible and are unlikely to be signifiers in the same way and therefore are less likely to be must-see or must-do activities. Broadway and the West End have, though become 'signifiers' of New York and London.
- Heritage is usually specific to the place visited whereas performing arts often are not. Potentially, the same plays, musicals, etc. may be found anywhere.
- Theatre-going often involves more organization than visiting heritage. Theatre tickets usually have to be bought in advance and, once capacity is reached, tickets are not available. Museum and heritage site visits, however, can be more spontaneous, entry is usually cheaper (sometimes free) and even where not, it does not usually require pre-booking. It is relatively unusual for heritage sites to be 'full'. There are not one-off performances per period of time that are either seen or missed and the timing is more flexible.
- In many productions in theatres there will be a language barrier for foreign tourists though less so for musicals (or music concerts, opera and ballet) or for North American tourists. There is less of a language barrier for heritage sites.
- Heritage sites are easier to enjoy in that there is more freedom to pursue own activities. Watching a production in a theatre is a more constrained activity. In addition different aspects of heritage are more likely to appeal to several members of a family.
- It is more difficult to market the arts to tourists than it is to market heritage as most heritage is stable and unchanging. The stability enables long-term marketing campaigns to be developed and tourists also know that the sites and buildings will be there during their visit. Arts performances change regularly and this makes it more difficult to integrate into long-term marketing. Arts production details are often not known or cannot be guaranteed far in advance.

Heritage and the arts are not, however, directly competing activities. For some visitors, heritage and the arts will both feature in the tourist visit. In addition, visits to heritage sites and museums and to the theatre may be non-competitive in that the arts may be regarded as supplements to the main purpose of the visit and as evening activities (see Chapter 7).

Chapter summary

There has been a connection between culture and tourism ever since tourism first developed. This was particularly noticeable in the Grand Tour that characterized Europe, in one form or another, for about 300 years through to the nineteenth century. Motives relating to gaining knowledge of the arts and history dominated tourism at this time. Even though 'pleasure' invariably featured in the Grand Tour, this has become more obvious with the growth of mass tourism in the twentieth century. The motives for tourism have become less instrumental and more obviously related to enjoyment, relaxation, escape and change without a particular educational or developmental purpose. Sun and sea have featured heavily in modern tourism.

Nonetheless tourism with a cultural motive continues and is believed to be increasing in significance almost as an inevitable next stage in the progress of tourism. There are, however, problems in determining developments because of confusion surrounding the term 'cultural tourism'. It is applied to a variety of tourism trips and not always consistently and, in particular, it is used to cover visits to a diverse range of venues including museums, art galleries and theatres and, occasionally, other less obviously related venues. It is, in addition, applied to such visits regardless of why the tourist is there in the first place and whether as a result of a deliberate decision or by chance. It would be more meaningful to focus on a particular aspect of culture, such as theatre, rather than deal with all as a single entity.

From a focus on the performing arts (including entertainment) it is suggested that people who are in audiences whilst tourists may be there for one of two reasons. They may have a particular interest in arts and entertainment and are there solely because of them. These people are termed 'arts-core'. Others may be in audiences as a result of being in a place for some other reason. They may visit a town for business reasons or for a holiday primarily for sun and sea or for heritage. Theatre is not the sole or main reason for being in that town or city but it features as part of the tourist visit. These people are termed 'arts-peripheral'.

The tourists may be further classified according to whether or not the trip is considered to be a holiday but whether this is so is something that only the individual tourist can decide. Both arts-core and arts-peripheral tourists may be on a trip that is classified by them as a holiday. Equally both can be on a trip that is non-holiday. The arts-core tourist may travel and stay in order to see a play or concert and not consider the trip to be a holiday and the arts-peripheral tourist may be visiting friends or relatives or on business.

There are a few studies that suggest the existence of tourists whose trips are the outcome of a desire solely or mainly to see and visit cultural attractions, though not particularly the performing arts. These culture-core tourists are considered to be a relatively small number of all culture-related tourists. Most tourists at cultural attractions are likely to be culture-peripheral. The terms cultural tourist or arts tourist are probably best reserved only for culture-core or arts-core.

In explaining the apparent interest by tourists in culture, higher incomes and increased leisure time enabling more people to go on holiday and others to go on more holidays are frequently referred to. The interest is also explained by other factors. The pace of change in modern society with the consequent dislocation of identity has led to a desire for more 'meaningful' leisure activities. There is a reaction against the less-involved sun and sea holiday. In addition, there is a continuing search for new experiences, spurred by the consumerist society. The developments are associated too with the growth of the service or middle classes and the reduced significance of manual or working classes. The tradition of seaside holidays perhaps meant more to working class and manual workers as an identity-reinforcing activity and as divisions in society have become less distinct this form of holiday has become less meaningful and desirable. The purchase of culture-related or arts-related holidays may be especially meaningful for the service classes as such holidays indicate particular status and they differentiate the service classes from others. They have the education and background, which others do not, that suggests they would wish to experience such holidays. Increasing levels of education and of access and exposure to the arts and heritage are likely to have contributed to the demand. Finally museums, heritage centres and theatres have been actively encouraging visits by non-locals in the search for new markets. A similar strategy has been adopted by cities anxious to find means of regenerating their economies.

These explanations would appear to relate more to a tourist interest in heritage than in the arts though they do help explain interest in the latter as well. There are nonetheless a number of reasons for believing that heritage may be the more popular attraction.

5

The arts-related tourism product

Introduction

In the previous chapter the nature of arts-related tourism was discussed and a framework was developed to explain why there might be tourists in audiences: the demand. In this chapter the focus is shifted towards the supply: what is on offer to these tourists and what might attract them. The discussion in the previous chapter pointed out how there have been shifts in holiday-making so that there has apparently been an increased interest in culture-related and arts-related tourism. Despite this, most tourism remains sun and sea based and holiday-makers seek diversion on holiday. There is discussion of seaside resorts in this chapter as these, in the past, have been the most obvious and important places to offer entertainment to tourists – usually as arts-peripheral tourists. They continue to be the places (both domestic and international) to which most people go on holiday though the popularity of particular places, states and countries has changed. Arts and entertainment elsewhere, such as in cities, have been less aimed at tourists though this is now changing.

The chapter includes:

- a classification of arts and entertainment according to how far they aim at tourists and how far they are successful in attracting them;
- entertainment associated with holidays in the past and how that influence lingers; this extends the historical discussion in Chapter 4;
- a consideration of the current holiday entertainment situation especially with respect to seaside holidays;
- an examination of the importance of local government in holiday-related entertainment;
- arts festivals as recent developments with significance for tourism.

Classification of products

There is no particular form of the arts or entertainment that is specific to tourism and it is difficult to identify what will and what will not have an appeal to tourists, whether arts-core or arts-peripheral. The seaside variety show is, however, often thought of as being a typical holiday tourist form of entertainment. This includes a range of different acts such as dancers, magicians, 'comics, singers, sand-dancers, conjurors and men who balanced girls in swimsuits on their noses' (Hudson, 1992: 55) and is 'light' and undemanding. Even this, though, has not been confined to the seaside and derives from the music-halls of the late nineteenth and early twentieth century cities. Much has been made of the decline of this form of seaside entertainment but it is still a common feature of many seaside holiday towns especially in Britain (see later this chapter). Nonetheless any arts performance in any location may have tourists in the audience. Two simple reasons for tourists being in audiences were identified in Chapter 4. They were a decision to travel to see a production (arts-core) and as part of some other experience such as a sun and sand trip or business trip (arts-peripheral).

From the production side, events can be classified according to whether or not they set out to attract such tourists – their orientation – and according to their likely success in attracting tourists – their drawing power. These two aspects are shown in Figure 5.1.

Tourist orientation may be:

(a) **strong:** in seaside towns, shows (such as variety shows) will be deliberately designed for a tourist audience that is already in a destination. A wide range of productions, and not just the variety show, may however appeal to holiday-makers and a strong tourist orientation is not confined

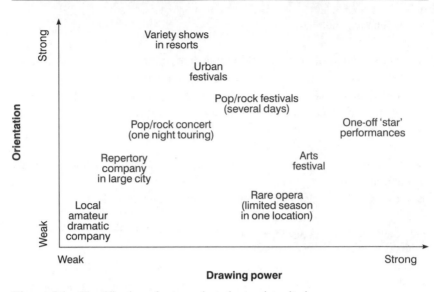

Figure 5.1   Classification of arts products by tourist criteria

to seaside towns. The theatrical scene of long-playing musicals and classic plays in London's West End and New York's Broadway is partly due to a strong tourist presence. Some productions may be established in areas that are not usually associated with tourism in order, partly at least, to encourage tourism. This may be particularly true in the case of old industrial cities that hold festivals.

A strong tourist orientation may exist too in the sense of arts managers wishing to widen catchment areas. Productions may be mounted that will appeal to a wide geographical audience without the concept of tourism as such entering into the consideration (see Chapter 6).

(b) **weak:** a production may be completely artistically-driven rather than established as a tourist attraction. A company may wish to produce a rarely performed opera simply because it has not been performed before. A company in a large city may also have little concern to satisfy a tourist audience as the size of the local population is such as to provide adequate audiences and revenue. Part of the mission statement of many is the desire to serve the local population. Community arts groups, by definition, will have little interest in tourism.

Is there a link between the 'reasons' for tourists being in an audience (Chapter 4) and tourist orientation? Productions with a strong tourist orientation are also likely to be those that audiences choose to see as part of the arts-peripheral holiday experience. The assignment of type of tourist to type of production is not, though, quite that simple. Some of the strong tourist-oriented productions in holiday areas may be unique and provide the only opportunity for certain performers or productions to be seen and thus some in the audience may have needed to travel if they wish to see them (arts-core). Other productions with a strong tourist orientation may be aimed at 'distant' markets rather than at holiday-makers and attract non-holiday-makers (arts-core, non-holiday).

In some cases there may be a change in orientation. Some of the productions in the weak orientation category may, in fact, need or desire to attract audiences from a widespread catchment area and in this sense they come to have a tourist orientation. An arts festival may be established in order to provide an opportunity for local plays and music to be performed and to encourage all forms of local community participation. Over time, there may be financial pressures that drive the organizers to look to a wider audience. This however was not their initial rationale, unlike entertainment in seaside resorts. Regardless of orientation – i.e. their initial rationale – the influence on tourism could be quite significant in practice in either case. Some will be more successful than others in drawing tourists (see Figure 5.1):

Tourist drawing-power may be:

(a) **weak:** it is quite possible that productions with a strong orientation may, in fact, have limited drawing power in isolation. The significance of entertainment amongst all of the many attractions of a seaside resort or any other holiday destination may be limited even though it is aimed at a tourist audience.

(b) **strong:** some productions will have a tourist appeal because of their uniqueness and limited availability and people have to travel in order to see them. Those productions and events to which no idea of tourism was attached when they were conceived (i.e. weak tourist orientation) may, in reality, attract a widespread audience and tourists.

The case where the arts or entertainment are of less importance than some other attraction may represent many coastal towns to which tourists are primarily attracted by sun and sea or, in the case of urban destinations, by heritage. It is difficult to be certain about what attracts tourists to many holiday destinations but it is likely that arts and entertainment are secondary considerations in most cases: arts-peripheral (see Chapters 6 and 7 for further discussion of this). The arts and entertainment are, however, a major or sole reason for travelling for some tourists and in these cases they are therefore 'primary' tourist attractions. This may be so in, for instance, London or New

York where some tourists are motivated solely or largely to see a play or concert despite the attractions of the city being many and diverse: arts core. Categories of production are not so easily identifiable or separately classified in practice. Any classification of the arts by tourist orientation and drawing power and allocation of type of tourist to each will therefore be arbitrary.

Elements of the product

Any play, show, concert, festival etc. that has the potential to attract audiences from a geographical area that is non-local (arts-core or arts-peripheral) is an element of the arts-related tourism product (see Table 5.1). Some may be more likely than others to attract non-local audiences but all have the potential to do so.

Table 5.1   Types of arts-related tourism product

- Plays, shows, concerts
- Arts festivals
- One-off performances and tours by 'stars'
- Buildings: theatres, concert halls, arenas
- In-hotel entertainment + bar and club entertainment
- Arts and entertainment-holidays (hotels, cruises)
- Related: entertainment in museums and heritage centres, theme parks; historical re-enactments
- Associated: entertainment on streets and in shopping malls

- 'Holiday shows' in seaside resorts will have a high proportion of visitors in the audiences. This includes shows in foreign countries deliberately aimed at holiday-makers or tourists, such as flamenco shows and mediaeval banquets in many coastal parts in Spain.
- Festivals that include a number of events and performers over a short period of time may be particularly successful in attracting such audiences.
- The occasional one-off concert by a star will have the same effect.
- Tours by pop and rock stars and groups to a limited number of towns and cities.
- Open air summer concerts and plays in Central Park, New York: they may not be decisive factors in drawing visitors to the city but there will nonetheless be a sizable proportion of visitors in the audiences.

- Concerts and productions in holiday areas: such as the summer programme at Saratoga Springs (New York State) which, in 1999, included the New York City Ballet and the Philadelphia Orchestra.

Buildings themselves (theatres, arenas and concert halls) can also be tourist attractions in their own right. Tours around theatres and of back-stage areas in particular can be very popular. This appears to be especially the case for new, distinctive or particularly famous buildings. London's Theatre Royal, Drury Lane (dating from 1663) advertises hour-long behind-the-scenes tours led by professional actors. The significance of many theatres is reflected in the fact that they have been identified as having particular architectural or historical importance.

- The recently opened (1997) **Shakespeare's Globe** theatre in London, reconstructed as it is believed to have been in Shakespeare's time, is itself a tourist attraction separate from the plays that are performed there.
- The **De la Warr Pavilion** in the small seaside resort of Bexhill-on-Sea (Sussex) is considered to be of great significance in the development of British Modernism architecture (Foster, 1999). This was built 1933–35 and includes a 1000 seat theatre.
- Some modern theatres would appear to be equally significant: the new 500 seat theatre in the seaside resort of **Ilfracombe, Devon**, (opened 1998) is housed in one of two white-brick cones.

Theatres and opera houses frequently feature in tourist guide books as buildings to see:

- **Vienna's State Opera House:** visitors are advised in the *Michelin Guide to Vienna* (1997) to 'admire the fine neo-Renaissance facade' of this 2200 seat theatre, originally constructed in 1869 (re-constructed 1956). Tours of the interior are also available.
- **Lincoln Center for the Performing Arts, New York**, which is home to American Ballet Theatre, Metropolitan Opera, New York City Opera, New York Philharmonic, etc. The Center, built in the 1960s, is, according to the *Insight Guide to New York* (1996), somewhere that 'even visitors with no interest in classical music should visit . . . especially at night'.
- **The Gran Teatre del Liceu (Barcelona):** the largest opera house in Spain (built in 1844) was burnt down in 1994 and prior to that had, according to the *AA Baedeker Guide to Barcelona* (1998), a 'plain facade' but 'magnificent auditorium'. A page of the Guide is devoted to this theatre and includes the observation that even the absence of the building is an

attraction! The building re-opened in 1999 but the re-building programme itself attracted many visitors.

■ **Sydney Opera House, Australia:** this building is widely recognized and has become a signifier of Australia as a whole as well as of the city. It is described in the AA guide *Essential Australia* (1998) as 'an architectural masterpiece; . . . one of the world's most distinctive and unusual buildings'. There are guided tours around the building.

In addition, entertainment is often provided in hotels for many reasons (see Chapter 7) and is a further element of the product. A very large proportion of holiday entertainment may now be experienced in hotels, clubs and bars. Other holiday entertainment in many seaside resorts includes outdoor 'band' concerts and children's beach entertainers.

Entertainment may also feature as an element of other tourist resources such as theme parks, museums and heritage centres. These, such as Wigan Pier (Lancashire) and the North of England Open Air Museum at Beamish (County Durham) often include 'animated experiences'. They are provided by staff dressed in period costume and also by costumed staff participating with customers in 'mock' school or eating situations, for instance, that reproduce those of the historical period concerned. Colonial Williamsburg (Virginia, USA) is one of the earliest examples of this. It is made up of over a hundred original eighteenth and early nineteenth century buildings and has operated as a 'living museum' since 1932. Costumed historical interpreters re-enact and explain this period of US history.

Arts and entertainment are essential parts of many other 'tourist' products such as sports events (including the Olympic Games), conferences and trade exhibitions. They are not the main focus of the event but they are often considered to be valuable and necessary additions to the main activity.

Enactments of historical events such as battles are now quite common and, although not usually staged as tourist attractions, they may have that effect. The 'Grand Encampment' at the Fortress of Louisbourg, Cape Breton Island, Nova Scotia attracts over 1500 participants. The Fortress is a reconstruction (North America's largest) of an eighteenth century community and includes costumed 'actors' as part of the everyday scene of residents and soldiers. This is bolstered by the Grand Encampment, which includes volunteers from all over North America re-enacting ceremonies, parades and battles.

'On-street' entertainers similarly do not always have a tourist-attracting purpose but contribute to the animation of an area, especially in shopping centres and malls. This is not, of course, confined to tourist areas. Perhaps the most well-known in the UK are the entertainers at London's Covent Garden. This old market area in the centre of London, adjoining the Royal Opera House, has been transformed into a tourist zone of specialist shops and market stalls, cafes and restaurants and is regularly animated by fire-eaters, jugglers, living statues and the like.

Entertainment and early tourism

Travel before the twentieth century was largely done out of necessity, for trade, war, government, worship, etc. rather than for the 'non-instrumental', pleasure purposes of today. Some of these early journeys were however associated with the arts. Religious festivals in ancient Greece drew a large number of travellers. In addition to sacrifice and prayer, the festivals included athletics 'games' as part of the dedications to the gods (Casson, 1974). The most significant was probably the Olympic Games, held in honour of the god Zeus, at which spectators could also listen to readings and view works of art. The annual festival in honour of Dionysius was largely music-based and literature-based and with no athletics at all. Drama became increasingly important and theatre as such may well be considered to have started here. These larger festivals attracted audiences from outside the local area.

Even where the object of the trip was not to experience the arts, most tourism since its earliest days has been characterized, incidentally, by entertainment as a distraction along the route or at the destination itself (Feifer, 1985). For instance, pilgrims to the 'Holy Land' (from the thirteenth century onwards) would be entertained at inns by travelling performers who sang or recited. Those who went on the later Grand Tours (sixteenth through to the nineteenth centuries) found many diversions from their serious purpose, both en route and at their destinations. Theatres and concert halls in Italy and in Paris, for instance, were popular with tourists. Some Grand Tour journeys were planned so as to coincide with festivals and events of various sorts including religious festivals in Rome and carnival in Venice. For nineteenth century Grand Tour visitors to Paris, the Louvre was a major attraction but during evenings there was an active social life including literary salons and visits to the theatre as well as public promenading and display in pleasure gardens, boulevards and the 'new' restaurants (Withey, 1998).

Tourism in the early resorts, the inland spas such as Bath and Tunbridge in the UK and Saratoga Springs and White Sulphur Springs in the USA, existed under the pretext of the health cure. Bathing in and drinking spa water were believed to cure a great many ills. In reality, especially in the eighteenth century, there was considerable social activity based on coffee houses, gaming, theatre, etc. which was likely to have been a major attraction. 'Most successful spas served pleasure as well as health needs' (Towner, 1996: 54). The prime function of spas was to cater for leisure of their upper class clientele.

This social life was later copied in the seaside resorts that developed during the nineteenth century. These resorts had also developed as centres for health cures except that now it was sea water that was considered to have the curative qualities. The resorts initially differed little from the inland spas and facilities and activities mirrored those of the spas. Brighton, for instance modelled itself closely on Tunbridge. They included Assembly Rooms and a promenade for display and socializing. 'From the beginning the seaside, like the spas, catered for seekers after pleasure, recreation, novelty and status as well as votaries of health and rest' (Walton, 1983a: 156). The nature of the seaside resort has altered over time with, very broadly, their main customers shifting from being predominantly the wealthier classes in the early years through to a mainly working class clientele in the mid twentieth century. Each resort however has its own distinct nature. Some have an image of older and middle class holiday-makers whilst others are associated with a more working class holiday-maker. As a consequence, the entertainment in each has differed and still does differ but nonetheless most were characterized by a unique amount of entertainment (and other leisure activities). The facilities were not too different from those available in home towns but resorts were towns that specialized in opportunities for pleasure, and they were in locations free from the grime and congestion of industrial towns and free of the overtones of work.

Significance of the entertainment

What was established during the late nineteenth and early twentieth centuries persisted through until seaside resorts began to lose tourists in the latter part of the twentieth century (see Chapter 3). Holiday-makers in the 1920s and 1930s through to the early 1950s would find the same range of entertainment on offer with little change. The variety show, which developed from the concert party show, remained ever popular. Live entertainment remained a feature of the seaside resort in most countries right through to the early 1960s. During the 1950s and 1960s the 'traditional' forms of seaside entertainment began to wane as a result of many influences including television and pop music. Since this time, resorts have had to re-think their entertainment strategies (see later this chapter). The significance of this entertainment has been considerable:

- Much of the entertainment in seaside resorts is likely to have been 'incidental' since it would not have been the main reason for going on holiday. Audiences would be arts-peripheral. On the other hand, its significance could have been considerable in so far as it appeared to constitute a major form of diversion during the holiday. 'Throughout the period . . . the quality of a resort's range of commercial entertainment was an important competitive weapon' (Walton, 1983a: 157). Even in Monte Carlo, a place so obviously geared to the one function of gambling, it was necessary that developers should build 'superb hotels and sumptuous restaurants. They organised princely entertainments for which Europe's finest artists were engaged' (Pimlott, 1947: 200).
- From a different perspective, the seaside resort has been a key component of the arts and entertainment. An indirect assessment of the significance may be derived from the fact that, for instance, in the early 1980s professional theatres in English seaside resorts accounted for 40 per cent of theatre capacity in England outside London (ETB, 1982). Ominously, however, twelve of the eighteen theatres in England that closed between 1975 and 1982 were at the seaside, as were only five of the forty that opened.
- Regardless of any altered expectations that tourists now have of holiday entertainment, many resorts are left with a legacy of theatres and halls built with a very different market in mind. Many of the theatre and concert hall buildings were built in the early part of the twentieth century. They may well have an attraction in themselves as being particularly appealing in their design, structure and decor but the facilities are not always appropriate to meet the expectations of present-day audiences. The age of many of these buildings has also presented problems in terms of maintenance, heating and air conditioning as well as technical problems in stage production.

Entertainment and seaside resorts' decline

It is believed that there has been a decline in seaside entertainment since the 1960s. In England, for instance, a tourist board study of seaside entertainment reported in 1984 that the traditional summer show (large star-centred and theatre-based) was disappearing. In nineteen coastal tourist towns surveyed, the number of summer shows had fallen from 30 in 1974 to 21 in 1983 (English Tourist Board, 1984).

The decline in seaside entertainment has been associated with a general decline of the seaside resort in the UK as a long-stay destination (see Chapters 3 and 4). There has been a similar decline in other countries, which has been associated with shifts in holiday destinations. As 'old' coastal destinations have declined in popularity so too has the provision of entertainment. In the case of the UK and several other European countries this affected the country as a whole as the old destinations were domestic but the new ones were in foreign countries. In other places such as USA the shifts have been internal. As some resorts have declined so, inevitably, has the audience for seaside entertainment (see Figure 5.2). Entertainment is provided in new resorts and destinations but even here there has been a change in the type, quantity and quality of the product.

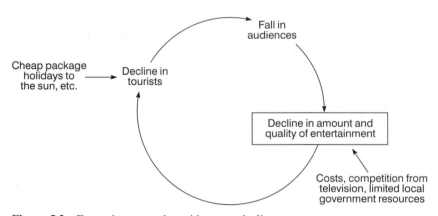

Figure 5.2   Entertainment and seaside resort decline

In the resorts the entertainment product declined for many reasons (see Figure 5.2):

- a fall in staying visitors resulting in falling audiences;
- falling audiences led to reduced income from which the product and the theatres could have been upgraded;
- theatre (and cinema) generally have experienced the effects of direct competition from television since the 1960s so that people stay in for their entertainment rather than go out. To some extent this has happened in resorts in the same way as it has at home, though live entertainment and 'going-out' are unlikely to have been replaced entirely by television as a holiday experience;

- the influence of television has been more indirect though considerable. Holiday-makers often expect to see shows performed by 'stars' with whom they are familiar from television. The fees required by such stars for appearing in summer shows are, however, considered to be excessively high. Performers who previously would be willing to commit themselves to a full summer season may be less willing to do so now because of opportunities elsewhere. At one time the summer season was a major source of employment and income for many performers. Television has also altered the public's expectations of entertainment and encouraged them to expect 'quality', professionalism and technologically-based productions;
- costs of providing the traditional spectacular show have risen greatly;
- local governments have had a considerable role to play in the summer show but have experienced overall financial difficulties. As a result, they have been unable to finance the type and quality of show that holiday-makers now expect and have been unable to contribute to the renovation of old theatre buildings;
- all this has been combined with a certain degree of inertia and reluctance to change. The nostalgia for the traditional show amongst many policy-makers has inhibited their willingness to adapt the product to new tastes.

As well as the decline of resorts leading to the decline in entertainment, it is possible that there has been a reverse effect. The change in entertainment has itself contributed to the decline of holiday destinations (Figure 5.2). Resorts no longer provide 'spectacle' and the 'extraordinary' and it is this that might have contributed to their decline. Resorts were, at one time, unique, distinct places where entertainment and pleasure were concentrated (Urry, 1990). This is no longer the case as cities have developed as places of leisure consumption rather than of production. In addition, the development of theme parks and of home-based entertainment through television, video and computers have reduced the attractiveness of resorts as places for leisure. In the past, the distinctiveness of resorts lay in being the places of leisure and pleasure that contrasted with inland towns and cities, which were places of work and production. Live entertainment and shows in seaside theatres and concert halls contributed to that uniqueness.

The outcome has been a continuation of poor quality shows (and theatres) which, in turn, has continued the spiral of decline in terms of failing to capture audiences. At the same time there has been considerable growth in other forms of competing entertainment in resorts such as cabaret and variety-type entertainment in hotels themselves and in clubs and pubs. The overall picture is one of a 'vicious circle: a cumulative effect of fewer visitors causing smaller audiences leading to less income and therefore poorer product and deteriorating theatres which in turn led to smaller audiences and to fewer visitors.

The re-establishment of the special extraordinary nature of the older seaside tourist town is a difficult task but there has been a feeling that restoration of holiday entertainment is important in this. Concern in the 1980s about the continuation of live shows as part of the tourist product led the English Tourist Board to establish a Working Party to identify problems and provide suggestions for the way forward. Their view was that live shows were in decline and facing 'a major crisis' but that 'it is essential for the well-being of the resorts that this expectation (of live entertainment) is fulfilled' (English Tourist Board, 1984: 11).

Current situation

Some form of live entertainment aimed at the holiday-maker does survive however in most seaside holiday towns. There was, for instance, a programme of entertainment offered in 60 out of 69 UK seaside resorts during the 1994 summer season (Hughes and Benn, 1997a). The entertainment took many forms but most common were 'variety shows' and 'children's shows' (see Table 5.2).

A visit to the theatre to see a summer show has been a traditional part of family holidays. This does not however mean that holiday entertainment should not change nor that the holiday show is necessary for the well-being of seaside resorts. It may be that the live show or the theatre-based show are no longer sufficient. Spectacle and the extraordinary are sought in other forms such as funfairs, theme parks, amusement arcades and inter-active virtual reality galleries with their associated technological products. There may, in fact, be only a limited role for the live show or theatre-based show as part of the holiday in the future.

Summer entertainment in resorts is in the process of change, though given the inter-relationships identified earlier (Figure 5.2) it is proving difficult to carry through. The 'traditional' variety show does continue especially in those resorts that cater for the more traditional holiday-maker. It is noticeable however from Table 5.2 how a number of other types of entertainment are offered during the summer season.

Many seaside theatres, concert halls and arts centres are able now to draw upon a wider audience base than previously. Car ownership means the

Table 5.2 Types of live entertainment at seaside resorts in the UK (1994 summer season)

	Per cent of resorts in which performances of each were offered during 1994
Variety shows	64
Childrens' shows	61
Plays	58
Musicals	52
Jazz	45
Folk/country music	44
Classical music concerts	44
Comedy	41
Pop/rock concerts	25
Cabaret	25
Pantomime	23
Opera	23
Circus	17
Ballet	16
Contemporary dance	10

Source: Hughes and Benn, 1997a

catchment area for any one resort theatre is larger and as a consequence many have re-programmed to aim at a target audience that is not specifically holiday-makers. Being in relatively isolated locations (at least not in large urban conurbations), resorts provide the only theatre or concert hall within a considerable radius and thus they can act as centres for the surrounding populations. Seasons of classical music, drama and musicals are as much aimed at a 'local' audience (including day-visitors) as at staying visitors. In some cases the year's productions are programmed and budgeted largely on the basis of audiences who are non-holiday-makers. Theatres are regarded by management as receiving theatres that happen to be in a resort and programming is planned on the basis that they are year-round venues, with the summer season as a relatively minor consideration.

Local government

Local government has long had a role to play in the provision of the arts and entertainment (see Chapter 2) and in seaside resorts this role has been critical.

The English Tourist Board Working Party (1984) implied that local authorities had an important role to play in ensuring live entertainment was provided in seaside resorts. The 1994 survey referred to earlier in this chapter asked about local government support for entertainment in seaside holiday towns (Hughes and Benn, 1997a). The provision was often a mix of local government and commercial but in just over half the towns with any theatres or concert halls (33 out of 60) it was only local government that provided such facilities. Commercial provision as the only form occurred in only in a small number of seaside towns (8 out of 60). Local government was itself directly responsible for planning the entertainment programme in some theatres and concert halls. This was the case in two-thirds of seaside towns with some live entertainment.

Local government support for arts and entertainment is not a requirement. In the UK it remains discretionary and is usually a net cost. Throughout the country, income was only about 50% of current expenditure on performance venues during the 1980s (Audit Commission, 1991). The Audit Commission (1991) reported that 'on average only 32% of seats in resort theatres owned and managed by local authorities are sold' (p.20). Most seaside holiday towns subsidize both promotions and the fixed costs of venues. The link between entertainment and tourism has long been recognized by seaside local governments and they have felt justified in using public finances to support arts and entertainment in this link (see Chapter 2).

In the nineteenth and early part of the twentieth centuries, for many towns and cities it was often a matter of civic pride for local government to provide theatres or encourage the arts for the benefit of local residents. In nineteenth century British seaside towns, however, the motive of local government was usually more related to generating tourists for the resort and was thus more commercially oriented than that in cities. Entertainment was considered necessary to attract visitors and therefore local governments either provided it directly or encouraged others to provide it as an investment rather than solely as a service for local residents (see Roberts, 1983 and Walton, 1983b for discussion of Bournemouth and Blackpool respectively). The resort towns were in the forefront of seeking parliamentary permission to provide entertainment prior to legislation that granted a universal but limited right to provide. This was itself the result of pressure from tourist local governments (Hodson, 1986).

The tourism dimension has therefore always featured strongly in the arts or cultural policies of local governments at seaside towns. More recently the governments of inland urban areas and cities in particular, have also encouraged cultural policies with a tourism angle. This development in many cities has been, in part, a response to economic decline. Tourism and cultural policies have both been regarded as means of regenerating cities and the tourism potential of the arts and entertainment has been recognized as having particular significance (see Chapter 8).

Festivals

Tourism has been a consideration, at least in part, in the formation and early development of a number of arts festivals. The term 'festival' is applied to many activities but essentially festivals are 'special events' where there is a particular concentration of activities over a short period of time. This is most often over a weekend but also, in the case of larger festivals, over several weeks. They are often regular in that they occur every year though some are less frequent. Festivals take many forms, including rock, pop, folk and world music festivals such as Glastonbury, Reading/Leeds, WOMAD and Guildford. It was estimated that there were about 520 festivals with an arts focus in the UK in 1991–92 (Rolfe, 1992). Many of these include a range of arts such as music, plays and film but most are concerned with a single art form. A fifth of UK arts festivals in 1991 were 'folk music' festivals and others focused on jazz, classical music or opera, etc. Because of their short-term nature, most festival organizations rely heavily on unpaid volunteers for their functioning.

The nature and size of festivals ranges greatly. The Notting Hill Carnival, an annual two-day event in London, attracts between 1 million and 2 million spectators (Smith and Jenner, 1998). Audiences at the 1996 Edinburgh International Festival numbered 400,000 with a further 900,000 at the Festival Fringe (Jones Economics, 1996). The 1996 Adelaide Arts Festival (South Australia) had a total attendance of 700,000 (Smith and Jenner, 1998). The majority of festivals however operate on a much smaller scale with, for instance, over 60 per cent of arts festivals in the UK having ticket sales of less than 5000 (Rolfe, 1992). Half of all festivals include non-arts activities such as talks and social and recreational activities and 70 per cent occur during the May–August period, the conventional tourist period. A very large number are located in rural or coastal parts of the country (rather than inland cities) and in areas that are already attractive to tourists because of heritage or natural scenery.

Aims

Even though there some long established festivals such as the Three Choirs (1713) the majority have appeared since the 1960s. Arts festivals have been established for many different reasons including (see Figure 5.3):

- 'artistic vision' reasons include a desire to 'celebrate' and to promote awareness and increase understanding of a particular art form or culture. This may be especially so when opportunities for performances are otherwise limited;
- to enable arts attendance by local residents in small towns or rural areas where there are few other opportunities;
- the drive to establish a festival may come from enthusiasts across the country wishing to come together to share a common interest;
- for many of the more recently developed festivals the tourism potential has been an important consideration. Two festivals in Ireland, for instance, the Temple Bar Blues Festival (Dublin) and the Clifden Country Blues Festival (Galway), were established with a view to attracting visitors to their respective locations. In both cases 'music . . . is simply packaged into the most tourist-friendly product possible' (Quinn, 1996: 392).

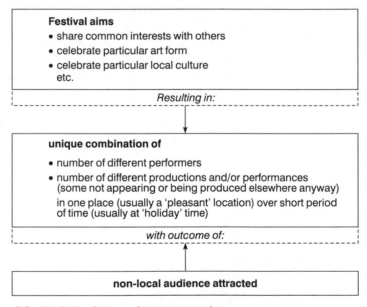

Figure 5.3   Festivals: features that attract tourists

As with the arts and entertainment generally, many festivals receive financial support from local government and would be unlikely to exist without it (Rolfe, 1992). This once more reflects the views of local government about the role of the arts generally but also specifically in tourist areas. The object may be:

- to provide opportunities, that would otherwise not be available, for locals to attend arts events;
- to improve locals' access to the arts;
- to encourage community coherence through participation;
- to foster a community spirit and the 'feel-good' factor;
- to develop residents' pride in the town or city;
- to increase awareness of the town or city outside;
- to improve its image outside.

These two latter 'external' objectives are associated partly with tourism. Awareness and improved image will attract tourists not just for the festival itself but at other times also. The awareness and image factors are also, however, aimed at making a town or city attractive enough to encourage businesses to locate there and people to live and work there. These issues have been of particular importance to cities that have been anxious to develop strategies for economic regeneration: to find solutions to unemployment and low incomes and their related social problems (social deprivation, physical environment, crime, housing, etc.). Although many cities now host annual festivals of varying degrees of significance, some of the more significant have been one-off festivals such as Glasgow's designation, by the European Union, as European City of Culture for 1990. Unlike most other such cities Glasgow decided to hold a large number of events over the entire year. For the year 2000, the European Union designated nine 'Cities of Culture' as representing the rich diversity of culture of Europe. The nine were Reykjavik (Iceland), Bergen (Norway), Helsinki (Finland), Brussels (Belgium), Krakow (Poland), Prague (Czech Republic), Avignon (France), Bologna (Italy) and Santiago de Compostela (Spain).

Tourist appeal

Not all festivals have a tourism dimension and some are anxious to preserve a more community-based focus. For many festivals however, attracting tourists has often become a consideration even though it was not an initial one. By their very nature arts festivals are usually short-term, 'special' events offering unique opportunities to see and hear performances, activities and performers under exceptional circumstances. This critical mass is the essence of a festival:

- a relatively large number of artists and performances,
- together in one place,
- over a concentrated period of time.

For the 1999 Glastonbury Festival, bands such as Manic Street Preachers, REM, Fun Loving Criminals, Beautiful South, Super Furry Animals as well as Lenny Kravitz, Ian Dury, Fat Boy Slim and Courtney Pine and many others were brought together over three days. Reykjavik's year as City of Culture (2000) includes Bjork, the San Francisco Ballet, 'Icelandic Music in the Twentieth Century' and a jazz festival.

In addition to such distinctive combinations of artists and events on the one hand and place and time on the other:

- for certain performances (or artists), festivals may be the only occasion when they are seen or heard;
- the particular rationale of some festivals may be to introduce music or plays that are not commonly heard or seen and may appeal only to a limited local audience, e.g. contemporary music. By placing them in a festival concept (such as the annual Huddersfield Festival of Contemporary Music in Yorkshire) they may succeed in appealing to an audience from further afield and make their production more viable. The Brighton Festival (Sussex) also has a philosophy of introducing new artists and works;
- major artists, orchestras or companies may not be seen in small towns or rural areas because they cannot generate the audiences. Holding festivals in such locations may expand the potential audience (and local residents benefit).

Festivals are therefore likely to raise more awareness than an on-going arts or entertainment programme in a theatre, arena or concert hall and they come to the notice of a widespread number of people. Festivals can exert considerable drawing power and attract large numbers of non-locals to the audiences (Figure 5.3). They are then frequently actively promoted as tourist attractions if not by the festival management then by others such as local tourist boards.

Levin (a well known author, playwright and critic), in his descriptive and anecdotal consideration of festivals, inextricably linked festivals and tourism. He considered that most festival towns are in places pleasant enough to visit any time and are of a size small enough to be dominated at festival time by the festival. Apart from the attractions of the location, he saw festivals as having a special attraction for tourists because of the holiday atmosphere generated. 'How much sweeter music sounds at the end of a day of walking, bathing, sunning, sipping, than of a day of working! Music, of course, *is* a holiday in one crucial sense: a holiday from the mind' (Levin, 1981: 14).

Pre World War II, the Salzburg Festival (Austria) was actively promoted to foreign visitors and has continued to be so ever since. In the 1920s and 1930s

American and European tourist agencies were encouraged to prepare Festival packages and special arrangements were made by the Austrian government to ensure foreign visitors obtained visas. As early as the 1920s there were complaints about the artistic integrity of the Festival being sacrificed for the purposes of attracting tourists (Gallup, 1987). The founders of the Edinburgh Festival, 1947, desired to establish 'a centre of world resort for lovers of music, drama, opera, ballet and the graphic arts' (quoted in Bruce, 1975). This was not a strategy to encourage tourism as such but was a deliberate attempt to reinstate civilized values and foster understanding and peace through the arts in the aftermath of the Second World War. The appeal was to be, therefore, to the widest possible audience. Cheltenham was the first of the post-Second World War festivals to emerge in the UK (1945), though with less grand ambitions than Edinburgh. It too was intended as a festival that would bring in visitors from all over Britain, if not from abroad, to listen to English music in a holiday environment and atmosphere (Howes, 1965).

Pros and cons of festival tourism

If a festival does succeed in attracting non-local audiences it is usually considered favourably:

■ Audience spending by tourists is a net injection into an area (Figure 5.4). Most spending by locals on tickets and associated services adds nothing and may only be diverted from spending on other local goods and services. It is a re-circulation of local money unless it can be shown that the locals would have spent that money outside the area (see Chapters 6 and 8).
■ The festival may also create good publicity and create a good image for the area – with two possible effects (see Figure 5.4):
   – tourists at non-festival times;
   – encouragement of other non-related businesses to locate in the area (inward investment).

There are, however, a number of potential problems associated with festival tourism:

■ Not all festival tourists are an 'addition' to an area. Some visitors may have visited anyway (their expenditure is 'deadweight') and others may have brought forward their visit (time-switching) (see Figure 5.4). The festival has brought no real benefit here.
■ Some regular visitors to the area may have been put off coming by the event and the festival tourists are therefore only replacing them, with little or no addition to overall numbers.

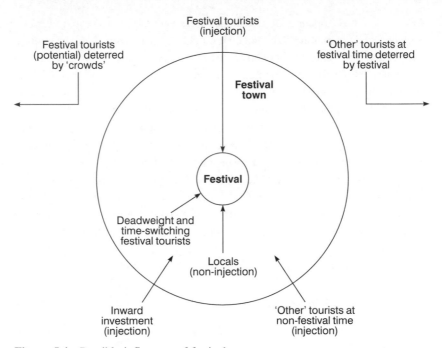

Figure 5.4   Possible influences of festivals

- Tourism during festivals may sometimes be less than anticipated, partly because of people's beliefs that it would be over-crowded or that they would be unable to obtain tickets or book accommodation. The very popularity of a festival may be counter-productive.

By their nature the impact of festivals would seem to be short-lived. As a result there are issues relating to the productions and to the influx of visitors. There may be performance spaces available for a festival as many theatres will be 'dark' during summer months and may welcome the extra business. The use of existing venues appears logical but they do not always exist or they are inadequate. Some festivals may therefore require additional venues if performances are to occur:

- The building of new venues for short-term events such as festivals could only be justified if long-term use could be assured. The restoration of a theatre, such as the Opera House at Buxton (Derbyshire), with a view to it being the focus of a festival has led to problems relating to its long-term future and use at other times. Nonetheless in that particular case, the Buxton Arts Festival can claim some credit for initiating the restoration of this 1903 Matcham theatre prior to the first festival in 1979. This has enabled local residents to have access to a local receiving theatre ever since.

■ No-one will develop additional performance capacity simply to cope with a short-term increase in demand and a problem may remain if capacity does not exist:

Festivals frequently use existing unconventional buildings such as stately homes, churches, museums, art galleries, market halls and assembly rooms as performance spaces or they resort to temporary buildings including marquees. Performances of Gilbert and Sullivan's 'Trial by Jury' were held in Bow Street Magistrate's Court during the 1999 ROC Covent Garden Festival in London.

Open-air performances are common especially in the grounds of stately homes and as such require only temporary performance and audience facilities. In many cases, audiences are required to bring their own seating (or not as they wish).

Street performances obviously reduce the need for venues. Some festivals are entirely street based.

Similarly there needs to be sufficient accommodation (and other associated tourist facilities) for any extra tourists. Problems with accommodation are often alleviated by relying on hotels in nearby towns and villages, by recommending guest houses in addition to hotels and by encouraging local residents to host visitors in the residents' own homes.

Nonetheless for most festivals, audiences are primarily local or regional and are not drawn from a wide catchment area. This is the case for even the largest festivals. Jazz and folk festivals in the UK are those most likely to have non-local audiences (Rolfe, 1992). For further consideration of festival audiences and drawing-power see Chapter 6. For a view on the wider issues of the impact of festivals see Chapter 8.

Chapter summary

It is obvious that there is no one particular type of tourist arts or entertainment as such. Any play, show or concert may have tourists in the audience. Some managements will however have set out to attract such an audience and others will have aimed at largely local audiences. Whatever the aim, the 'success' in actually attracting tourists may vary greatly. Some productions and events may be produced for reasons quite unconnected with tourism but may experience high proportions in their audiences. An instance of this is the production of a rarely-performed play, a decision which might have been made because it is felt that it has been a unjustifiably neglected piece and deserves public exposure. Similarly a 'star' artist or pop group may give only limited public performances. The desire to see these may be such as to attract audiences from considerable distances.

Experience from the past suggests that most holiday-makers have always wanted some form of entertainment. The most noticeable instance is that of the holiday-maker at the seaside over the last 150 years, where the entertainment has been light and undemanding. The seaside holiday-maker has, in the past, been reluctant to engage in 'the arts' as conventionally defined and a vast entertainment industry developed to satisfy the demands of such tourists. This endured until the second half of the twentieth century when, with competition from 'new' sun-based resorts, older resorts in Britain, other north European countries and North America declined. Live entertainment itself has experienced many problems not the least of which have been associated with the growth of television in this post-war period. Costs of producing shows have risen as have audience expectations of quality and the performers they want to see.

A 'vicious circle' of fewer visitors leading to reduced audiences leading to less revenue, poorer product and, in turn, to reduced audiences and fewer visitors appears to have been established. Not only has the shift to new destinations caused problems for entertainment, the decline in entertainment may have made the older resorts less attractive. It would be unwise however to blame the decline of, for instance, British holiday-making on poor seaside entertainment as the causes are many.

Despite growing interest in 'culture-tourism' or arts-related tourism, most holiday-makers continue to seek sun and sea. This means that arts or entertainment do not feature as the focus of most tourist trips but that they (and especially entertainment) do feature as secondary or incidental activities. Most tourists who are in audiences in sun and sea destinations will be arts-peripheral.

Entertainment continues to exist in the 'older' seaside resorts and many seaside theatres are 're-inventing' themselves as year-round venues serving a wide catchment area. The summer programme targeted at tourists has become one element of a wider strategy that is primarily designed to develop local (including regional) core audiences. This non-holiday season may well attract arts-core tourists to audiences.

The situation in the UK has not been helped by the difficulties faced by local government. It has been responsible for a great deal of support for the arts and entertainment in seaside resorts to the extent that it really was the critical initiating and supporting influence. Recent financial pressures and a re-think of the role of local government has resulted in a reduction in that support. Any future developments will not be based on the levels of support that were experienced in the past and will have to rely on the commercial sector, either alone or in partnership with local government.

A recent development compared with seaside entertainment is the growth of arts (and rock and pop) festivals. Even though many may not have been established with tourist audiences in mind, their very nature – a range of performers and productions in one place over a short period of time – encourages audiences from a wide catchment area. In addition many are located outside cities in attractive parts of the world. Many cities are however now hosting festivals as part of their regeneration strategies. The impact of festivals is often considered favourably though it must be recognized that the inflow of expenditure associated with tourists may be less than initially believed and there may also be problems to do with ensuring venues for performances.

6

The arts perspective

Introduction

In the previous chapter the product on offer to the tourist or that was likely to appeal to the tourist was examined – the chapter looked at the supply of the product. This chapter, and the next (Chapter 7), continue with this examination of supply. Both the arts and tourism are seeking to attract customers. They may have different objectives and different types of organization and different strategies but their interests and activities overlap in arts-related tourism (see Figure 6.1). In this chapter the product and the arts–tourism relationship are examined from the point-of-view of the arts organizations and arts managers (the left-hand half of Figure 6.1). (In the next chapter, Chapter 7, the point-of-view shifts to the other element of supply – the tourism industry – the right-hand half of Figure 6.1.)

This chapter includes a discussion of:

■ the reasons that arts organizations and managers might have for trying to attract tourists;
■ the ways in which they attempt to attract those tourists;

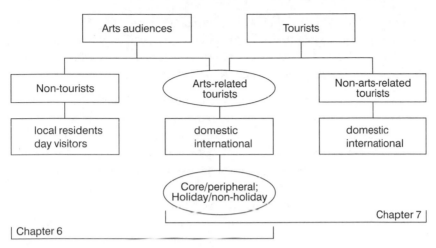

Figure 6.1 The perspective of chapters 6 and 7

- whether or nor there actually are tourists in audiences;
- a comparison of the tourist and the non-tourist in audiences;
- the influence of arts on the decision of tourists to visit a particular place.

Reasons

It is not immediately obvious why any arts organization would want to attract tourists into the audience. Where audiences are from and whether or not they are on holiday is, in many ways, of no concern as long as the artistic and financial objectives of the theatre are being met (Leader-Elliott, 1996). If productions are playing to capacity houses and the organization's income at least matches its expenditure then little else may be of interest. It may be of interest and use for arts managers to know where their audiences come from in order to focus marketing activity but the fact that some are tourists may be of little direct interest. (It is of more obvious significance for tourist bodies.)

There may, though, be a desire to extend the catchment area for audiences. The tourist market may be one of several they choose to explore and exploit in order to catch the more 'distant' market. The live performing arts are, like most services, only consumable at the point of production and the consumer needs to travel to the theatre or concert hall in order to consume the product. Each theatre has a geographical threshold (see Figure 6.2) from within which most of their audience comes. The threshold marks the distance beyond which the willingness to travel drops rapidly. For most audiences a visit to the theatre is 'a night out' and is similar to many other forms of localized leisure including eating-out, clubbing and drinking. Even the West End and Broadway have sizable 'local' audience cores: respectively, 70 per cent from London and South East England (MORI, 1998) and 54 per cent from New York city and suburbs (Hauser and Roth, 1998).

For people outside the threshold, any perceived benefit from seeing a production will be outweighed by the extra cost of seeing it: cost in the form of time, effort, cost of travel, perceived distance and so on. In Figure 6.2 the threshold is given by the break-even point where perceived benefit is equal to cost. At any point to the left of the break-even point, the consumer believes that it is worth travelling. To the right of the break-even point, the costs outweigh the benefits and it is not worth travelling. The aim of an arts manager will be to raise the level of perceived benefit (to raise B in Figure 6.2). This may mean 'adding-value' by promoting its special qualities (star performer, the only production, etc.) or offering as a holiday package. It may

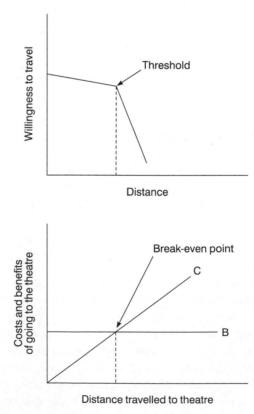

Figure 6.2 Audience threshold

simply be a matter of drawing the attention of the potential audience to the existence of the production. An alternative strategy is to reduce costs (lowering C in Figure 6.2) perhaps by offering a reduced price package of tickets and accommodation. The convenience of this may, in itself, be perceived as reducing the cost of the trip.

Some arts productions do attract non-local audiences and push back the threshold or break-even point with little or no effort on the part of management. In Chapter 4 it was noted that some people will travel and stay overnight in order to see a production because it is not available elsewhere or because it is of a high standard that cannot be seen elsewhere; they are arts-core. To see it at all or to experience that particular standard requires travel. Others are present because it is part of the holiday experience. For these (arts-peripheral), where the production is not the main reason for the trip, the threshold and break-even concepts apply to the decision to visit the destination rather than to travel to see the production.

Managers may however choose to target a tourist audience. This may be for several reasons. Tourists may be the 'obvious' market for some but in other cases there may be a need to fill seats from any source. Some arts organizations may not need to target tourists but feel that tourists are in some sense desirable or even preferable:

Principal market
- In some places tourists are the 'local' audience. Management of arts organizations may actively seek a tourist audience because the theatres and halls are located in holiday areas. Productions have a strong tourist orientation and are aimed at tourist audiences as there is a market to be exploited. Likewise some productions, especially festivals, are established (partly at least) as tourist attractions.

Need
- Need arises from the continuing desire to find sources of revenue in view of the fact that financial support from central and local governments is less generous than in the past.
- A limited local audience. In non-holiday places the audience may be limited in any one of several ways such as size, interest or ability to pay, and thus tourists are an extra source of revenue. It could reflect a wider disinterest in theatre as a result of the spread of other forms of entertainment.

    It could also be the outcome of production of particular art forms that have limited appeal in a relatively remote rural area where a large audience is unlikely to be found locally though it may well exist for other more popular art forms. Productions at the 'cutting-edge' of the arts, such as many modern music, dance or drama compositions, may have limited appeal too.

Certain productions (especially the 'high' arts) are likely to be characterized by high prices and this too limits the local audience. Those of a high standard may charge high prices.

Desire

- *Higher revenue.* Tourists may be willing to pay higher prices. If so, then the appeal of such an audience is obvious (see later this chapter).
- *An indicator of quality.* Many theatre managers point out how far some people in their audience have travelled and use this as if it were proof of excellence.
- *Justification for existence.* As with the previous reason many theatres point to the tourists in the audience as a contributor to the local economy. Claims for financial assistance from local government, arts boards, tourist boards or local industrial sponsors often refer to the ability of the theatre to attract tourists and therefore to be of benefit to others. The impact of tourists is claimed to be greater than that of others such as day visitors because of the expenditure on accommodation, eating-out and any other holiday activities they engage in during the stay. It may be undesirable for many in the arts to see justification for supporting the arts expressed in this way but it is common. Many believe that the arts are justifiable on their own merits without reference to such economic matters.

Strategies

When targeting a local audience, theatre management has the benefit of targeting a limited geographical area (see Figure 6.3). Because tourists are non-local, additional problems arise when targeting them. The market is:

- distant;
- dispersed.

The potential audience may be anywhere in the country or world and is unlikely to be concentrated in one particular place. Decisions have to be made as to how these problems may be overcome. It may be appropriate to target particular categories of people and/or particular parts of the country (or world). These decisions can only be made on the basis of market research that identifies who and where potential audiences are. Such information is increasingly available but much of the marketing effort is often based on guesswork and intuition.

Given these two dimensions to the target tourism market it is almost inevitable that the effort and cost involved in attracting non-locals will be high relative to that of attracting a more local audience. It is likely to be more of a scatter-gun approach than more localized efforts where market knowledge may be greater. The marketing message may have to be transmitted some distance and with a very wide circulation (see Figure 6.3):

(a) Distance: the greater the distance and the less local the market then marketeers are less likely to know about the markets and distribution costs are likely to be greater.

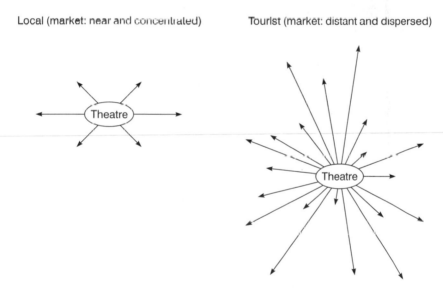

Local (market: near and concentrated)   Tourist (market: distant and dispersed)

Figure 6.3 Characteristics of local and non-local or tourist markets

(b) Dispersion: it may be considered more economic to convey a very broad message that appeals to the maximum number of (different) people in different parts of the country (or world). This may be cheaper than constructing a larger number of specific messages that appeal specifically to differences between people. Because it is so general, however, it may be less effective than the more specific approach.

'Most cultural marketing effort has been directed to local audiences. To bring in audiences from a wider base ... it is necessary ... to add techniques of tourism marketing to the more traditional marketing techniques' (Leader-Elliott, 1996: 57). Arts organizations may find it difficult to adopt 'tourism marketing' techniques because of their limited marketing expertise and limited financial resources (Silberberg, 1995; Canadian Tourism Commission, 1997b). It therefore seems appropriate to seek the assistance of tourism boards and tour operators either in terms of expertise or in joint ventures (see below and Chapter 9).

The message transmitted to tourists will also differ from that aimed at more local audiences. Tourists, if arts-peripheral, are more likely to be seeking diversion and a 'night-out'. Many in the potential market may be unfamiliar with theatre in their home towns but regard a visit as part of the holiday experience and will respond to a less formal publicity and booking strategy.

Promoting the arts to tourists may hit a particular 'time' problem however. The decision time of the tourist may be such that the arts are not able to supply detailed information about their programmes at the time. This has frequently been the case where the tourism trade has been unable to obtain detailed information in time for the marketing campaigns carried out by them. This is especially the case for (but is not confined to) receiving theatres. Tour operators and tourist boards and city and resort marketing bodies, for instance, may prepare their brochures 12 to 18 months ahead of the relevant season whereas, at that time, many theatres and concert halls have not finalized their programmes. This problem has arisen partly because of uncertainty about government funding. The arts and entertainment can therefore only be promoted in general terms in tour and resort brochures. The arts world is frequently implored to provide information to tourist bodies as soon as possible (Leader-Elliott, 1996).

Approaches to promoting the arts to non-local audiences include the following, each of which is discussed further below:

■ promotion, inside the destination, of the arts;
■ promotion, outside the destination, of the arts (including joint marketing);
■ promotion of the destination itself.

Promotion inside the destination

This would usually be aimed at arts-peripheral tourists. The most direct approach involves reaching out to tourists who are already in a town or city (especially a holiday town) or to those who are considering a destination. Marketing messages will be transmitted using channels similar to those used for a local population (see Figure 6.4). The approaches may be modified to include the distribution of flyers and posters to hotels and the encouragement of hoteliers and key persons such as receptionists, concierges and porters to promote the entertainment. A strategy of familiarizing staff of hotels and tourist information centres with local theatres through tours and talks will increase knowledge and hopefully also enthusiasm for the arts and therefore for encouraging tourists to buy tickets. Some resorts and tourist cities produce specialist entertainment brochures that give details of productions for a period of time such as a week or a summer season. These are circulated to hotels, tourist information centres and other tourist businesses including restaurants and taxi and coach companies and other tourist attractions.

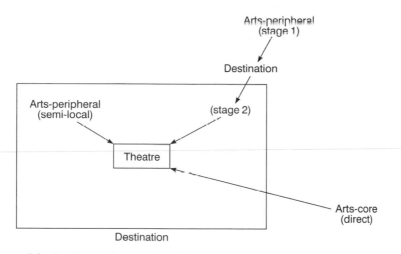

Figure 6.4 Tourism and promotion of the arts

It may be effective to cultivate locals not only as an audience but also as a publicity vehicle. This will apply not only to hoteliers and others in the tourism sector but also to the wider population. People visiting friends or relatives may be persuaded or taken by their local hosts to see a show or hear a concert. The use of the local media for generating good publicity will be important as will generating good public relations through a variety of community involvements. Word-of-mouth recommendations from local residents can be very effective.

In addition, if it is known where holiday tourists usually come from, then some of the promotional effort can be directed to the catchment area. Theatres in Yorkshire seaside resorts may advertise in papers in Leeds and Sheffield.

Promotion outside the destination

The approaches here are largely directed at the arts-core tourist and are aimed directly at the potential tourist wherever he or she lives. Some of these outside-destination strategies will also, however, be relevant for the arts-peripheral tourist.

For arts-core tourists, the production is more important than the location or the intent to go on holiday and then see a show (see Figure 6.4). It is the production or performer, rather than the destination, which is the key element in the marketing strategy. Approaches include:

- **advertising** in specialist 'arts', music and theatre magazines and periodicals and relevant newspapers. This approach may also be more suitable for urban tourists;
- **mail shots:** circulation of publicity material through the mailing lists of other arts companies. This approach makes the marketing less scatter-gun and more focused by directing material to those who have already shown an interest in the same or similar type of production. Mail-shots may be directed at relevant target groups individually or collectively through interest groups and group organizers. 'Membership lists of clubs and associations can be a powerful marketing tool and local clubs and associations can be used to promote the event to their wider membership' (Getz, 1991: 245). The mailing lists of local hotels can also be used in order to distribute promotional material and priority booking and special discounts at theatres given to hotel guests. This will enhance the product offered by the hotel.
- **reviews:** many arts-lovers will be attracted (or not) to a production by the reviews written by critics in newspapers and journals. It may be that some people are not even aware of certain productions until reviews are read. It therefore could be beneficial to obtain the widest coverage possible of productions by the newspapers and magazines read by the target audiences.
- **tourist information centres:** distribution of promotional material to tourist information centres in the region is appropriate, as is use of these centres for the booking of theatre tickets. Many already provide accommodation-finding and booking services. One-stop booking of accommodation and theatre tickets may be a particularly attractive proposition for tourists.
- **packages:** theatres can make more use of own mailing-lists by enclosing details of selected accommodation and a contact number of an accommodation bureau. One step further is the development of packages linking accommodation with theatre tickets. There is some potential for theatre, etc. as a component of such holidays offering transport, accommodation

and performance tickets at an 'all-in' price (see further discussion in Chapter 7). These, to date, have had only limited success in the domestic market with exceptions such as 'theatre breaks' to London. Trade fairs are held to bring together the arts and tourism with a view to develop such packages. As part of the same strategy, the Society of London Theatre (SOLT) publishes a 'Guide to London's West End theatres' as a manual for the travel trade with details of theatre capacities, seating arrangements and contact names and numbers.

■ **contact with the travel trade:** it is relatively difficult to aim successfully at overseas visitors. They are usually interested in a limited range of arts activity and in visiting 'pleasant' places. They are also difficult to reach in their home countries through marketing campaigns. They may be reached by distributing material through the foreign offices of national tourist boards, though in many cases it would probably be more cost-effective to target foreign tourists once they are in the destination country. Even then, it may be most productive to target the travel trade including coach operators, group travel organizers, incoming tour operators, conference and incentive tour operators by means of direct mail shots and the like. Targeting the organized package tourist is likely to be more productive than targeting the independent tourist and links with in-coming tour operators may therefore be particularly useful.

For both foreign and domestic tourists it may be effective to target 'organizers' in a similar way, rather than target individual tourists. The arts product offered may be made more attractive through 'value-added' elements such as backstage tours, talks, meetings with artists and backstage staff, meet-the-cast parties, receptions, etc. In all of these instances where arrangements are made with others, hotels, tour operators, travel agents and other booking agents will usually expect theatres to allocate blocks of tickets and offer discounts and commission. Arts organizations may not be prepared to do this if they do not feel confident about a return in the form of overall increased revenue. The advice pack published (1997) by BTA and the Arts Council for England suggests that the travel trade is most likely to be interested in arrangements that potentially involve a sizable number of people if they are to be financially worthwhile. Computerized theatre booking services through travel agencies would also make the arts a more attractive tourist resource for the trade.

Joint marketing

Marketing campaigns aimed outside the destination, whether the domestic or foreign market, arts-core or arts-peripheral, may be more effective and economic if carried out on a joint basis. It may include a variation of an 'arts-card' scheme whereby tickets may be purchased at discount prices. Joint marketing may be especially relevant for several arts organizations to promote the arts attractions where it is not certain, far in advance, what the programmes will be (see above). A joint effort can focus on the generic aspect and the fact that the destination is a centre for a variety of arts and entertainment without specifying any one particular show or concert. The Festival of Arts and Culture 1995 initiated by the BTA was such a generic campaign and 'by pooling funds to present Britain as the world's leading and liveliest cultural destination, generic campaigns provide a backdrop of cultural awareness and a platform from which individual providers and consortia can project their sector-specific image and develop their own marketing tactics' (Varlow, 1995: A95). Many festivals in the UK have contributed to a joint marketing effort organized by the British Arts Festivals Association that promotes all without indicating individual programmes. This effort is particularly targeted at foreign markets and brochures are distributed through the BTA overseas network. The diverse nature of the arts, including both the 'high arts' and entertainment, may however make such co-operation difficult in practice. In addition, many arts organizations may be reluctant to contribute to such activities if it is believed they will benefit competitors.

Campaigns such as 'British Arts Cities' and 'Arts Cities in Europe' are an example of a combination of destination marketing (see below) with this direct appeal to those with a primary interest in the arts. Cities in Britain such as Glasgow, Newcastle, Liverpool, Cardiff and Manchester are promoted as centres for the enjoyment of 'culture'. The brochures feature theatre and dance, music, art and heritage in each city along with descriptions of the cities and of hotels. In reality, however, the 'British Arts Cities' campaign has not been a great success in terms of take-up.

During 1999, tourist boards in Britain recognized an opportunity to capitalize on the 'foreign connection' of specific theatrical productions in promotion of the country to overseas visitors. About one-third of advance bookings for the Abba-based show 'Mamma Mia' were from Scandinavian visitors. A large number of Germans were also booking to see 'Chicago' which had a number of German leads including Ute Lemper.

The co-operative ventures may extend beyond the destination (whether town, city or country) to include 'competing' destinations. Theatres in several resorts or other potential tourist destinations may find economies of scale in combining to organize joint programming, funding and marketing of productions. They may also co-operate in the development and promotion of special events and promotions.

Co-operation with other non-arts attractions for development of joint products and promotion may also be vital as the arts are often not the main reason for a tourist visit (Leader-Elliott, 1996). 'Probably the most important form of partnering and packaging is among cultural and non-cultural tourism products . . . It offers the variety of experiences that most people are seeking and greatly widens the market' (Silberberg, 1995: 364). It may take the form of joint advertising or a 'passport-type' package allowing discounted entry to several attractions both cultural and non-cultural. As with joint arts efforts, the fact that competitors may benefit without any guaranteed benefit to the arts organization itself may mean they are reluctant to contribute. This strategy, like so many others, is not new as evidenced by this comment from the US Department of Commerce:

> Tourism has tended to segregate the elements of cultural resources in its promotional efforts and market identification. Yet it is the totality of vehicles through which a community releases its cultural energy that creates the unique metabolism of a place . . . A comprehensive approach to cultural resources uniting the arts, humanities and historic preservation should be more thoroughly explored.
>
> (Wiener, 1980: 6)

Packages that offer admission at a discount to several attractions (arts and other) can add to the appeal of a destination as well as increasing the possibility of increased revenue for any one attraction.

Promotion of the destination

This would be most appropriate in seeking to attract arts-peripheral tourists. In addition to promoting the arts and entertainment themselves it might be productive to contribute towards any strategies that market the town as a tourist destination and thus encourage tourists in the first place (see Figure 6.4). In seaside resorts and many cities the visit to the theatre is often secondary to the decision to go on holiday. Sometimes the visit is an 'accidental' one in that there was no intention to visit the theatre at all when the holiday decision was made so getting tourists into the resort or city in the first place is vital.

In addition, informing potential tourists through destination marketing that arts and entertainment exist in a location may influence the choice of holiday destination. It is also possible that a production or performer may be a primary cause of a decision to go on holiday.

Reviving domestic tourism in the UK may be extremely difficult but, at least, the short-break market offers considerable potential for both coastal resorts and for inland cities. Arts organizations may therefore:

- contribute to the general marketing of a place (whether town, city, region or country);
- influence the place-marketing so that it recognizes the significance of arts and entertainment.

The contribution of the arts sector can be to either finances or policy-making, or both. The process will be important even in the non-holiday situation as the willingness of people to travel and stay in order to see a production will be influenced by the image that people have of a place. This influence may be exercised through lobbying or through membership of tourist boards and similar place-marketing organizations. These often have a strong local government connection and input and it may therefore also be helpful to lobby local government to bring about desired results.

As part of the process, arts managers may need to raise the awareness of the significance of arts and entertainment as part of the holiday experience among tourist boards, city and resort marketing bodies and local and national government politicians and officials. They need to be made aware too of the potential for attracting long-distance audiences in the cases where it is less of a holiday experience (often arts-core). It follows that arts managers should ensure that the availability and range of the performing arts is given appropriate prominence in tourism marketing strategies as in the examples above in 'joint marketing'.

Audience composition

There are not many published studies that provide clear information about whether or not there are tourists in audiences for the arts and entertainment. There are two possible sources of information (see Figure 6.5):

1 **Arts studies:** audience surveys may determine whether or not there are tourists in audiences and 'why' tourists are present in those audiences. This approach catches those tourists who attend the arts and not those who don't and therefore cannot determine extent of or reasons for non-attendance. It may miss some tourists who do attend the arts but are not in the audiences on the occasion of the surveys (represented by the left-hand part of Figure 6.5).

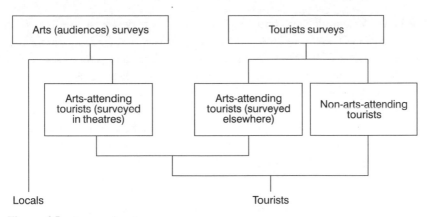

Figure 6.5   Approaches to surveys

2 **Tourism studies:** these range more widely and will include people who are
not arts-attenders. Surveys of tourists will indicate the existence of those
who attend and those who do not attend arts performances while tourists
and how far tourists are attracted by the arts to visit a destination.
(Represented by the right-hand part of Figure 6.5.) This second approach is
examined in Chapter 7.

The remainder of this chapter deals with arts studies (1 above) rather than with
tourism studies. There are not many published studies of audiences in popular
tourist destinations such as seaside resorts and most studies relate to urban
areas that are not particularly associated with tourism, with the exception of
London and New York. Some audience surveys confirm that there are tourists
in theatre audiences though the number of surveys that provide clear
information is limited. Most tend to identify how far audiences have travelled
and/or their home area or specify that they are 'out-of-region'.

Some studies that do give relevant information include those below. The
number of overseas visitors in audiences is more often identified than is the
number of domestic visitors (probably reflecting the economic dimension to
most studies). See Table 6.1 for a summary of some of the more significant
figures.

■ **Broadway:** in 1997 international visitors were 11% of audiences (from 9%
in 1991). Domestic visitors were 35% (down from 41% in 1991). The
Broadway audiences were increasingly 'local' with residents of the city
accounting for 24% of audiences in 1997 (from 22% in 1991) and residents
from the suburbs accounting for a further 30% in both years (Hauser and
Roth, 1998).

- **New York and New Jersey:** people from outside the region and from outside the USA were 36% and 13% respectively of attendances at theatres *and* museums (1992) (Port Authority of New York and New Jersey, 1993). This study, like the Broadway study above, did not distinguish staying from non-staying visitors.
- **Adelaide Festival 1996 (Australia):** 18% of audiences were out-of-state (South Australia) and, of these, over four in ten were from Melbourne or Sydney and one in eight were from overseas (Market Equity and Economic Research Consultants, 1996).

Table 6.1 Proportion of audiences that are tourists: summary of some of the studies

- **Broadway (1997):**
  international visitors 11%
  domestic visitors 35%
- **New York-New Jersey (theatre and museums) (1992):**
  outside region 36%
  outside USA 13%
- **Adelaide Festival (1996):**
  out of state 18%
- **Adelaide Ring Cycle (1998):**
  out of state 66%
- **West End (1997):**
  UK from outside London 43%
  international 18%
- **Edinburgh International Festival (1996):**
  UK from outside Scotland 30%
  international 21%

- **The Adelaide Ring Cycle:** this cycle of Wagner's operas, the first in Australia, attracted audiences that were 66% out-of-state including 12% of all audiences from overseas (South Australian Tourism Commission, 1998).
- **West End theatres in London:** audiences have been regularly surveyed since the early 1980s (Society of West End Theatre, 1981). Surveys showed an increase, between 1982 and 1985–86, in the percentage of West End theatre audiences that is from overseas (from 32% to 37%). Such visitors had been responsible for most of the overall increase in attendance over this period (Gardiner, 1982, 1986). The 1990–91 survey concluded that some of the 1986 results might have been temporary as overseas visitors were

down to 32% of the audiences (Gardiner, 1991). By 1997, the share of overseas visitors in audiences had fallen to 18%. There had also been a fall in their number (MORI, 1998).

The 1990–91 survey identified domestic visitors. A third of attendances were by UK residents from outside London, most (61%) were on day trips but over a third were staying at least one night, i.e. were domestic tourists (Gardiner, 1991). By 1997, UK residents outside London had risen from 33% to 43% of the total. The proportion that were staying overnight was about half (Martin, 1998) but it would appear that it has fallen reflecting the increase in the number of 'locals' from the south east of England (MORI, 1998).

- **London:** the PSI report estimated that 40% of theatre and concert audiences were tourists (i.e. both domestic and foreign with an 'over night stay') (Myerscough, 1988).
- **Outside London:** in audiences elsewhere in Britain, the proportion of tourists is often low. The same PSI report identified tourists as being only between 2% and 8% of theatre and concert audiences in Britain, elsewhere than London (Myerscough, 1988). In Northern Ireland, tourists (from outside of N. Ireland) were only 2% of theatre and concert audiences but 18% of visitors to museums (Myerscough, 1996).
- **Edinburgh Festivals:** between 43% and 67% of the 1990–91 audiences were tourists (domestic and foreign) (Scotinform, 1991). At the 1996 Edinburgh International Festival, over half of audiences were from outside Scotland (including 21% from outside UK) and just over half of the visitors were overnight visitors (Jones Economics, 1996).
- Although they did not focus on the arts as such, some related studies have also identified 'tourists'. Visitors to 'cultural' sites in Europe covered by the 1992 ATLAS survey were classified as international tourists (60%) and domestic tourists (25%) (Richards, 1993). Nearly 80% of respondents surveyed at heritage sites in the Isle of Man (1988–91) were 'holiday tourists' (Prentice, 1993).

Tourists are therefore identified in some audience studies and it is evident that in some urban areas and festivals the proportion can be quite high. There is little information about the number of tourists in audiences in seaside resorts and other holiday areas but it is likely to be high here too. Elsewhere, most audiences are probably local.

There is, of course, no necessary connection between a person being in an audience and the influence of that show or concert on the decision of that person to visit the town, city or seaside resort. It is possible that the influence may be very slight but many tourists nonetheless go to see a show once at a destination. This influence, the drawing power, is discussed later in this chapter.

Few if any surveys ask if audiences are on holiday as such but they do often show the proportion that are on other particular types of visit. In the West End 8% of audiences were in London on business, work or study trips and 9% were visiting friends or relatives (MORI, 1998). The New York-New Jersey study showed that 22% of the audiences had come to the region for business reasons and 8% to visit friends and relatives (Port Authority of New York and New Jersey, 1993).

Audience composition: by type of production

Some of the London West End surveys also indicate the composition of audiences in particular types of production. For many types of production such as drama, classical play, comedy, opera and ballet, the number of London residents in the audience does dominate, but for musicals and thrillers, visitors (including 'day-visitors') dominate (MORI, 1998).

Non-locals, from the rest of the UK outside London and the south east and from foreign countries, are high proportions of audiences for musicals (34% of audiences) and for thrillers (44%). They are only low proportions of the audiences for opera and ballet (11%) and classical plays (18%). Within this there are differences between foreign and domestic visitors. Musicals had the highest percentages of domestic visitors: 35% were from the south east of the UK and 16% were from the rest of the UK. Thriller audiences had the highest percentages of foreign visitors (33%) and drama audiences the highest percentages of North Americans (13%).

It is significant that there are high proportions of non-locals in musical and thriller audiences though this has not always been the case. In 1990–91 non-locals were in the majority in most audiences (and in the minority in opera and dance audiences only) (Gardiner, 1991). Some of this change can be accounted for by the fall in the number of foreign visitors in audiences by 1997. Nonetheless musicals and thrillers would appear to be the types of production at which the greatest proportions of non-Londoners are to be found, whether local day-visitors from the South East or visitors from elsewhere in the country or from other countries. Certain types of production are therefore likely to have a high tourist component.

This does not, however, indicate what tourists prefer or what most of them attend. The fact that the proportion of overseas visitors in audiences for musicals is greater than that in audiences for classical plays does not mean that more foreign tourists go to musicals than go to see classical plays. Productions such as musicals and thrillers certainly have audiences with the highest proportion of visitors from outside London and it may perhaps be assumed that these are the sort of production that they prefer but it is not certain. Londoners are apparently more attracted by other types of theatre such as drama, opera and ballet.

Tourists and non-tourists

It was noted earlier how arts managers might want to target tourists for several reasons including the hope that they might pay higher prices than others. Although some surveys do identify tourists, there are very few that identify differences between the tourist and non-tourist in the audiences. Such studies would not only confirm (or otherwise) the view about ticket prices but could potentially yield information that would assist the marketing activity, by not only showing their demographic characteristics and where they come from but also where they obtain information about theatres and concerts, how and when they book and the type of productions they prefer. Below are some of the few studies where differences are recognized:

- **Broadway:** visitors and non-visitors were not compared but it was noted that 60 per cent of tourists purchased theatre tickets before arriving in New York (Hauser and Roth, 1998). International visitors, however, were more likely to purchase after arrival, which suggests that they were less concerned about what they saw. The very fact of having visited Broadway and of having seen a Broadway production is probably sufficient for most.
- **London West End theatres (1990–91):** although the domestic staying visitor was not distinguished from the day-tripper, domestic visitors generally paid more for their tickets than did Londoners (or overseas visitors). A significant number were in large groups and they were more likely than others to have booked their theatre tickets in advance. They were also the most likely group to have booked through a ticket agency. Press advertising was a particularly important source of information for them.

  With respect to overseas visitors, USA visitors were the single largest group (44 per cent of overseas visitor sales). Overseas visitors were the group most likely to book tickets on the day of the performance (43 per cent of sales) and to buy tickets at the box office. They were less reliant upon the press and media for information and the most important source of information was the London Theatre Guide. The average price paid was more than that paid by Londoners but less than that paid by domestic visitors (Gardiner, 1991).

- **London West End theatres (1997):** this confirmed that overseas visitors were more likely than others to book on the day of the performance (40 per cent compared with 21 per cent of all ticket sales). With respect to ticket prices, however, the situation was apparently different from that in 1990–91 with overseas visitors spending more on average than UK theatre-goers did. Visitors (domestic and overseas) were also more likely to eat out in connection with their theatre trip (MORI, 1998).
- **ATLAS:** this study did not compare tourists with others (locals) at cultural sites but it did report the characteristics of the tourists. They had high levels of educational qualification and a surprisingly high proportion were young (over 30 per cent were under 30 years old). They were usually heavy consumers of culture at home and many were themselves employed within the cultural industries (Richards, 1996).

There is, therefore, little in these studies that gives a clear picture of significant differences between tourists and non-tourists in audiences. The fact that international visitors to New York and London tend to buy their tickets after arrival, and particularly on the day of the performance, suggests that what is seen is relatively unimportant.

Drawing-power: arts perspective

In Chapter 4 it was seen how tourists in audiences could be categorized as arts-core or arts-peripheral. Some would be drawn to a particular city or seaside resort in order to see a certain performance whereas for others the main reason for being in a place could be sun and sea and going to see a show would be an afterthought. In the first case the influence of the arts in bringing a person to that city or seaside resort was considerable but in the second it was insignificant. This ability of the arts to attract tourists – 'drawing-power' – is difficult to determine but can be assessed, at its simplest, by asking audiences to indicate the importance of the arts in the decision to visit the town. In the few relevant audience surveys, audiences are usually asked:

- whether or not the performance is the main reason for the visit to the destination, sometimes as a choice of several alternatives
    e.g. 'What was your one main reason for visiting . . .?
    – to go to the theatre
    – business
    – sightseeing
    – shopping, etc.

■ to rate theatre in 'importance' as a reason for the visit to the destination. This is usually done in isolation in that the same is not asked about other possible influences.

e.g. 'How important a factor was theatre in your decision to visit . . .?
– sole reason
– very important
– quite important, etc.

In some cases, both questions are asked but in others only one.

The surveys do not, however, usually link the reason for the visit to the section of the audience who are tourists. The reasons are applied to the whole audience or to visitors without identifying tourists as such. Studies that do include relevant information on the influence of the arts on tourists in the audience include the following (see Table 6.2 for a summary of some of the more significant figures):

■ **New York and New Jersey:** in the case of the performing arts, over half (58%) of the audiences from outside the region indicated that 'attending cultural activities' was the main reason for the visit to New York-New Jersey. (They were termed 'arts-motivated' visitors.) A further 20% indicated that they had extended their visit in order to attend arts and cultural events (Port Authority of New York and New Jersey, 1993). These figures include non-staying, more local visitors as well as tourists. The

Table 6.2 Drawing power of the arts: summary of some of the studies

■ **New York-New Jersey (1992)**
  main reason: 58% of all visitors
  extended stay: 29% of all visitors
■ **Adelaide Festival (1996)**
  main reason: 52% of all visitors
  residents 'diverted': 20%
■ **West End (1997)**
  sole reason: 48% of all visitors
  main reason: 61% of all visitors, 30% of international visitors
■ **Edinburgh Festivals (1990–91)**
  sole reason: 39% of visitors from outside Scotland
■ **ATLAS**
  important or very important: 60% of tourists
  specific: 9% of tourists

drawing power of museums would appear to be less. Just over a third of those surveyed at museums said that cultural activities were the main reason for the visit to New York-New Jersey and visiting friends and relatives and sightseeing were more important than for the performing arts attenders. The visitors most likely to be drawn by cultural activities lived closer to New York-New Jersey than did others.

- **Broadway:** drawing power was not considered in the 1997 study.
- **Adelaide Festival 1996:** just over half of visitors in the audience said that the festival was the 'main reason' for the visit. In addition, 20% of Adelaide residents at the festival would have gone away on holiday if not for the festival (Market Equity and Economic Research, 1996).
- **London West End 1990–91:** a third of all visitors and 1 in 10 of overseas visitors in the audiences said that theatre was the sole reason for the visit to the city. The draw therefore was greater for domestic visitors than for overseas visitors. In response to a separate question about what was the 'main reason' for the visit, 50% of all visitors specified theatre (business: 16%, sightseeing: 13%). Theatre was the main reason for 32% of overseas visitors (sightseeing: 25%) (Gardiner, 1991).
- **London West End 1997:** the same questions were asked in the 1997 survey and 48% of all visitors said that theatre was the sole reason for the visit to London (overseas visitors: unspecified). The percentage stating theatre as the 'main reason' for the visit had risen to 61% (sightseeing: 9%) though for overseas visitors it was little changed at 30% (MORI, 1998).
- **Edinburgh Festivals 1990–91:** 39% of attenders who lived outside Scotland indicated that the Festivals were the sole reason for the visit to the country (Scotinform, 1991). For a further 17% it was 'very important'. (This was not done in the 1996 study.)
- **Northern Ireland:** a quarter of tourists in theatre and concert audiences gave the event they were at as the main reason for the visit to the province (Myerscough, 1996).
- **ATLAS study:** nearly 60% of visitors indicated that the attraction was 'important' or 'very important' in the decision to visit the city/location. It was also estimated that 'specific cultural tourists' were only '9% of tourists visiting cultural attractions' (Richards, 1996: 314). This was assessed on the basis of those who travelled to the destination specifically to visit the attraction.

For many it would appear, therefore, that the arts do have an important influence on the decision to visit festivals or a city especially with concentrations of theatres. Those tourists would not be there but for the arts. Audience surveys seem to suggest that there are a high proportion of arts-core tourists in audiences. For instance, it would appear that at least 48% of visitors in West End theatre audiences in 1997 are arts core by reference to 'sole reason', or 61% by reference to main reason. This and other surveys did not however distinguish tourists within the visitor category.

There are, nonetheless, noticeable proportions of arts-peripheral tourists in audiences. At least 29% of visitors in West End audiences considered theatre to be only 'quite important' or 'not at all important' in the decision to visit London (MORI, 1998). If judged as not being the 'main reason' then nearly four in ten of visitors in audiences in New York-New Jersey and just over half of visitors in audiences in Adelaide would appear to be arts-peripheral. There are a few problems, however, with such surveys.

Some problems with audience surveys

Where a distinction has been made between members of the audience who are local and those who are not, the studies usually (see Figure 6.6):

■ do not identify separately the day visitor and the staying visitor (tourists);

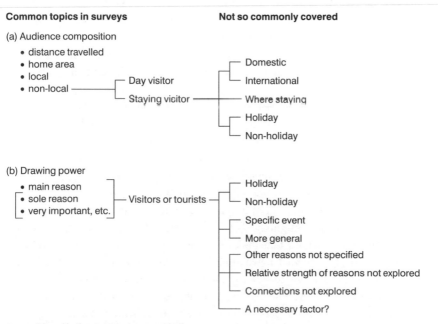

+ considered in theatres and concert halls

Figure 6.6 Audience surveys: characteristics and weaknesses

■ do not show whether staying visitors are staying in the area of the performance or elsewhere.

Even those surveys that do distinguish between visitors and tourists:

■ do not relate tourists to other questions such as production attended and ticket prices paid or to 'drawing-power';
■ do not differentiate between tourists who are on holiday and those who are not.

In addition, the exact nature of the drawing power remains unclear and drawing power is often overstated:

■ Surveys do not always indicate whether the decisions to attend related to specific events or to a more general desire to attend the performing arts.
■ The answers of tourists surveyed in audiences may be distorted or biased. Their assessment of 'importance' may be influenced, however unconsciously, by being in the theatre or concert hall at the time. If they were interviewed elsewhere their answers may be given with equal consideration of all possible factors and therefore be less distorted.
■ The answers may be distorted further by surveys asking about the arts and entertainment in isolation, such as asking 'how important' the arts were in the decision to visit. Surveys do not present this question for the other possible reasons for the visit and the survey respondents focus only on the arts without consideration of other factors. The significance may therefore be exaggerated.
■ Even where audiences are asked to consider other reasons – such as to choose the main reason from several – there is no indication of the 'strength' of that main reason compared with the others. The arts may be the main reason for a visit to a town but this could range from being only slightly more important than other reasons, such as sight-seeing, through to being totally dominant over any other possible reasons.
■ Associated with this is the fact that surveys do not indicate what connections there might be between reasons for the visit. Some in the audiences may claim that the arts were the main reason for the visit but the reality may be that it was only so in combination with others. There will be instances where the arts alone are the reason for the visit but for some in the audiences it may be a combination of reasons and these may be interdependent. A person may visit a town with a 'main reason' of going to the theatre but only if some other attractions are also available. Equally, the main reason for a visit may be sea or sight-seeing but the

visit only occurs if entertainment is available. Holiday-makers would not visit if there was no entertainment available, even though it was not a main reason. Decisions to visit a town or a country are often based on a combination of factors and any one by itself may not be a critical influence.

- For some people arts and entertainment are not a necessary part of the visit and their complete absence may have little effect on the decision to visit. Other factors, even though none by themselves may have been as important as the arts, may in combination be sufficient to encourage visitors. Some people claim they would visit a place anyway despite having claimed that the arts were 'very important' in the decision to visit. On occasion, this has been assessed by asking visitors in audiences what effect an absence of entertainment would have had on their decision to visit. This sort of question is rarely asked but in such an imaginary situation of 'no theatre', over 60% of overseas visitors surveyed in London audiences would have visited the city anyway (Myerscough, 1988). Nearly half of visitors in Adelaide Festival audiences would have come to the city anyway if there had been no festival (Market Equity and Economic Research Consultants, 1996). (See also Chapter 7.)

- Tourist spending which is due to the arts is exaggerated by 'claiming' the spending of anyone who stated the arts were of any importance at all (of 'some importance', 'very important' or sole reason). In the PSI study it was claimed that 68% of all spending by foreign tourists in London who attended the arts was due to the arts (Myerscough, 1988) though the study established that only 15% of foreign tourist audiences in London gave the arts as the sole reason for the visit. In the case of the International Edinburgh Festival nearly three-quarters of the tourists' expenditure was considered to be Festival-related (Scotinform, 1991). These estimates were derived by weighting the expenditure of tourists in audiences by 'importance' in their decision to visit the town:

  - all of the spending by tourists whose sole reason for the visit was the arts is attributed to the arts
  - the percentage of each tourist's spending that is attributed to the arts is reduced as the importance of the arts as a reason for the visit becomes less; e.g. none of the spending by those for whom the arts were 'not a reason at all' and perhaps 50% of the spending by those for whom the arts were 'of some importance'.

- The material gathered in audience surveys is sometimes wrongly applied to all tourism. There is a temptation to claim any results are about all tourists when, in fact, they apply only to tourists in audiences (see, for instance, Myerscough, 1988).

Despite these problems in determining drawing power and in overstating the power, it is important to appreciate that the arts and entertainment may have considerable indirect drawing-power and influence that are very difficult to determine precisely. The influence of the arts and entertainment may be more subtle than surveys can suggest. Factors such as arts and entertainment create atmosphere and act as a 'signifier' or marker of a place as a place for a holiday even though people may not have any intention of attending a show when choosing their destination and may not even attend when on holiday (see Chapter 7).

The information in this chapter about drawing-power has come from audience and site surveys. This is a relatively narrow approach, which may give a misleading impression. It was noted above that those surveyed in theatres and concert halls may give 'biased' answers. In addition the studies obviously relate to those tourists who actually attended performances rather than to tourists in general – they are audience studies – and may not give a complete picture of arts-related tourism. An alternative is to consult more general surveys of tourists conducted at a range of other locations which include theatres and concert halls but also other places where tourists might be found such as hotels, restaurants, historic sites, beaches and shops (see Figure 6.5). This is explored in the next chapter.

Chapter summary

There are no compelling reasons why arts managers should want tourists in audiences as the source of revenue is largely irrelevant. Knowledge of audience composition and expectations is, nonetheless, important if only because who is in the audience will influence the arts experience offered. A holiday audience at a seaside resort will be looking for an experience that is different from that of regular, keen, theatre-goers in their own home town. The arts manager in holiday areas will often be looking to the tourist market for a significant proportion of the audiences. Elsewhere, there may be an interest in the tourist market because arts managers are looking for new sources of audiences and to push back the threshold from within which audiences are prepared to travel.

Targeting tourists, who are usually some distance away, may require approaches that differ from those aimed at more local audiences. Part of the approach is to ensure that particular places are marketed successfully as holiday places and ensuring they have a pleasant and positive image. This will usually involve collaboration with tourist boards and local government. In addition, arts-core tourists may be targeted directly through mail shots and advertising. Offering the experience as a holiday, especially as a 'package' may have the effect of pushing back the threshold and persuading some people to travel to see the arts. This will apply to both arts-core and arts-peripheral tourists. These approaches may be best undertaken on a joint basis with other arts organizations or with the tourism industry. Tourists who are already at a destination may be targeted with a modified range of local-market approaches including targeting hotels and the production of general 'what's on' entertainment brochures.

There is evidence from audience surveys that there are tourists in audiences. There is only a limited number of relevant surveys where tourists are actually identified but the proportions of tourists in audiences can be high. It would appear that tourists are particularly interested in certain types of production, such as musicals, but there is mixed evidence about whether they are high spenders. Many of these tourists also claim that their visit to the destination was largely due to the arts and entertainment. There are, in some cases, high proportions of arts-core tourists though whether or not they consider their visit to be a holiday is not evident. There is little to show the composition of audiences in coastal holiday towns, in particular, where it might be expected that tourists will be a high proportion of the audience. It is not known just how important arts and entertainment are to such tourists and whether they are arts-core or arts-peripheral.

There is not always a clear identification of tourists in some of these surveys and data sometimes relate to both staying and non-staying visitors. There are a number of other drawbacks of audience surveys including the fact that there is little recognition of the possibility of combinations of factors attracting tourists to a place. Arts and entertainment tend to be evaluated in isolation and also, at a practical level, are evaluated by tourists when they are actually in the theatre or concert hall. This, in itself, may give rise to a distorted judgement. Surveys of tourists as a whole may give a clearer picture.

7

The tourism perspective

Introduction

The previous chapter was concerned with the supply side of the arts–tourism relationship, from the arts perspective. This chapter continues the same theme but from the tourism perspective (the right-hand half of Figure 6.1). The tourist industry has always taken an interest in the arts but there has been a particular interest in recent years. It was seen in Chapter 5 how the ETB had expressed concern in the early 1980s about the state of live entertainment in seaside resorts. There has been little obvious concern for this since and the attention has shifted to the 'arts' in the wider sense and to cities and to foreign tourists coming to Britain.

The structure and content of this chapter are similar to that of Chapter 6 but topics are regarded from the tourism studies perspective rather than from that of the arts. This chapter includes a discussion of:

- arts and entertainment as part of the range of tourist attractions;
- reasons why and the ways in which the tourist industry is involved;

- whether or not people do go to see arts and entertainment when they are tourists;
- a comparison of the tourists who attend the arts and entertainment and those who do not;
- the influence of the arts and entertainment on the decision of tourists to visit a particular place.

A classification of tourist resources

Many in the tourist industry see value in the arts as a means of encouraging tourists. They are seen as an attraction of a tourist destination. Tourist destinations may be analysed by examining a number of features of the destination: the 'four As' (see Figure 7.1):

- **Attractions:** the features that cause a tourist to visit. They have the ability (either by themselves or together) to attract visitors and may also be termed 'primary tourism factors'.
- **Amenities:** features, such as shops and restaurants, that do not themselves attract visitors but which add to a destination's attractiveness and may also be termed 'secondary tourism factors'.

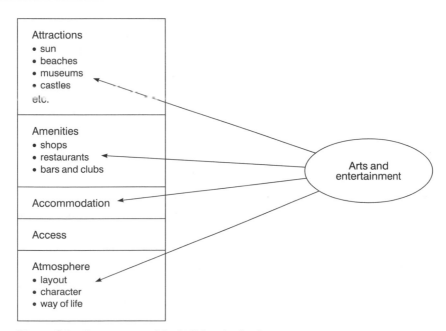

Figure 7.1 Components of the holiday destination

- **Accommodation:** its amount and quality are influential in determining numbers of tourists and is also a 'secondary tourism factor'.
- **Access:** this can take many forms including number and quality of roads, car parking, number and frequency of air flights or train services and also cost of travel. This is one of the 'additional tourism factors'.

It is not too clear how certain sights and sites become tourist attractions but they have been 'marked' somehow through guide books, films, books and a cumulative popular mythology as being significant (Britton, 1991). What might be considered by a tourist to be an attraction can be a local amenity for residents. Museums, art galleries, theatres and cathedrals may be patronized by locals as well as by visitors and classification as a tourist attraction is often problematic especially given that locals may feel they have a priority claim. Where attractions occur in 'clusters', in close proximity to each other, it gives added drawing power to a destination.

Putting any feature such as the arts into the 'attraction' or 'amenity' category depends on the motivation of the tourist. As noted previously, the arts can be a primary interest of a tourist and as such they are a major attraction of a destination. For other tourists, the arts are of lesser importance and they are not the attraction of a destination but an 'amenity' which makes the decision to visit more likely but is not critical. Thus arts appears under both attractions and amenities in Figure 7.1. It appears also under the fourth A, 'accommodation'. Entertainment is often provided in hotels (and bars, clubs and restaurants) and hotel-based entertainment probably features in many tourists' experiences. It may be relevant to the choice of destination, however incidentally (see later this chapter).

Whatever the significance of the arts and entertainment in attracting tourists, they may make a significant contribution to arts-peripheral tourist experiences. Holidays may have a focus of sun-bathing or visiting museums and historic sites but they invariably involve evening activities that complement these primary elements of the tourist trip. There is likely to be a demand throughout a holiday for visits to restaurants, bars and clubs, cinemas and theatres, usually in the evening. Going to the theatre is but one of these secondary activities. A 1991 survey is one of the few to provide information about evening activities. It showed that, for overseas visitors to the UK, 'leisurely meal in a restaurant' was the most common evening activity (75 per cent of visitors) followed by 'strolling around' and 'visits to pubs' and then 'theatre or classical music concerts' by a third of visitors. Visits to discos, night-clubs or to a pop or rock music concert were made by only a relatively low percentage of overseas visitors (BTA, 1992).

Entertainment may also feature however in many bars, clubs, restaurants and hotels as well as the more obvious and explicit visit to the theatre or concert hall. All of these 'amenities' are essential and critical elements of the holiday product so that their absence or perceived poor quality could affect the number of tourists though the significance of any one of them may be unclear.

A person away from home to visit relatives or friends may also look for evening entertainment as part of the trip and business travellers may look for diversions in the form of entertainment. It is widely expected that conferences and conventions will include a programme of entertainment for delegates and partners as a standard part of the experience.

Figure 7.2 shows the relationship between this classification of tourist resources and the classification of the arts-related tourist. For the arts-core tourist, the arts and entertainment will undoubtedly be an 'attraction'. For the arts-peripheral tourist with incidental intent, the arts are less important than other attractions but could be either an 'attraction' or an 'amenity' dependent upon the strength of the intent. For the accidental arts-related tourist, the arts will not be an 'attraction' but could well be an 'amenity'.

Arts-related tourist	Arts and entertainment as tourist resources
Arts-core pre-interest in attending; main purpose	attraction; primary element
Arts-peripheral (incidental) pre-interest in attending; secondary purpose	attraction or amenity; primary or secondary element
Arts-peripheral (accidental) no pre-interest in attending; not a purpose	not an attraction, possibly an amenity; not a primary element, possibly secondary
Unintentional no pre-interest in attending; not a purpose; no deliberate decision to attend	not an attraction or amenity; not primary or secondary element
Non-arts related tourist no pre-interest in attending; not a purpose; does not attend	indirect attraction or amenity; indirect primary or secondary element

Figure 7.2   Relationship between 'type' of tourist and tourist resources

Jansen-Verbeke's (1986) classification of tourist resources is important for differentiating between the 'activity place' and 'leisure setting' aspects of a destination. This draws attention to the fact that a town or city's overall layout and character and the way-of-life of its inhabitants can be powerful elements in attracting tourists. The attraction of a destination can often be character and atmosphere that amount to more than the physical buildings or activities in them. Performances in theatres, concert halls and elsewhere (including on-street) can contribute considerably to this atmosphere as do cafes, restaurants, bars and clubs. It may be regarded as a fifth A – 'atmosphere' (see Figure 7.1) – which includes layout and character of a town, the way-of-life of its inhabitants and the whole feel of a place – its 'buzz', whether it is vibrant, exciting and sleazy or calm and refined. In the case of Amsterdam, for instance, it is the place as a whole and the free-and-easy atmosphere rather than any impressive individual buildings or attractions that are the appeal of the city (Ashworth and Tunbridge, 1990). Towns and cities where things are happening and there is plenty of night-life, in particular, may prove particularly attractive for tourists. The very presence of 'fun things to do' may draw tourists even though not all will go to the theatre or clubs or eat out.

This is especially evident in the fact that the existence of arts and entertainment may draw visitors even though those visitors have no intention of attending and do not in fact do so. The arts and entertainment are ingredients that symbolize a holiday atmosphere and identify a tourist area as such or as a particular type of tourist area. They are one part of the collection of attractions that need to be present if an area is to achieve a critical mass for viability as a tourist destination. Visitors may be drawn by this overall attractiveness. This indirect influence on the decision to visit is difficult to measure.

In a related way, the presence of 'high arts' that are prestigious may identify and give a sense of identity to a location. This may enhance the attractiveness to tourists even if they do not visit the event or facility. There is probably a tourist spill-over effect from an event such as the Edinburgh Festival. It creates an image of the city that is 'attractive' and increases general awareness of the city so that people visit it at non-Festival times.

Arts and entertainment can therefore feature as a tourist resource in several ways. Apart from the case where they are the main attraction they may occur in other tourist experiences, however incidentally or accidentally or even 'unintentionally' (see Figure 7.2). Some tourists may not make a deliberate decision to see arts or entertainment but experience it as a result of a visit to a club or restaurant or a stay in a hotel.

Any tourist destination (actual and potential) would therefore want to ensure the provision of arts and entertainment of the appropriate form and in the appropriate quantity and quality if it is to succeed as a destination. In the case of the UK as a whole it may be that the arts are a strength of the 'product' in which case this becomes even more important. This is also true for most seaside towns in this country. For destinations with other resources, such as climate and scenery that are attractions, the arts and entertainment become less important.

Reasons and involvement

Because of its significance in the tourism experience it is not surprising that the tourism industry has become involved in several ways with the arts and entertainment, including encouragement, using them in tourism products and direct provision. There are several components of the tourism industry (see Chapter 3) and each sector will have its own reasons for being involved with the arts and entertainment.

For commercial organizations it is obvious that the potential for earning profit is important but for other bodies such as local government and tourist boards this is less important. There is optimism about cultural tourism generally because it is regarded as:

- an **additional market**: it is 'new' and it exists in addition to (or instead of) other forms of tourism in that it satisfies motives not satisfied by the sea and sun based type of tourism. There is a demand for such a form of tourism which provides an opportunity for commercial exploitation.
- a **growth market**: not only does a demand exist, but there is a great deal of optimism that tourism related to culture generally and to the arts in particular will continue to expand.
- a **'premium' market** which can be more profitable than mass-market, low-margin package holidays to the sun.

In addition it may be seen as having growth potential in the sense of there being groups of consumers with interest who have not been yet been targeted in marketing strategies. The arts as part of cultural tourism and as part of the activities of other tourists are also regarded favourably.

Tourist boards

It was seen in Chapter 6 that marketing approaches for encouraging theatre audiences could take several forms including marketing directly to tourists at a destination and also, more indirectly, marketing the destination itself. Tourist boards or visitor bureaux (and local councils) are involved with this second process. Tourist boards (local, regional and national) who encourage tourists to a destination have no direct involvement in arts provision and can only encourage the arts and entertainment industry to provide.

The tourist boards' role is largely to facilitate the commercial activities of others. Part of this function is to identify the particular strengths of a destination that may be identified as being in the arts (see Figure 7.3). They

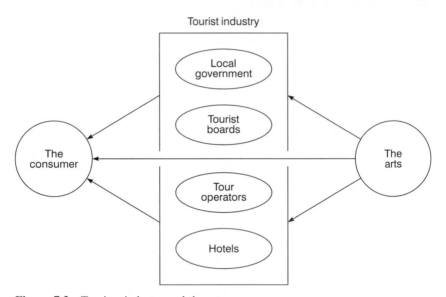

Figure 7.3   Tourism industry and the arts

also, through their market research, may identify a demand for arts-related tourism. In this way tourist boards provide assistance to the arts industry encouraging it to exploit the perceived advantages through product development and/or own marketing. Tourist boards may go further and provide advice and assistance in marketing or in product development. Tourist boards such as the BTA and ETB have recognized the link for many years (BTA, 1983) and encouraged the relationship in a number of ways. Following its report on seaside entertainment in 1984 (see Chapter 5) the ETB launched a major promotion 'England Entertains' in the following year. This was designed to encourage live entertainment. The ETB published the *Arts Tourism Marketing Handbook* in 1993 and, with the BTA, has organized a series of seminars bringing together arts managers, tour operators, travel agents and tourist boards. Additionally the BTA has published (1997) a 'Tourism and the arts advice pack' aimed at arts managers and a regular 'Tourism and the arts' newsletter. The BTA distributes promotional material through its overseas offices.

The Festival of Arts and Culture was launched by the BTA in 1995 as an umbrella, or generic, campaign highlighting music, literature, theatre and art as a tourist attraction. This was basically a promotional campaign with the detail of what was being offered being left to the arts and tourism worlds. It is estimated that it generated an extra £150 million of spending by overseas visitors (Smith and Jenner, 1998).

Marketing strategies may focus in whole or part on the arts. It has already been noted that the UK may have a particular strength here and in heritage (see later this chapter). Other countries similarly have significant cultural assets that they utilize as tourist resources. The tourist boards would be likely themselves to feature these strengths in their own marketing of destinations.

Tourist boards may produce material aimed at the specialist arts segment – calendars of events, brochures and specialist maps indicating places of interest with artistic connections.

Some marketing campaigns are joint efforts between tourist boards, local government and local arts boards.

Local government

Local government will often be directly involved with the provision or financing of arts and entertainment (see Chapters 2 and 5). Regardless of that, it does have a responsibility for the well-being of its citizens and, as such, will encourage activities such as arts-related tourism that are regarded as being economically beneficial (see Figure 7.3). The arts may be regarded as a special strength of the destination in terms of tourism potential (as in many cities). In other cases, such as seaside tourist towns, it may be regarded as a necessary complement to several other strengths. Many local councils (especially in cities) have developed tourism strategies and arts strategies that are linked with each featuring the other. Tourism strategies include the arts as a tourist attraction and arts strategies include tourism as a particularly beneficial outcome (see Chapter 8). Such tourism strategies may take the form of encouraging others (the arts and entertainment industry) to provide the product and of offering assistance in marketing. It was noted in the previous chapter how arts managers distribute leaflets through the Tourist Information Centre network in the UK (a network financed by local government).

In addition, however, many local councils also accept responsibility for marketing their towns and cities as tourist destinations. For some, the arts will feature as a particular strength. Coastal local councils have been in the forefront of place-marketing of seaside towns, and cities have followed with city-imaging partly to attract tourists. Local councils may undertake place-marketing themselves but increasingly it is undertaken jointly with the private commercial sector. Local councils are, of course, not the only bodies to engage in these activities as tourist boards do so also. Local regional tourist boards in particular have a strong local council membership.

Local councils will encourage the arts in order to stimulate their economies and to create income and employment. They will also be interested in the potential of the market as:

- **a quality or prestige market:** the product, whether 'high arts' or pop festival, may enhance the status of the town, city or country and encourage civic or national pride;
- **a profile-enhancing market:** the product may have the ability to attract considerable media attention.

Both of these will be significant for their ability to stimulate not only tourism related directly to the arts product but also tourism at other times as well. They are considered important too for their potential in encouraging other economic development and 'inward investment' including the location of other non-related businesses in the area.

Tour operators, travel agents

Even if the competitive advantage of a particular place is in the arts and entertainment, it does not mean that an arts-related tourism product will be offered by commercial organizations. A specific involvement such as a tour operator providing or a travel agent selling arts-related products usually follows from the potential of earning profits and from recognition that the arts-related tourism market is a 'new' growth or a premium market (see above). Tour operators use the arts and entertainment product in developing a 'package' of performance tickets and accommodation (and sometimes transport), which is then marketed to the public (see Figure 7.3).

These commercial organizations are generally thought of as offering and selling sun- and sea-based packages for holidays to foreign countries. There do exist, however, a number of small specialist operators:

- **Packages to foreign countries.** Most of these companies are relatively small and specialize in a particular country or art form such as theatre or opera. The sort of package offered includes a 12 day visit to the USA taking in concerts at Tanglewood (Massachusetts) with the Boston Symphony Orchestra and opera at Glimmerglass (New York State). 'Travel for the Arts' is advertised as 'the opera travel specialists' and offers, for instance, packages to the Salzburg Festival, to the New York Metropolitan Opera, Paris Opera Weekends and Aida performed in Egypt at the Pyramids.

  Packages are not confined to theatre but also extend to pop and rock concerts. Mondial Tours, for instance, offered a package to see Tina Turner perform in Cologne (in 2000). This included coach (and ferry) travel, hotel accommodation and concert tickets with optional Rhine Valley cruise and wine tasting. Argon Events offer packages to concerts (such as Sting in Paris), sporting and cultural events and to European rock, pop and metal festivals such as Dynamo 2000 (Netherlands) and Gods of Metal (Italy).

- **Packages to the domestic market:** arts-related visits to places such as London, Stratford and Edinburgh. There are occasional offers to other centres, such as to the seaside town of Scarborough (Yorkshire) to see plays by Alan Ayckbourn. All of his plays are premiered and directed there by the author himself.

  There are a number of independent operators who buy tickets and rooms from theatres and hotels (usually on a 'sale-or-return' basis) and offer pre-packaged trips. Some maintain flexibility and avoid pre-booking by offering to obtain tickets and rooms for whatever show and in whatever hotel a client prefers. This is usually from a list of hotels with which relationships have been established. The London visits in particular include an option to include rail travel in the package.

  The market for London visits is dominated by relatively large operators (though not in the league of the mass market outward package operators). Some are specialist arts tour operators such as Theatrebreak ('your passport to the performing arts'). Others such as Highlife and Superbreak are short break specialists who also offer theatre packages in the cities in their programmes. Rainbow Holidays is a market leader for such short breaks and is also part of First Choice, one of the largest tour operators in the UK.

  Both theatre and hotel companies also provide packages. The theatre company Stoll Moss, for instance, has offered packages to London of theatre tickets (not only Stoll Moss) and accommodation (3-star plus in central locations). The company has also operated theatre breaks on behalf of Thistle Hotels. Radisson Edwardian hotels have operated as 'the official partners to SWET' and through the associated company, Centre Stage, offered theatre and concert breaks in London using the Edwardian up-market hotels.

133

An associated development is that of 'clubbing weekends'. The local tourist association in Leeds (Yorkshire) arranges weekend packages of hotel accommodation and guest list entry to six clubs including 'Liquid' playing 'hip hop, funk and soul' and 'Majestyk' playing 'funky house, garage and disco mixed with a little soul'.

These domestic and foreign packages or offers are advertised in a variety of ways. Direct mail to existing clients is important but they also include advertisements in local and national newspapers and in the specialist arts press. Some are offered as part of a readers' travel club or a more general readers' discount club in association with the newspaper or magazine itself. One independent tour operator is part of an independent travel agency and has operated several of these clubs for magazines as well as operating its own 'theatre travel club' and 'arts travel club'. A particularly important target is party or group organizers. They are usually enthusiastic amateurs rather than professional organizers and regularly organize theatre and concert visits for their own school parties, work groups, clubs and societies. They have the advantage of being a relatively small segment to target.

■ **In-coming tour operators** (or ground handlers) offer arts-related packages (ready-made or tailored) to foreign visitors to the UK.

There are relatively few arts-related packages in this country offered by domestic tour operators largely because most domestic tourism is individually organized and is not in the form of inclusive packages. Most tourists are content to make their own arrangements (accommodation, transport and entertainment) for domestic holidays. Compared with foreign holidays it is a relatively easy task. Most of the interest in domestic arts-related tourism comes from destination marketing bodies and incoming operators and from the arts and entertainment providers themselves. Packages exist as the products of the arts organizations rather than of tour operators.

The reasons why arts organizations become interested in tourism have been considered in the previous chapter. Many have taken the initiative and offered packages of accommodation and theatre tickets. One of the earliest of these schemes was the Royal Shakespeare Company's 'Stop-over'. This scheme was administered by the RSC itself and offered tickets at the Stratford theatre, dinner and accommodation. Other similar packages such as that at Chichester Festival Theatre (Sussex) have been joint efforts between theatre and the local council and hotel association. It is more common for theatres or festivals to indicate in their brochures how accommodation might be booked along with a list of recommended and participating hotels that usually offer a reduced room rate. The hotel bookings are usually done directly.

Hotels

Hotels are in the business of providing accommodation (and associated services) but many also offer an arts-related product (see Figure 7.3). Entertainment in hotels (and in bars and clubs) is likely to appeal to many as it does not have the same overtones as going to the theatre. It is more informal and casual and, in many cases, it is on-site and free.

■ **Entertainment as a part of the hotel experience.** The extent and nature of the entertainment will vary and in some cases it is offered as a regular activity in the hotel itself as a unique selling proposition. There is, for instance, a chain of UK hotels branded as 'Entertainment Hotels' (ex-Butlins Holiday Hotels) whose tariffs include accommodation, meals and 'live cabaret every night'. Most hotels do not give quite the same emphasis as this but nonetheless it is common for hotels to offer some entertainment on the premises on a regular basis. In Blackpool, for instance, about one in five of all shows seen by holidaymakers were in hotels, pubs and clubs. It is also estimated that at least one in five of all hotels in the town provide some form of live entertainment. Apart from discos and live music for dancing, the entertainment was dominated by singers, live music, cabaret, variety acts and comedians (Hughes, 1999). It was usually provided as an addition, rather than in competition, to the entertainment available in the rest of the town.

   The US 'resort', a hotel complex which is positioned as a destination in its own right, often includes some form of entertainment as well as many recreational and leisure activities such as golf, swimming or skiing, and gymnasium. A particular type of resort hotel, the casino hotel, puts an emphasis on entertainment. These are especially associated with Las Vegas (Nevada) where casinos are usually based in hotels that also provide live entertainment in order to attract and retain customers. In fact, most entertainment in Las Vegas takes place in hotel complexes.

■ **Arts (often music) breaks on an occasional basis,** such as weekend breaks with the performances in the hotel. These can be on a one-off basis or as part of a more regular 'Special Interests Weekend' programme which might include, at other times, activities for gourmets or sports, literature, hobby and film enthusiasts.

■ **Accommodation as part of 'theatre packages'** arranged by arts organizations or tour operators. Some hotel companies, as noted above, offer their 'own' packages.

Why do hotels do this?

135

- to fill empty rooms at weekends and during the slack season (summer in cities);
- to familiarize the public with the hotel group in the expectation of future bookings for other purposes;
- to reinforce the image that the hotels wish to promote – perhaps a classical string quartet recital for up-market country hotels or a folk music weekend for other types of hotel.

There is little reason however to believe that, generally speaking, people choose their hotels on the basis of entertainment offered. Nonetheless in Blackpool where hotel entertainment is widespread, hotel owners believed that it was important in the choice of hotel by holidaymakers there. They felt obliged to provide it because others were doing so. It also acted as a boost to bar revenue (Hughes, 1999).

Tourist activities

In order to decide whether or not tourists do go to see the arts or entertainment it is necessary to examine studies that show what people do whilst, for instance, they are on holiday or on business trips.

There are a number of reports and studies, usually carried out by tourist boards, which look at the arts (or theatre in particular) within the context of tourism. The material discussed in Chapter 6 was collected through surveys of audiences. In this chapter most of the information comes from surveys that have been conducted amongst tourists (see right-hand side of Figure 6.5). These will cover tourists who have attended the arts and also those who have not. They should therefore give a more complete picture. Tourists in general, when surveyed, are less likely to focus solely on the arts and will be able to assess the arts in their visit within the context of all of their activities and motives.

Relatively little is known about what holiday-makers do whilst on holiday but some indication of the relative importance of arts and entertainment can be gained from a breakdown of tourists' expenditure. Domestic and overseas visitors to the UK spent 4% of all their expenditure on 'entertainment' (1998), compared with 35% on accommodation, 20% on shopping and 23% on eating-out (BTA, 1999a). On domestic trips within the USA 'entertainment and recreation' accounted for 7% of expenditure, compared with 35% on personal transportation, 10% on lodging and 21% on purchases (Waters, 1998). Inbound holiday tourists to Australia (1998) spent 2.6% of their total expenditure on 'entertainment and gambling' compared with 13% on shopping (Australian Bureau of Statistics, 1999b). Arts and entertainment are obviously only minor parts of total tourist expenditure.

Studies relating to activities include the following (see Table 7.1 for a summary of some of the more significant figures):

- Domestic tourists:
  - **Canada:** the Canadian Travel Survey shows that attending cultural events (plays and concerts) occurred on 3% of trips and visits to museums or art galleries occurred on 4% in 1996. Shopping and sightseeing occurred on 28% and 22% respectively of trips (Statistics Canada, 1997).
  - **Australia:** a survey of domestic tourism 1990–91 showed that eating out and swimming or surfing were the most popular activities (by 46% and 39% of tourists respectively). Heritage visits were made by 13%

Table 7.1 Proportion of tourists who attend the performing arts: summary of some of the studies

Domestic
- **Canada (1996)**
  cultural events: 3% of trips
- **Australia (1990–91)**
  theatre: 3% of tourists
- **USA (1998)**
  cultural events or festivals: 10% of travellers
- **UK (1997)**
  performing arts: 3% of holiday trips
- **England (1985)**
  live entertainment: 38% of holidays
- **Blackpool (1994)**
  seen a show: 71% of holiday-makers

International
- **New York-New Jersey (1992)**
  concerts, plays or musicals: 29%
- **Australia**
  performing arts: 12% of all international visitors (1994)
  performing arts: 12% of all cultural visitors (1996)
- **Britain (1995)**
  theatre: 32%
- **London (1995)**
  theatre: 20%–31%

of tourists, museum visits by 6% and visits to live theatre by 3% (Spring, 1991).

- **US domestic travellers:** a third went shopping during the trip whereas 15% visited an historic site or museum and 10% went to a cultural event or festival in 1998 (TIA, 1999).

- **UK:** the most popular activity on domestic holiday trips by UK adults in 1997 was 'hill-walking, hiking, rambling, orienteering' which occurred in 16% of all holiday trips (English Tourist Board *et al.*, 1998). Visiting museums, art galleries and heritage centres occurred on 6% and visiting castles, monuments and churches on 14% of holiday trips. 'Watching the performing arts' occurred on only 3% of domestic holiday trips. This included 'visits to theatre, concert, opera or ballet'. It is unlikely that respondents who had attended variety shows and similar holiday entertainment (perhaps in clubs and bars as well as theatres) would identify this with 'watching the performing arts'. It is probable, therefore, that the extent of participation in entertainment is under-stated in this tourist board data. The list of activities in these surveys is limited and activities such as 'shopping', 'beach activity', 'visits to pubs and clubs', 'window-shopping', 'just strolling' are not identified.

- An 'old' survey dating back to 1985 is one of the few that specifically included entertainment though confusingly it used the word to refer to all forms of the popular arts and the high arts including opera, ballet, circus, disco, variety shows, ballroom dancing, watching sport, pop concerts, etc. (Research Surveys of Great Britain, 1985). The study related only to British holiday-makers in England. On over a third of holidays in England, holiday-makers had gone to see some form of live entertainment. This was more likely in the case of seaside holidays (49%) than for those visiting cities (24%) and more likely for those in manual occupations. The most popular activities were visits to discos and watching variety shows, each 'seen' on about a quarter of holidays when any live entertainment was seen. People were much more likely to go to variety shows (and most other forms of entertainment) when they were on holiday than when they were at home (only a third of those who went to see variety shows on holiday also went to variety shows when not on holiday).

- In **Blackpool**, the largest seaside tourist town in the UK, seven out of ten of holiday-makers had seen (or intended to see) live entertainment during their stay. A quarter had seen three or more shows during their stay. Those most likely to see live entertainment were those on longer stays, the older age groups and those on 'main' rather than 'second' holidays. Holiday-makers accompanied by children were least likely to see a show (Hughes and Benn, 1997b). Only about half of the holidaymakers went to the theatre when at home and a third went whilst on holiday but did not go at all when at home. This supports the view that, for many, live entertainment is a holiday rather than a non-holiday experience.

- International visitors:
  - **Overseas visitors to New York-New Jersey:** some of the most important activities were shopping, eating-out and sight-seeing (each by over six in ten of overseas visitors) followed by visits to art galleries and museums and to historic places (about four in ten). Nearly three in ten went to concerts, plays or musicals (Port Authority of New York and New Jersey, 1994).
  - **UK visitors to USA:** nearly 30% visited an art gallery or museum and 17% went to a concert, play or musical (Prohaska, 1995).
  - **International visitors to Australia:** 28% of all international visitors to Australia had been to a museum or art gallery and 12% to the 'performing arts' during their stay in 1994 (Spring, 1995). Foo and Rossetto (1998) estimated that 60% of all international visitors to Australia visited at least one cultural attraction during their stay. Heritage buildings and sites (30% of all such cultural visits) and museums and art galleries (27%) were more popular than the performing arts (12%).
  - **International visitors to Britain, and to London in particular,** are more likely to visit historic sites and houses and museums than the performing arts. Over six in ten overseas visitors to Britain visit heritage sites (including museums) during their stay compared with three in ten going to the theatre (BTA and ETB, 1996). The situation in London is similar but not identical: over half visit museums, over three-quarters visit historic buildings and between two in ten and three in ten go to the theatre (LTBCB, 1995). Theatre itself tends to be more popular than opera, ballet or classical concerts. Nearly one in three went to theatre compared with one in twenty who attended ballet or opera performances and one in ten who went to classical concerts.
  - **ATLAS:** this was a 'site' or audience study and not a tourist study, but, for those surveyed, visits to heritage were more likely than were visits to the performing arts when on holiday. Just over half of those surveyed visited museums on holiday compared with just over 20% who attended the performing arts. Although not a tourist study, it does tend to confirm that heritage tourism is more important than arts tourism. It was also concluded in this study that attendance at the performing arts and heritage on holiday was similar to attendance when at home (Richards, 1996).

This finding in the ATLAS study contrasts with the conclusions of the much earlier survey of entertainment in England and the Blackpool study (see above) and also with Light and Prentice (1994) who concluded that 'visiting heritage sites is something undertaken more when on holiday . . . than in the area of permanent residence' (p.104). It may be that for some, such as the service classes, theatre-going and museum-visiting are part of usual (non-holiday) leisure activities. For others, perhaps the non-service classes in particular, this is not the case but it is a generally accepted part of being on holiday for them to go to see a show. It is seen as a holiday rather than a 'home' activity.

There is no clear picture about going to see arts and entertainment when on holiday, especially with respect to domestic tourists. Studies do suggest however that going to see arts and entertainment are activities that tourists participate in and, in some cases, the proportion that goes is high. Overall however it would seem that most people do not go to the theatre when tourists. Going to the theatre or concert hall may not be the most popular pursuit but nonetheless the arts and entertainment are significant tourism resources. 'Heritage', in the form of historic buildings (including churches) and sites, and museums and art galleries, is undoubtedly more popular with overseas tourists. The picture with respect to domestic tourists is not so clear.

It is possible too that there is a large number of visitors who visit both heritage and the theatre. Most tourist visits involve more than one activity and it is likely that a good many of those who visit historic sites also go the theatre and vice versa. The surveys do not indicate this connection and the extent of multi-activity.

Drawing-power: tourism perspective

Drawing power was examined in Chapter 6 from the evidence of audience surveys. Many of the audience surveys showed that the arts were an important influence on the decision to visit a destination (usually a city). Here, tourism surveys are examined to determine drawing power though once more there are only a limited number of surveys to draw on. See Table 7.2 for a summary of the more significant figures. Relevant studies include:

■ **New York-New Jersey:** a survey of American and Canadian 'travellers' showed that for those who had not yet visited the area, the arts and sight-seeing were of equal importance as a 'main reason' for a possible visit. They were each mentioned by 45% of travellers, theatre and musicals by

Table 7.2   Drawing power of the performing arts: summary of some of the tourism studies

- **New York-New Jersey (1992)**
  theatre and musicals as 'main reason': 35%-38% of American and Canadian travellers
- **Australia (1996)**
  'specific interest' in cultural attractions : 28% of international cultural visitors
- **Outbound from UK (1996)**
  particular interest in cultural activities: 40% of cultural tourists
- **Britain (1995)**
  theatre as important or very important: 37% of international visitors
- **UK (1997)**
  performing arts as main reason: 1% of domestic holiday trips
- **London (1995)**
  'possibility of enjoying' musicals or plays encouraged the visit: 32% and 23% (respectively) of overseas visitors
- **England (1985)**
  live entertainment as most important reason: 15% of holidays
- **Blackpool (1994)**
  entertainment as most important reason: 29% of holiday-makers

35% and museums and art galleries by 22%. The arts, however, were much more important than sightseeing for attracting repeat visits by those who had been to the area before. Arts was a main reason for 50% and sightseeing for only 22%; theatre and musicals 38% and museums and art galleries 18% (Port Authority of New York and New Jersey, 1994).

- **International visitors to USA:** an early study showed that several clusters could be determined. 'Culture and comfort' was a significant cluster and included tourists who were particularly interested in heritage, art and theatre. The cluster accounted for 18% of the market from France, 21% from Germany and 19% from UK (Prohaska, 1995).
- **International visitors to Australia:** were classified as 'specific' cultural visitors if they had a specific interest in visiting the attraction or if they worked in 'culture'. They accounted for 28% of cultural visitors. (The questions posed related to the influences and motivation for visiting the attraction and not to visiting Australia though the discussion suggests that this is what is intended (Foo and Rossetto, 1998).)
- **Outbound tourists from UK:** a study of tourists showed that 69% participated in at least one cultural activity during their visit to a foreign country (Alzua et al., 1998). Of these, two categories were identified as

placing particular emphasis on heritage and culture in choosing a holiday. These two ('heritage, younger, backpacker' and 'heritage, middle age, family') accounted for 40% of the cultural tourists identified.

■ **International visitors to Britain:** the BTA has asked about the importance of the arts in the decision of overseas visitors to visit this country since as early as 1978. In subsequent years there was not always reference to the arts in the annual Overseas Visitors Survey (OVS). The 1995 survey did compare the drawing power of the arts with that of other non-arts attractions and also included a further arts attraction, arts festivals, in the prompt list (BTA and ETB, 1996). Previous surveys had asked about the relative importance of each of the arts but without reference to any other type of attraction. The inclusion of these in the 1995 survey meant that visitors were asked to assess importance not in isolation but thinking also about the range of other attractions. Theatre was rated as 'very' or 'quite important' in the decision to visit by 37% compared with churches and cathedrals by 59% and historic buildings and castles by 70%.

■ **London:** here too, heritage is more important than the arts in attracting overseas visitors (LTBCB, 1995). Over half of overseas visitors to London indicated that the 'possibility of enjoying' historic buildings had encouraged them to visit the city compared with a third who specified musicals and a quarter who specified plays. (The questions in the London surveys were structured differently from those in the OVS.)

■ **Domestic tourists in the UK:** no particular activity is specified as the main reason for the vast majority (80%) of domestic holiday trips by UK adults in 1997 (English Tourist Board *et al*, 1998). In addition hardly any one of the activities identified in the annual tourist board surveys is apparently of great significance. 'Hill walking, hiking, rambling and orienteering' is the single most important 'main reason' at 47% of all domestic holiday trips. Watching the performing arts is the main reason for only 1% of such trips.

■ In the 1985 survey mentioned earlier (Research Surveys of Great Britain, 1985) none of those interviewed mentioned, in an open question, that live entertainment had been considered when deciding where to go on holiday. It was only on a list of prompted factors that live entertainment assumed any significance in the decision to choose a particular holiday destination. For 15% of holidays it was the 'most important' reason. It was, however, more important for those holidaying at the seaside (22%). Other factors such as 'interesting places in the area to visit', 'easy to travel to' and 'beautiful scenery' were each rated more highly.

■ In **Blackpool**, the largest seaside tourist town in the UK, nearly 30 per cent of holiday-makers rated entertainment as 'the most important factor' in the decision to visit the town (though the town does have an image associated with spectacular entertainment). This factor was mentioned by more people than was any other single factor. As such, it was the most popular 'most important factor'. It needs to be recognized however that over 70 per cent of people considered a number of other factors to be the 'most important factor' for them. Entertainment was more important for older age groups, for those on longer stays and for those not accompanied by children on the holiday. Despite the fact that so many rated it as the most important factor (out of a prompt list of several possible factors), when asked to state how important it was, by itself, in the decision to visit, most (88%) rated it as only 'fairly', 'not very' or 'not at all' important (Hughes and Benn, 1997b).

Tourism studies do suggest that the arts have the ability in themselves to attract some tourists to a destination who are therefore equivalent to arts-core tourists. Nonetheless, even though culture, heritage or the arts rate highly, for instance, in reasons for visits to New York-New Jersey or to Britain, theatre does not dominate as a reason.

Unfortunately, in published survey results, the views on drawing power are not usually linked to those who do participate in the arts/theatre but are views expressed by tourists as a whole (with exceptions such as Alzua *et al.* and Foo and Rossetto). It is obvious from the earlier part of this chapter that most tourists are neither arts-core nor arts-peripheral as most do not go to the theatre. For those who do go, the relative importance of arts-core and arts-periphery is not known because of this failure to link participation and drawing power. It cannot be assumed that all of those who expressed a view on the importance of the arts in the decision to visit also participated. It is in audience surveys that the link is made (Chapter 6) though, of course, they are not directly comparable with tourist surveys.

The role of theatre in domestic tourism is relatively unknown. This limited number of surveys suggests that, on the whole for domestic tourists, entertainment is of little importance in the choice of destination in comparison with other factors. Certain resorts in the UK have a more positive image than others among visitors in terms of live entertainment and, in those cases, arts and entertainment will be of greater importance. Most resort surveys do not, however, permit the assessment of the significance of entertainment in the choice of resort since reasons for visits are frequently classified as 'been before' or 'like the area' and do not refer to specific attractions.

Foreign visitors when rating theatre as important in the decision to visit often do not rate its influence as highly as other 'attractions' of a country. In the case of Britain in particular, heritage aspects are more important in terms of influencing the decision to visit (and in terms of actual places visited). The arts appear to be a significant draw and activity but not the most important. Within the arts, it is theatre that is more important (influence and participation) than concerts or opera and ballet. The role of the arts in encouraging people to visit a particular destination appears to be significant though not decisive. For some, of course, it will undoubtedly be the sole reason for the visit.

Tourist surveys cover people who don't visit the theatre as well as those who do. As a consequence, it might be expected that they demonstrate that theatre is of less importance than is suggested in arts surveys. There are, however, a few problems with tourist surveys (see later this chapter).

Arts-related tourists

There is a common view that cultural or arts-related tourists, especially those who are arts-core, are highly educated, high income, high spending, frequent travelling, hotel-staying, older individuals (Leader-Elliott, 1996; Canadian Tourism Commission, 1997b; McDougall, 1998).

Although there are tourists who are drawn to a destination by the arts, it has already been noted that it is not easy to distinguish arts-core and arts-peripheral tourists as such, from tourist surveys. The New York-New Jersey study was an audience survey that showed that 'arts-motivated' visitors to New York-New Jersey only stayed an average of 2.9 days in the region compared with the average of 4.1 days for all arts visitors. The spend per day was also less at $137 compared with $146. These are tourists for whom the arts are the focus of the visit and it is perhaps not surprising therefore that the visit is shorter. Those who extended their stay because of the arts did so by an average of 2.3 days (Port Authority of New York and New Jersey, 1993).

The Policy Studies Institute study (Myerscough, 1988) concluded that arts-tourists (widely-defined) in London had a longer length of stay and a higher average spend per trip than did other tourists in London. The same study confirmed similar features of the Glasgow arts tourist and also that the arts tourists were older and more likely to be from service and professional occupations than were other tourists.

International cultural visitors to Australia (also widely defined) were more likely to be teachers, lecturers or students than were all inbound visitors. They also stayed longer in the country (average of 32 nights compared with 24 nights) and were more likely to be on their first visit to Australia (Foo and

Rossetto, 1998). In Canada, cultural and heritage travellers (also widely defined) accounted for only 12 per cent of all domestic leisure trips but had an average stay that was longer than that of other leisure travellers (4.8 nights compared with 3.0 nights). They travelled further and average expenditure was greater (double that of other leisure travellers) (McDougall, 1998).

Some studies distinguish between different types of cultural tourist. Alzua *et al.* (1998) divided cultural tourists into five categories with two of them being particularly 'strongly focused on cultural tourism': cluster 1 'heritage, younger' and cluster 5 'heritage, middle age'. Tourists in cluster 1 were typically young and highly educated and were frequent travellers. Cluster 5 were older and generally less well educated than members of the other four clusters. In terms of tourist spending, the two culture clusters spent less on average than, for instance, the resort and sun cluster (but more than the friends and relatives cluster). The two culture clusters were also more likely to spend longer away from home on their trips than the other clusters.

Although not identifying the cultural or arts related tourist as such, a study of domestic tourists in Australia suggested that the proportion of cultural activities in all tourist activities increased with age (Spring, 1991). Similarly cultural participation was more frequent for tourists with higher levels of education. There was not, however, the same obvious relationship with income as the highest proportion of cultural activities occurred in the lowest income groups.

From these studies it is evident that there is, in reality, very little information about the characteristics of the arts-related tourist. The common view that they are 'high-spenders' is not well documented.

Some problems with tourist surveys

Drawing power is a complex concept and these survey approaches may be too simplistic. As was suggested in Chapter 6, the exact nature of drawing power remains unclear and tourist surveys, as well as audience surveys, have limitations. Some of the issues are similar to those identified as being problems with audience surveys (see Figure 7.4):

- Tourist surveys do not usually link the people who go to the theatre whilst tourists with views on the importance of theatre in the decision to visit the destination. Arts-core and arts-peripheral tourists cannot be identified.
- Most, including the Overseas Visitor Survey (UK), do not distinguish holiday from non-holiday tourists. This applies to the business and friends and

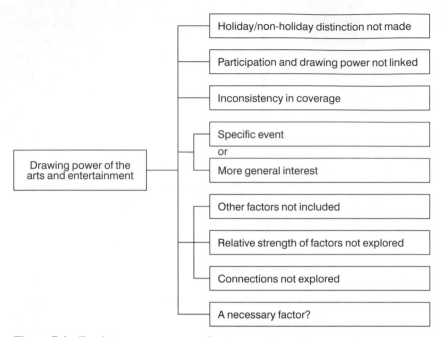

Figure 7.4   Tourist surveys: some weaknesses

relatives tourists as well as to the concept of the instrumental, non-holiday visit that is undertaken solely to visit the arts (see Chapters 3 and 4).

■ There is not a clear picture for domestic tourism in particular of activities undertaken.

■ Surveys have not been consistent in their coverage of importance or participation. Some surveys have related to broad categories such as 'performing arts' or 'arts and entertainment'. The effect of having such broad categories is that it is difficult to identify attendance at theatre and its drawing power or to track influence and participation over time. The category of 'theatre' itself covers a diverse range of activity.

■ Theatre may well be important to many visitors but surveys (like audience surveys) do not usually indicate whether the decision to attend related to a specific performer or production or to a more general wish just to go to the theatre. The relative importance of certain productions in particular in the decision to visit a destination as a tourist is rarely identified. Many productions in London or New York are not unique to those cities or countries and can be seen in many places. This suggests that it is not a case of specific demand (desire to see a particular show) as the show could have been seen elsewhere. It is, for some, a case of 'seeing a show' in London or New York both of which are attractive destinations for many reasons.

Often the show may be irrelevant. The fact that theatres in London and New York theatre are numerous and concentrated in a small area means that there is a possibility of accessing a large number of shows within a stay (Travers, 1998). It also increases the likelihood of a visitor being able to see a show without prior consideration or choice.

Nonetheless demand in the West End or Broadway can, at times, be specific. There may, of course, be a desire to see a particular show or concert but specifically in London or New York. There may also be a desire to see a 'West End' or 'Broadway' production of a particular show even though that show can be seen elsewhere. There may too be a preference to see a West End or Broadway production of any show.

- As with audience surveys, the various 'art' forms are not always evaluated against a full range of other factors. In some they are evaluated against each other only and in others, against 'non-arts' activities. A restricted prompt list has limitations in indicating the relative importance of influences on the decision to visit.

- In respect of participation the very nature of the surveys (non-diary) has meant that rates include 'intent to visit' which may not, of course, turn into an actual visit.

- Where a full range of factors is included there is usually no indication of the relative 'strength' of each (see Chapter 6). For example, 40% may rate arts as the main reason for a visit to a destination and 30% may rate scenery but for those 40% how much more important is arts than scenery or any other factor?

- The studies do not always indicate what connections there might be between reasons for the visit (similar to audience surveys). They do not show whether theatre is an important reason in isolation or only with other arts. Joint availability may be critical. For example, heritage may be shown to be 'very important' to, say, 70% and arts to 25% but it is not known how many of the 70% also find the arts very important. They do not, either, indicate whether theatre and the arts are important only within a wider package of other attractions. More people may have rated heritage than anything else as important, but does the visit depend solely on heritage or on that and other factors? It may, in practice, be difficult or impossible to identify the relative pull of attractions. The absence of any one, such as theatre, may reduce the pull of others such as shops or museums and vice versa. It may be that it is a combination of attractions rather than any single attraction that influences the visit decision, but this will not be evident unless surveys are more discriminating and focused. It is more than likely that heritage exercises such an influence only because it is available in combination with other attractions such as theatre.

■ As was noted in the discussion of audience surveys it is possible, confusingly, for people to rate the arts highly in the decision to visit a place even though they believe that the arts are not necessary to ensure a visit. A few tourist studies ask tourists what effect an absence of the arts would have had on the decision to visit. A survey dating back to the mid-1980s asked foreign visitors' reactions to an imagined absence of certain features in Britain (BTA and ETB, 1985). If theatre had been absent from Britain then 58% of visitors would have come anyway but if historic buildings and towns were absent only 31% would have come and if scenery and countryside were absent only 20% would have come. Theatre would appear to have rather less influence than many other attractions.

In Blackpool, despite entertainment being the single most important reason for people choosing it as a destination, 84% of people would have come anyway in the absence of entertainment (Hughes and Benn, 1997). Entertainment was the most popular 'most important' reason but other attractions mentioned may, in combination, have had an overwhelming influence (71% found a number of other factors to be 'the most important'). Similarly, many may rate arts or entertainment as 'very important' in the decision to visit a destination when asked to respond to a question asking about the importance in isolation. Many other factors could though also have been rated as 'very important' and it is the ranking and comparisons that are important but these are not determined.

None of the audience and tourist surveys demonstrates clearly the existence of arts-core or arts-peripheral (or incidental or accidental) arts-related tourists nor, as indicated above, whether interest is specific or general (see Chapter 4).

There are problems in determining drawing power but it is obvious that the influence of the arts and entertainment can range considerably from being the most important factors or resources (by themselves or with others) through being important but secondary factors (also by themselves or with others) through to being of no importance at all. Regardless of the influence in the destination choice decision, visits to arts and entertainment whilst on holiday are common. It was noted earlier that for some, attendance at arts and entertainment occurs even though they did not feature in the destination choice decision (the 'accidental' arts-related tourist). Similarly, for others importance in the destination choice decision was not followed by actual attendance, for whatever reasons. The OVS of 1995 demonstrated that 'very large numbers of those reporting an arts sector as important simply do not attend' (BTA and ETB, 1996: 35). This 'non-attendance' was greatest in the case of the performing arts whereas the reverse was the case for museums and art galleries: higher proportions visited them than had indicated they were important in the decision to visit. This presumably is because of the relative 'ease' of visiting museums compared with theatre, which has limited capacity. Even though visitors may have intended to go to the theatre they may not have been able to buy tickets or had changed their minds once here if only because of the relative prices of visiting a museum and going to the theatre. Participation and influence are not necessarily connected.

Chapter summary

The arts and entertainment are seen by the tourist industry as having the potential to attract tourists. In some cases, for arts-core tourists, they can be the sole or main attraction whereas in others, for arts-peripheral tourists, they are less important and may be amenities rather than attractions. The actual provision of arts and entertainment is, of course, largely left to that industry but the various parts of the tourism industry may be involved in several ways. Tourist boards and government may utilize and emphasize the arts and entertainment in marketing a town or a country. Government, especially local, may encourage and financially support the arts because of the tourism-generating potential. More direct involvement may come from tour operators who put together inclusive tour packages of accommodation, theatre tickets and transport. The most direct connection is through hotels, which, apart from the inclusive tour involvement, often provide some form of live entertainment themselves.

Given that there is an interest by tourists in arts and entertainment, then surveys of tourists might be expected to show how many actually do go to see a performance of some sort. In terms of total tourist expenditure the arts and entertainment do not seem particularly important in comparison with shopping, accommodation or travel. In terms of participation it is usually only a minority of tourists who go to see the performing arts but nonetheless the proportion of tourists that does attend a show or concert can be quite high. In some cases, it is the only occasion when visits to the theatre are made and going to the theatre is a holiday experience for some people. It is evident however that for many tourists other attractions and activities, such as heritage, are more popular. Some tourists indicate that arts and entertainment are important factors in visiting a destination, though, again, it is often other factors that are important for a greater number of people. The existence of arts-core and arts-peripheral tourists is difficult to determine because participation in the arts and the importance of the arts in the visit-decision are not linked in published surveys.

Like audience surveys, these surveys have a number of other weaknesses. In particular, there is little recognition of the inter-connection between reasons for visiting a destination.

8

Impact

The two previous chapters have included a discussion of two issues: first, the extent to which people go to the theatre or a concert when they are tourists and second, how important the arts are in attracting people to a destination (whether it be town, city or country). Both of these were looked at, first, from the viewpoint of the arts and then from the tourism viewpoint. It was seen that there can be large numbers of tourists in some audiences and that the arts can play an important role in attracting tourists to a destination. It looks therefore as if the two (arts and tourism) are mutually beneficial. The continuing interest, by tourism and arts organizations, in the arts–tourism relationship suggests that there may be some benefit for both in the relationship. The beneficial aspects of the relationship were recognized early by the American Council for the Arts (1981). The English Tourist Board considers that the arts and tourism 'have a complementary relationship and are heavily reliant upon each other' (ETB, 1993: 4). The Port Authority of New York and New Jersey (PANYNJ), as the body responsible for transportation and port facilities in the region (including the airports), clearly has an interest in tourism. It has carried out major studies of tourism in the region but also, significantly, of the relationship with the arts. The Port Authority's most recent study showed they are 'closely intertwined' (Port Authority of New York and New Jersey, 1993, 1994). In the Policy Studies Institute report mentioned in previous chapters, it was stated that 'it is self-evident that the arts and tourism enjoy a complementary relationship. The arts create attractions for tourism and tourism supplies extra audiences for the arts' (Myerscough, 1988: 80).

It is the issue of 'benefit' that is examined in this chapter. There may well be a relationship between the two but is it in their best interests to have this relationship? Importantly, are there disadvantages (or costs) arising from the relationship?

This chapter includes a discussion of:

- the effects of tourism on the arts;
- the effects of the arts on tourism;
- some of the more undesirable effects;
- the significance of the two for regeneration of cities;
- the effects of this joint promotion;
- the economic aspect of arts-related tourism with special reference to multiplier analysis.

Tourism's impact on the arts

In the case of New York it has been observed that 'arts-motivated visitors . . . are critically important to the arts industry' (Port Authority of New York and New Jersey, 1993: 4). Tourists have also been considered to be important for the well-being of London's West End theatres. In the early 1980s it was believed that 'if it were not for the visits by several million tourists each year, the West End theatre would be in serious difficulties' (Society of West End Theatre, 1982: 6) and it was doubtful if, in particular, theatres could remain open throughout the summer. The significance continues to be asserted: 'In earlier years, midsummer was usually the period in which there were large numbers of theatres closed but as overseas tourism levels have been improving, more theatres have been staying open during the summer' (Gardiner and Dickety, 1996: 8). Theatres in seaside resorts and other holiday destinations are almost wholly dependent upon tourists for their existence. Tourism can provide another source of audiences

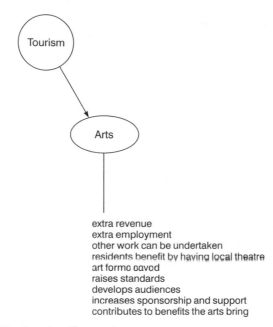

extra revenue
extra employment
other work can be undertaken
residents benefit by having local theatre
art forms saved
raises standards
develops audiences
increases sponsorship and support
contributes to benefits the arts bring

Figure 8.1 Tourism: its effect on the arts

and revenue for the arts (see Figure 8.1). It can therefore support artistic life and activity and contribute to the existence of the arts. 'Tourism provides a significant opportunity for cultural and heritage organisations to attract more visitors and increase revenues. This, in turn, will help them thrive and prosper' (Canadian Tourism Commission, 1997b: 10). Tourism can contribute to the survival of live theatre, which, of course, has experienced considerable problems related to the growth of the home-based leisure technology of television, video and the computer.

At its simplest, tourists are just another potential market that can be targeted and which can therefore generate extra revenue. There are also a number of other possible impacts of tourism.

Extra revenue

Extra revenue may be the result of:

■ audiences over and above those previously attained (extra ticket sales);
■ higher ticket prices paid by tourist;
■ greater tourists' spend on theatre souvenirs and merchandise.

Assuming that additional revenue does result then there are several possible outcomes, dependent upon the initial situation. Some companies would exist and survive anyway and the tourist revenue is a 'bonus'. For others it may make the difference between survival and extinction. Theatre companies in coastal tourist towns and some tourist cities will depend almost entirely on such tourist revenue for their survival. Tourism can therefore make a difference in that, in some cases, the arts are able to continue when they otherwise might not have done so (perhaps in the West End and on Broadway) and in other cases arts are initiated when they otherwise would not have existed (in seaside holiday towns).

Tourism may also make some productions viable or more profitable because an extended run is possible. A production in a city such as New York may have an extended run because of tourists or a production may tour to a holiday area in summer months as well as being in a city for the rest of the year.

Employment

Extra employment may also result. There is a greater number of jobs because some companies survive that otherwise would not do so. In some cases jobs would have existed for a while but employment is lengthened because the companies stay in business and/or because production runs are longer. The employment effects are therefore twofold:

- increase in number of people employed;
- same number of people employed but opportunity for individuals to obtain longer periods of employment and to be employed throughout the year. There is continuing employment for individuals if theatres in cities remain open during the summer (as has been claimed for West End theatres). There are also opportunities in seaside entertainment for those employed in theatre but who would have been unemployed during the traditionally 'dark' season in many towns and cities. (This seasonal cycle of employment is probably less than it used to be.)

These extra jobs and more secure jobs attract people into the profession and they also mean that people may stay in the profession. By providing more employment opportunities and continuity of employment, many who work elsewhere – in city theatres, in television, radio or film – may be able to survive and continue. For some performers, such live theatre is welcomed as an alternative to their more usual employment in the recorded media.

Other work

The extra revenue generated by companies that are already profitable may enable them to carry out activities which are desirable but were previously impossible. This will include educational work, outreach and experimental work.

Residents

Because of the survival of the arts, local residents benefit by being able to visit the theatre or hear a concert. They benefit by having the opportunity to see productions that would not exist if reliant wholly on a local market. Some arts activities including many festivals were established because of tourism (or have become dependent on tourism) and the ability to experience these would otherwise not be available. There is also a benefit to the locals through the income and employment generated.

Vulnerable art forms

Survival may be especially important where it is felt that a particular art form may have been in danger of disappearing or particular venues lost (Prohaska, 1995). Tourism may therefore allow the continuance of productions, art forms and venues that are considered to be important enough to survive but whose financial position is weak. Certain cultural activities and venues, once lost, may never be recovered. Limited interest may mean productions are unviable but the plays may be considered to be so important as to be preserved. The tradition of performance and knowledge about the plays are preserved so that others may have the option of attendance at some later time. If, for instance, Shakespeare plays were not performed currently, it would be less likely that there would be an opportunity for future generations to experience them. Current production at least offers the opportunity for those who are currently uninterested to become interested and to pass on that interest to others.

In the same way, if theatres do not succeed they may be demolished or turned to new uses meaning less opportunity for future generations to experience live theatre and concerts.

Undoubtedly some experiences would not exist at all but for an original strong tourist-orientation on the part of companies who produce in order to attract tourists (such as seaside entertainment and some festivals). The survival of variety and its components of dance, song, comedy, magic, etc. is due largely to seaside entertainment. This has been particularly associated with the seaside and despite there being audiences for this elsewhere, seaside holiday venues and audiences have contributed significantly to ensuring its survival.

Standards

There is not just a contribution to the survival of live performance but there may also be an effect on standards. In order to attract tourists (long-distance audiences) the production may need to be particularly 'professional' in content (and marketing approach). It may need to be particularly spectacular and/or 'unique'. The ETB (1993) considers that visitors, as outsiders, may 'bring a new perspective' to the arts and thus 'can challenge and enrich everyone's perspective'.

Audience development

Seaside entertainment also has a specific significance in audience development. It was seen in Chapter 7 that a visit to the theatre is, in some cases, a common holiday experience and that some people are more likely to see a show or concert whilst on holiday. It is possible that such visits could lead to the development of visits once back home. In this way the holiday can be an 'easy' introduction to the performing arts.

Sponsors and support

Although tourism is similar in its effects to any other additional source of revenue, the very fact that this market segment is made up of tourists may bring additional benefit:

- **Sponsorship:** the ability to attract tourists may make the arts more attractive to sponsors as it gives a wider geographical spread to their message. Sponsors may also be attracted by a high-spend audience and by the prestige of being associated with high quality productions, performers and events, which might be evident in the case of some festivals in particular. High-profile events such as festivals may result in considerable leverage of private sector finance for the arts.
- **Wider support:** hoteliers, bar and restaurant owners benefit from tourism and therefore look favourably on the arts. They may offer financial support to the arts, they may themselves sponsor productions and may lobby on their behalf. As noted in Chapter 6, this wider impact may strengthen the case that the arts make for support from local government and arts and tourist boards.

Benefits of the arts

If the arts are believed to be beneficial and tourism contributes to the existence of the arts, then tourism can claim to have contributed to those benefits. The arts are believed to enrich people's lives and live performances have merits of their own such as social interaction and community, escapism, a sense of contentment, fulfilment, happiness, satisfaction, etc. They can be more satisfying for many than television, recorded music and computer games and many other aspects of popular culture. The arts, more mundanely, are believed to contribute to the regeneration of cities (see below). Tourism can claim some credit for these and many other positive aspects of the arts through ensuring the survival of the live arts. More particularly, these attributes of live performances would not be experienced by some people if it was not for tourism. For some, seeing a show on holiday is more likely than seeing one when at home. Without theatres and shows in holiday destinations a large number of people would not experience these particular satisfactions.

The arts' impact on tourism

It is undoubtedly claimed that the arts stimulate tourism (see Figure 8.2). Reports on the West End and Broadway are quite clear in believing this to be the case. 'Broadway is the strongest tourist attraction in New York' (Hauser and Lanier, 1998: 1) and 'We know that the West End theatre is a key driver of in-bound tourism' (Travers, 1998: 9).

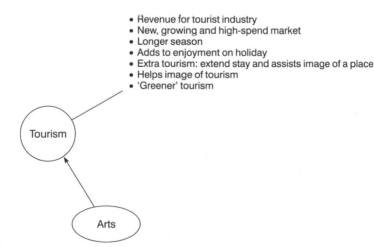

- Revenue for tourist industry
- New, growing and high-spend market
- Longer season
- Adds to enjoyment on holiday
- Extra tourism: extend stay and assists image of a place
- Helps image of tourism
- 'Greener' tourism

Tourism

Arts

Figure 8.2 The arts: their effect on tourism

The case for the arts is increasingly made in terms of 'tourism' generated. As arts organizations have been faced with growing difficulties in obtaining government funding they have pointed to their income, employment and tourism effects as justification for their existence and for further support. (This is also 'evidence' of the perspective of the arts as an industry, which is discussed later in this chapter.) In the economic impact study of the Adelaide Festival it was stated that 'cultural events such as festivals are not only a significant promoter of a destination for interstate and international tourism but also provide a significant injection to the local economy' (Market Equity and Economic Research Consultants, 1996: 7). The Port Authority of New York and New Jersey first published a report on the arts in 1983. Its stated interest as an organization was to 'bolster economic activity in this region, including the promotion of tourism and travel . . . The arts industry . . . draws millions of people here from all over the world' (Cultural Assistance Center and Port Authority of New York and New Jersey, 1983: 1). This view of the arts was confirmed in their more recent study where Broadway was identified as 'one of New York city's most enduring tourist attractions' (Port Authority of New York and New Jersey, 1993: 3).

In the mid 1980s the Arts Council of Great Britain advocated an increased public 'investment' in the arts partly because 'the arts are a substantial tourist attraction and foreign currency earner' (ACGB, 1985: 6). It is significant that the 1988 Policy Studies Institute study should have been of the economic importance of the arts and, within that, a whole chapter was devoted to the arts–tourism connection (Myerscough, 1988). The Wyndham report on London's West End theatres was commissioned specifically to identify the impact on the London and UK economies and a significant part of that impact was considered to arise from tourism and the industry was therefore a 'significant contributor to our balance of payments' (Travers, 1998: 5).

Extra revenue

As noted above, the arts may generate extra tourists and revenue for tourism businesses. In Chapters 6 and 7 it was seen that the extent to which the arts could attract tourists was not always clear cut but nonetheless they do have some drawing power. The arts therefore stimulate a flow of business for tour operators, travel agents, hotels and restaurants, etc. This spending (on hotels, food, etc.) is known as 'ancillary spending'. In the case of the West End, for every £1 spent on tickets there was a further £1.76 spent on meals (43p), accommodation (46p), transport (62p), programmes and souvenirs

(20p) and other items (5p) (Travers, 1998) (see Figure 8.6). It was estimated that international visitors to the Adelaide Festival spent A\$5.60 on accommodation, meals out, transport and the like for every A\$1 spent on tickets (Market Equity and Economic Research Consultants, 1996). Arts-motivated visitors to New York-New Jersey spent nearly 60% of their expenditure on hotels and meals, 19% on air fares and 11% on shopping (Port Authority of New York and New Jersey, 1993).

New markets

Tourism related to the arts is believed to be a new and expanding market made up of high-spend and up-market consumers. In the case of urban tourism, for instance, it is considered that such tourists are 'typically well-educated, affluent and broadly travelled, (and) they generally represent a highly desirable type of upscale visitor' (Holcomb, 1999: 64). In Chapter 7 it was noted that this tourism market is regarded as additional, growing and a premium one. The tourism market is becoming less of a mass market and more segmented. Arts-related tourism is part of the product differentiation, which fits with this segmentation and with the new demands for more meaningful tourism (Jansen-Verbeke, 1996). It is claimed, too, that satisfaction levels and willingness to repeat are high (Myerscough, 1988). Because of these features, the arts are considered favourably by the tourist industry.

Extends season

The arts extend the tourist season as they are less dependent on the weather. 'Dedicated music-lovers ... will attend events at any time of the year to satisfy their desire for special experiences' (Getz, 1991: 7). In some cases, events are deliberately planned as a strategic response to seasonal problems (Hall, 1992).

Fulfilment

Tourism also benefits in a less direct way as the arts can add to the meaning and satisfaction derived from a holiday. Arts and entertainment are often considered to be part of the holiday experience and for some they are only experienced on holiday. For some tourists therefore they are an essential part of the holiday experience. Their absence would, for these people, either reduce the likelihood of taking a holiday or of the holiday being pleasurable.

Extra tourism

Not only do the arts create extra business for the tourism industry directly they may succeed in doing so in a less direct way. It was seen in Chapter 6 how people who visited New York for non-arts reasons (perhaps business or visiting friends or relatives) extended their stay because of the arts. It was estimated that 16% of 'visitors' to the Adelaide Festival had visited South Australia for other reasons and extended their trip in order to attend the festival (Market Equity and Economic Research Consultants, 1996).

In a similar way tourists may combine an arts-based visit with a stay in other places. It is claimed that the Edinburgh Festivals result in more visits to the rest of Scotland than would otherwise occur. Nearly a third of International Festival tourists spent at least one night (average 6 nights) in another part of Scotland. 'The Festivals are a major attraction of tourists to Scotland. These tourists not only spend time in Edinburgh but also take the opportunity to ... holiday elsewhere in Scotland' (Gratton and Taylor, 1992: 40). The Festivals are therefore regarded as a catalyst for a greater flow of tourism. Around 40 per cent of visitors to the Adelaide Festival stayed overnight elsewhere in South Australia and/or took day trips elsewhere in the state (Market Equity and Economic Research Consultants, 1996).

The arts also raise the profile of a place and this may lead to tourism indirectly. The arts influence the image of a place and define a place, which may, in turn, attract tourists (Weiner, 1980). Music is considered by Cohen (1997) to be a particularly significant element in the production of 'place' such as in the case of the Beatles and Liverpool and jazz in New Orleans. Liverpool, a place of many and often contradictory images, is particularly associated with the Beatles and this has been used as a tourist resource. This has not been without contention however, as there are those who believe that it detracts from the contemporary practice and production of music in the city (Cohen, 1997).

Public relations

Tourism may benefit through a public relations aspect. The contribution to the survival of the arts can be used to support the case for tourism and counter-act any adverse publicity such as that associated with some of the worst excesses of mass tourism and with environmental damage in the countryside.

'Sustainable tourism'

It is claimed that arts-related tourism is 'greener' than other forms of tourism (ETB, 1993). It is in the interests of tourism that the heritage and the performing arts should continue and tourism contributes towards the continued existence through the revenue generated to providers. In addition, consumption of these is not so obviously damaging as are some forms of tourism. Some rural and coastal tourism may diminish or destroy the physical environment on which it is based. The ETB goes on to point out that tourism fits in with the growing trend for individuals to seek more learning and enrichment whilst treating the environment more responsibly. The UK government in a recent strategy for tourism states that 'tourism is largely based on our heritage, culture and countryside and therefore needs to maintain the quality of the resources on which it depends. Tourism can provide an incentive and income to protect our built and natural heritage and helps to maintain local culture and diversity' (DCMS, 1999: 8). Myerscough (1988) considered that cultural tourists are themselves likely to press the case for preservation and sensitive development. They are articulate and powerful enough to press this case successfully.

Nonetheless art forms can be modified by tourism and, in this sense, the performing arts are not sustained (see later this chapter). Heritage is also similarly altered so that a particular view of the past is preserved. It is also evident that the numbers of tourists in some heritage sites, whether battle-fields, castles or churches, can erode the physical fabric of the site and building and also 'spoil' the experience for those seeking a more personalized, less crowded or managed, interaction with the past. The success of cultural tourism 'has generated costs that can no longer be dismissed as a marginal and acceptable inconvenience ... Continued success threatens the quality and even continued existence of the resources' (Ashworth, 1993: 13). These comments were directed particularly at heritage tourism but nonetheless they may be equally relevant for the performing arts. There is, of course, the particular issue of entertainment and re-enactments in heritage centres and heritage theme parks. This very process is considered to be part of the process of trivializing and commodifying history and its conversion into the heritage industry. The performing arts play a significant part in it.

The benefits of tourism

It was noted earlier how tourism could claim that any intrinsic benefits of the arts could be attributed in part to it because it helped sustain the arts. Similarly the arts may be viewed as sustaining tourism and therefore any benefits that it might have are partly due to the arts. Invariably these benefits are stated in economic terms (see later this chapter).

Some problems in the relationship

Despite the many benefits claimed for both the arts and tourism from the relationship, there are a number of problems that need to be recognized. Most of the problems relate to the influence on the arts rather than on tourism (see Figure 8.3).

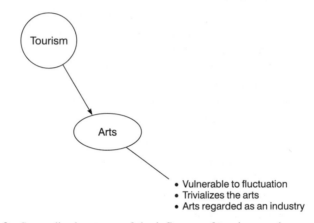

Figure 8.3 Some disadvantages of the influence of tourism on the arts

In the less industrialized parts of the world, tourism is often accused of destroying local cultures, arts and traditions so that a society's identity is altered. These arguments are not so extreme in industrialized countries such as Britain, Australia or the USA but nonetheless have some relevance. Tourism may cause problems for the arts such as:

Vulnerability

The flows of tourism can work against the arts. Any company that is dependent on tourism will prosper only so long as the tourism flows occur. A downturn or slowing down of growth in tourism will cause problems. The high proportions of overseas visitors in West End theatre audiences mean that those theatres have been, in the past, vulnerable to any changes in the number of tourists visiting the UK. There are 'strong correlations between the trends in theatre attendance and those for overseas visitors to the UK' (Dunlop and Eckstein, 1995: 4). It is noticeable that whereas increased ticket sales for West End theatres had come from overseas tourism during the 1980s, by the mid 1980s this was no longer true and sales to overseas visitors were falling (Gardiner, 1991). The number of overseas visitors in West End audiences continued to fall between 1991 and 1997 (MORI, 1998) though there were years such as 1995 when there were large increases in overseas visitor sales (Gardiner and Dickety, 1996). These changes are beyond the direct influence of the theatres as they are determined by many complex factors including air fares, relative exchange rates, prices in competitive destinations and fear for personal safety.

Regardless of year-by-year fluctuations in tourism it is obvious that much tourism is seasonal. The establishment of a strong local core audience may be necessary for long-term viability. Despite the many references to the beneficial effects of tourism on West End theatre it is recognized that the nurturing of a strong core local audience is desirable for the long-term stability and well-being of the industry. Such a core does exist in both London and New York. New York residents accounted for nearly a quarter of all Broadway ticket sales in 1997 (from a fifth in 1991) (Hauser and Roth, 1998). As a result, despite the vulnerability to tourism shifts, 'fluctuations in levels of overseas tourism tend to have less effect on theatre than on other tourist attractions such as museums' (Gardiner and Dickety, 1996: 64). The vulnerability of the arts to fluctuations in tourism is most obviously seen in the fate of traditional seaside entertainment discussed in Chapter 5.

In addition, the ability of the arts to attract tourists is often dependent on 'heritage'. It was noted in Chapter 7, in particular, that heritage was the factor within the UK that was most often cited as influencing the decision to visit. Theatre was of lesser importance for most. Theatre itself is not sufficient to attract most of these overseas visitors. The decision to visit the theatre is often a 'secondary' one dependent on the ability of heritage to attract in the first place or a joint one also dependent upon the ability of others to attract. If the decision to visit the theatre is tied in with the decision to visit other attractions then the fortunes of theatre are reliant upon the quality and marketing strategies of those heritage and other organizations.

Trivialization

The process of attracting tourists may lead to pressure to produce 'popular' artistic works and the product may become in some way commercialized and trivialized. Artistic aspiration may clash with the requirements of a tourist market. Some producers and performers may resent the fact that they have to appeal to the widest possible audience and to present productions that are 'entertaining' and light rather than original and meaningful. In some cases those in the arts have expressed concern about the fact that their work is not appreciated by tourist audiences who regard it as 'a night out' (Leader-Elliott, 1996; Canadian Tourism Commission, 1997b).

Although not directly referring to the performing arts, 'tourist art' in Craik's (1997) view involves some degree of modification of indigenous art so that outputs are standardized and simplified. Objects that had a function become separated from that function and become decorative. In the same way, performing arts that are new, experimental, dissenting, are of minority interest or performances that are community-based may be discouraged since they may not be the sort of production that appeals to the tourist audience. These art forms are already under pressure as they are unlikely to generate large audiences and revenues. The tourism dimension adds to this pressure.

The upsurge in beach-related tourism in Spain from the 1960s onwards was accompanied by tourist shows that included flamenco dancing. This is an Andalusian or Castilian art form and is 'foreign' to Catalonia. Performances in Catalan resorts on the Costa Brava and Costa Dorada were staged solely to conform with North European tourists' perceptions of Spain. They did not represent authentic Catalan culture and were purely tourist spectacle.

Theatres in London and New York have been criticized as being geared towards a tourist market leading to standardization, blandness and emphasis on spectacle (Hughes, 1998b). The West End has been termed a 'theatrical theme park' as it is regarded as part of the circuit that the tourist believes it necessary to visit whether or not he or she really has a liking for the theatre (Brown, 1996). The effect has been to make it more difficult for new, innovative and experimental productions to be mounted in the West End.

This trivialization occurs because leisure tourism continues to be predominantly a 'mass' phenomenon made up of packaged collective experiences, despite the suggestion in earlier chapters of this book that there is a move away from mass tourism. Even though there is increasing diversity in the tourism market in the form of adventure holidays, special interest holidays, heritage and arts holidays, etc., most tourists still seek amusement and diversion rather than profound experiences. The holidays are standardized, predictable and 'safe'. This was their original attraction and it remains so for many people today. Because of this standardization and the similarity to much of the fast-food industry, tourism is said to have been 'McDonaldised' though the term has been amended to be 'McDisneyised' (Ritzer and Liska, 1997). It is spectacle and signs that tourists desire rather than underlying authentic and meaningful experiences.

Not only are the products of the tourist industry standardized, so too are the arts. Leisure as a whole has become increasingly commodified in the sense that industry transforms many leisure pursuits into experiences that are bought and sold as commodities (Britton, 1991). Limited plots, spectacle and the emphasis on music and dance make musicals accessible to the more casual theatre-goer and to international audiences. They require little or no accumulated cultural capital for them to be enjoyed. The process has been encouraged by the view of the arts as having a role to play in attracting tourists. This has contributed to unadventurous cultural policy in cities (Bianchini and Parkinson, 1993). The arts and tourism are both made 'safe' and predictable through packaging and they require limited consumer involvement. The two industries offer superficial sensation without appreciation or understanding. Holidays and arts are packaged and choice is limited.

This trivialization is not always or necessarily the case however. This is most obvious in arts core cases where artistic events attract a significant tourist audience without any concession to popular appeal or loss of artistic integrity. A production is so 'good' that it attracts a widespread audience. It is possible that a minority-interest production, for instance, could only survive by appealing to a widespread audience. There may be few people in any one place with that interest but when added together across several places they can constitute a large audience. Such an audience is tourist more in the sense of being drawn from a large area rather than being 'holiday-makers'. Many high-arts festivals will fall into this category of tourist-oriented performances that are not trivialized.

It is also the case that many forces have been responsible for any trivialization that is believed to have happened. The influence of the mass media and television may be particularly relevant in this respect in creating a society that is interested more in inconsequential than in profound matters. The need for the arts to be more commercial in order to survive will have contributed to the process. Less financial support from government has meant a need to seek out new audiences perhaps by popularizing the product and presenting fewer limited-interest but meaningful productions.

Arts as an industry

The stress on the arts–tourism relationship may contribute to a view of the arts as an industry, as evidenced by statements such as 'London's West End theatre is a large and growing business' (Travers, 1998: 7). The arts are increasingly seen as a product (as evidenced by the title of Chapter 5 of this book!) and those who are involved in creating the product are in an industry like any other. This has the effect that the arts are seen as an activity that has no extraordinary distinguishing characteristics. Rather than seen as being worthy in their own right and for their own sake, the arts are regarded as important for the income, employment and balance of payments effects that are generated. The organization and packaging of the arts as a tourist resource is a significant contributor to this process. The arts remain favourably regarded until some other activity is shown to have more favourable effects. 'The problem with this justification is that the arts are asked to be something that they are neither designed nor intended to be . . . They may lose by these rules if another sector with a greater economic impact comes along' (Schuster, 1989: 14).

It has already been seen earlier in this chapter how the Arts Council, Policy Studies Institute and the Wyndham report had viewed the economic aspects of the arts in generating tourism to be of great significance. The Port Authority study of the arts perhaps overstated its case in saying that it sought 'to change the way people think about the arts . . . Too often we forget its importance to our economic vitality' (Port Authority of New York and New Jersey, 1993: 1) but nonetheless it is significant that it and many other studies choose to identify the economic consequences of the arts. The economic consequences identified invariably include discussion of its tourism impact. A recent Policy Studies Institute study barely mentioned tourism but was, significantly, entitled 'Culture as a commodity' with the sub-title of 'the economics of the arts and cultural heritage' (Casey *et al.*, 1996).

Tourist boards are not unaware of some of the dangers. The ETB, for instance, warns 'it should always be remembered that the desire to increase visitor numbers while sustaining the environment – physical and intellectual – that attracted them in the first place is a challenge and objective both spheres share' (ETB, 1993: 6).

The extent to which tourism contributes to this view of the arts needs however to be kept in perspective. In most towns and cities there are relatively few tourists in performing arts audiences (with the exception of tourist cities and festivals). It is also the case that it is only a few arts that attract tourists and which are affected by tourism. Tourism may influence the performing arts product but its influence is limited. The nature of the performing arts in most towns and cities is increasingly the outcome of commercial pressures regardless of the tourism dimension. Corporations in the arts have also themselves taken the initiative, seized the opportunities and exploited the tourism market and it is therefore not entirely the fault of tourism. Cultural policies may well though have intensified these influences by emphasizing the commercial and economic perspective through, in part, the tourism potential of the arts (see later this chapter).

Irrelevance

Arts aimed at non-local audiences face the criticism of not meeting the needs of locals. Some artistic events with a strong tourist input may be seen to lack local significance and they become open to charges of irrelevance and, in some cases, elitism. This may be the case with festivals, especially those that focus on the 'high arts' aimed at high-spending audiences across the country and the world.

Urban regeneration

As well as the effect of each upon the other, the arts and tourism have a joint effect, which is the effect of arts-related tourism upon urban regeneration (see Figure 8.4). Each activity – tourism and the arts – refers to the other in justifying its existence but, in addition, they both lay claim to very similar positive attributes. They are growth industries, they preserve culture and buildings, they create jobs and help regenerate inner cities. (See early statements of this in, for instance, ACGB, 1985 and ETB, 1981.) The connection between the arts and tourism is reinforced by the fact that both are seen as helping economic regeneration. Each is seen (individually) as helping regenerate cities but the regenerative effects of each are seen to partly depend

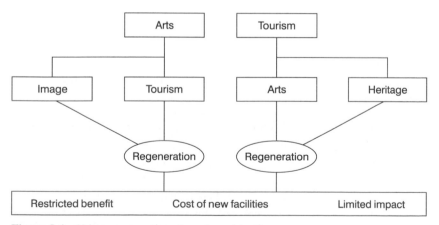

Figure 8.4   Urban regeneration, the arts and tourism

upon the other. Not only therefore do the arts and tourism industries see merit in their relationship, so too do those on the outside, such as local government, who have an interest in urban regeneration. They are both viewed, in cities in particular, as having the potential to assist in reviving run-down areas and to create prosperity where there was little before.

Many cities across Europe and North America have been facing the challenges of adjusting to the requirements of a world that differs greatly from the one when most of them were prosperous. Most cities are the product of nineteenth and early twentieth centuries and of industrialization. Recently their industrial base has diminished, associated with globalization and the international division of labour. The outcome is that inner cities in particular have experienced a fall in employment and a net population outflow (to the suburbs). Inner cities are often characterized by a high population density, poor quality housing, deterioration of infrastructure and environmental dereliction. All lead to high levels of ill-health and morbidity, a high incidence of social problems (including crime) and low educational achievement.

Encouragement of the arts and tourism in many cities has been, in part, a response to this economic and social decline and a desire to re-position themselves as centres of services and centres of consumption rather than of production and, in particular, as centres of consumption of leisure and pleasure: sports, shops, theatres, cinemas, pubs, restaurants, clubs (Hannigan, 1998). Prospering cities are those associated with services (though not solely leisure services) and information technology. Tourism strategies for urban areas have frequently been based on the regeneration potential of tourism, though how great an impact it can make is arguable. The English Tourist Board has been promoting the role of tourism in urban regeneration for some time (ETB 1980, 1981) largely based on early experiences in USA such as in Baltimore (Maryland) and Lowell (Massachusetts) (Falk, 1986). The possible role of tourism is recognized by the UK government (Department of the Environment, 1990). The arts and heritage are particularly strong tourist assets of many urban areas and the tourism promoted in cities is usually based on these (see Figure 8.4).

At the same time, regeneration has appeared in arts and cultural policies that have been developed in many West European and North American cities. Cultural policies may serve many purposes but serving the objective of urban regeneration is a relatively recent development (Bianchini and Parkinson, 1993). Cultural policies have shifted their emphasis from 'social welfare' or 'benevolent' provision for local residents and the development of local initiatives to economic ends and a concern for 'city-image'. In a study of local government in London it was concluded that there was 'a growing recognition of the value-added potential of arts and cultural input to urban and economic development' (Evans, 1993: 26). Culture may lead to urban regeneration in a number of ways including:

- **Improving the image of the city and using it in 'place marketing':** This hopefully will enable a city to compete in the international market for investment and encourage industry and commerce to locate in the city (Figure 8.4). The role of the arts in making a city an attractive place to live and work is emphasized by many. The New York-New Jersey study referred to the fact that 56 per cent of people who had moved to New York city cited the variety of cultural attractions as a major motivation (Port Authority of New York-New Jersey, 1993).
- **Attracting tourists:** The benefits of cultural policy are also expected to show themselves through tourism and the employment and income effects of an injection of tourist expenditure. The arts attract tourists directly and indirectly by influencing image (Figure 8.4). Tourism is itself dependent on a good image and this is helped by the arts provision. The artistic and cultural activities of a place will affect the image and perception of that place by those outside. Tourism is at the forefront of urban cultural policies though, for some, 'whether these facilities include significant numbers of tourists among their visitors . . . is less important than the perception that the leisured city, or the cultural city, is the successful city in the post-industrial world' (Voase, 1997: 237).

Tourism and the arts are regarded as contributing to each other's role in regenerating cities. They are each a necessary part of the other. Arts-related tourism is therefore regarded as being a significant contributor to reviving economic activity in cities. There has been widespread agreement about the role, so much so that the arts and tourism might almost be regarded as operating in a 'coalition', or informal linking. There has been a common view on the way forward.

Cultural policies have been designed with a view to encouraging inward investment and tourism but the middle or service classes have had considerable influence on them. What arts to develop in a city, along with other aspects of urban redevelopment, has been influenced by these particular classes. They have been able to express their wants more coherently and persuasively than others. They are often better organized and are able to influence those who make the re-development decisions, even though they will be fewer in number than others who live in cities. The outcome has been a 'gentrification' of cities, a

169

transformation into the work and leisure places for the middle and service classes (O'Connor and Wynne, 1996; Bianchini, 1999).

Gentrification has not always been welcomed. The jazz history of the Filmore district of San Francisco is being used as a catalyst for the district's regeneration. The opening of the Blue Nile club (a sister club to one in Greenwich Village, New York) and other jazz clubs is regarded as a final part of an extensive regeneration programme that will entail attracting visitors to the district. It has led to comments however that the local African-American community has been marginalized and their interests not being recognized (Wheat, 1999).

This 'gentrification' process has been assisted by the reduced influence of local government in urban regeneration strategies. Business interests have become more influential through the rise of 'coalitions' promoting urban regeneration (Shaw, 1993). This has been claimed to be so especially in the USA and, to a lesser extent, in the UK. Local government has become less important and their priorities have shifted from social welfare to economic development. The encouragement of private–public partnership and the establishment of development agencies outside local government have assisted in this process. The influence of such non-elected bodies on local growth has perhaps been greatest in the USA but business has influenced policy in a variety of informal as well as formal ways including through the pressure of interest groups and informal net-working.

'Business' and the middle classes have generally held similar views on which arts to develop and promote and on the need to promote cities as tourist destinations. In effect it is a 'coalition' of diverse groups who hold similar views. They may or may not operate together but their similar views and objectives ensure an outcome that furthers their common interests. Tourism, cultural and regeneration policies are the outcome of this coalition – basically representing a particular view of the world.

Some problems

Criticisms centre on three issues (Bianchini, 1993a, 1993b; Griffiths, 1993; Hannigan, 1998) (see Figure 8.4):

Restricted benefit

The argument has been that the emphasis has been on prestige projects and 'flagship' schemes at the expense of community-based schemes and of widening access to the arts. In particular, it is argued that local relevance and talent and the nurturing of long-term cultural development have been neglected and the emphasis has been on the high arts and prestige projects. Encouraging people to produce and perform themselves and promoting theatre-going by the local population may have been sacrificed in favour of providing buildings such as theatres, concert halls and event centres and arenas. Wider cultural activity may have been disregarded in favour of activity in theatres and concert halls. The focus has been on down-town, city-centre activity. Production by local cultural industries and artists may have been neglected as consumption of prestige activity has been encouraged. Temporary spectacle such as festivals may have been cultivated at the expense of longer-term artistic and audience development. Tourist and cultural policies have been supportive of only the safe and the prestigious in the arts. This may have been at the expense of more indigenous and adventurous cultural activity. In this way, tourism may have had a distorting effect on the arts encouraged in urban areas. Non-locals and local middle and service classes benefit most.

These views were expressed about Glasgow's year as European City of Culture in 1990 (Hughes and Boyle, 1992) and about the cultural development programmes launched in Barcelona in the years leading up to the 1992 Olympic Games (Dodd, 1999). The Spoleto Festival held in Charleston (South Carolina) since 1977 draws a high proportion of visitors into its audiences. The festival did not grow from the community and it could have been established anywhere. The General Manager of that festival has recognized that there are problems in terms of relevance to the local population. 'Charleston has a large black population and, in general, black populations in American cities are disenfranchised from the arts. This issue must be addressed' (Redden, 1989: 41).

New facilities

The pursuit of cultural policies and arts-related tourism has often led to the construction of new facilities (such as concert halls or arenas) or infrastructure. This has long-term consequences which are often not foreseen (or are ignored). New buildings and infrastructure require long-term financing and user programming. Many of these projects have been conceived and implemented as 'civic boosterism' in order to raise the status and profile of a city, without the benefit of rational, objective analysis and evaluation beforehand (Roche, 1994). Decisions have been the outcome of powerful leadership and power politics with justification and evaluation occurring afterwards. Alternative strategies may not have been considered. Projects have been activated without thorough evaluation or before the evaluation process is completed. It is possible that some favourable data is used to support the project and other data suppressed. The effects are over-estimated and, in practice, are difficult to determine with any degree of precision and 'the supply-driven approach to cultural tourism is allowed to thrive in a climate of boosterism' (Richards, 1999: 30).

The construction and development of any new facilities such as concert halls or arenas does create employment and income during the construction period and, in that sense, it is beneficial. It is, however, comparable to the building of anything else and the project can only really be considered beneficial if it generates revenue. Expenditure on construction is a 'cost' (rather than a benefit), which may or may not generate a 'return'. Facilities will be available for use by locals, they may act as a tourist attraction in their own right and it may be that the construction and associated infrastructure do act as a catalyst for some economic regeneration. If, however, facilities are under-used after an event such as a festival then there may be very real financial burdens. In addition, funds for construction are beneficial only if they are a net injection and not a diversion from other uses, perhaps with greater social impact including education and health (Loftman and Nevin, 1992). Prestige project elements of tourism and cultural strategies may have been misjudged and inappropriate.

Limited impact

Tourism and the arts are likely to have only limited impact as part of regeneration strategies. The nature of the world is such that action at city (local) level to reverse economic decline may be insufficient and international and national strategies may be necessary. It is also unlikely that tourism and the arts (separately or together) would be sufficient to revive cities and adequately replace their lost employment base. They will have only a limited impact given the magnitude of the problems faced by cities. It has already been seen that the extent to which the arts really attract tourists is not clear-cut (see previous chapters). In addition, what benefit there is, is likely to be focused down-town with little impact on city-wide growth.

Economic perspective

The benefits of cultural and arts-related tourism are often expressed in economic terms as the expenditure, income and employment generated. At the

Adelaide Festival, interstate and international visitors were 18 per cent of all ticket-purchasers but accounted for a quarter of all attendances (Market Equity and Economic Research Consultants, 1996). In the case of the Edinburgh Festivals the tourism impact is believed to be considerable. The Festivals generated extra direct expenditure of £44 million (in Edinburgh and the locality) of which £37 million was expenditure by tourists (Scotinform, 1991).

Estimates of the direct effects of any form of tourism are, however, difficult to calculate given limited comprehensive data and the necessity of relying on survey material for expenditure data (Sheldon, 1990). Figures of expenditure need always to be treated with caution because of the strong possibility that people may not be able to estimate future expenditure or to remember past expenditure accurately. Survey respondents may guess or even mislead.

It was seen in Chapter 5 that not all expenditure on the arts is necessarily beneficial. Expenditure by local audiences is not a net injection into the local economy in the same way as tourist expenditure is, as it may have been spent there anyway even if not on the arts (see Figure 8.5). It may well be diverted from one item of expenditure to the arts and as such adds nothing. To claim locals' expenditure as a benefit to an area can be misleading. It is conceivable, though, that the strength of the arts is such that locals spend locally rather than elsewhere. In the case of the Adelaide Festival, some adjustment was made for this. It was estimated that 20 per cent of the residents who went to the Festival had stayed at home to attend the Festival rather than go away on holiday (Market

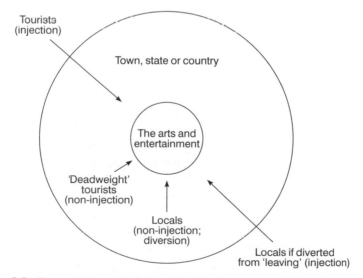

Figure 8.5 Economic impact of arts-related tourism

173

Equity and Economic Research Consultants, 1996) and their expenditure was therefore considered to be a gain. In a similar study, 12.5 per cent of Adelaide residents in audiences for the Wagner Ring Cycle 1998 would have gone away but for the Cycle (South Australian Tourism Commission, 1998).

The spending by visitors is more clearly a 'benefit' as it is an injection into the locality as opposed to a re-circulation of money (see Figure 8.5). Within a country, however, even expenditure by domestic tourists is 'local', though to any one particular town or city spending by domestic tourists is an injection. They bring money into a town from outside and it adds to the flow of expenditure and income. The expenditure of foreign tourists is an injection into a country. It is additional money which is an inflow on the balance of payments and which may create extra income and employment in the country concerned.

Unfortunately not all tourist expenditure is beneficial either. As has been seen in earlier chapters, there are problems of attributing tourism (and its consequences) to the arts and of making adjustment for any displacement of expenditure from other tourist attractions in the area. How certain can it be that the expenditure in the theatre might have not been spent in the area anyway in say museums or theme parks? Some expenditure, as noted in Chapters 5 and 6, is 'deadweight' as it is not induced by the arts and would have occurred anyway. An adjustment for this non-attributable element of the expenditure should be made, though this too is not easy to do.

Total expenditure generated by the arts needs to be adjusted therefore for:

- locals' (however defined) expenditure;
- tourists' expenditure that is displaced from other tourist attractions;
- tourists' expenditure that would have occurred anyway.

Earlier in this chapter it was seen that tourist audiences would spend on a range of other services in addition to tickets. These 'ancillary' purchases were usually on accommodation, transport, meals, souvenirs and the like (see Figure 8.6). There is however a further aspect of expenditure that can be examined and that is what happens to this expenditure after having been received by theatres, hotels, restaurants and taxi-drivers. There is further spending by, for instance, the theatre companies on supplies and to suppliers (and by them in turn) and further spending by employees of theatres, etc. A chain of further expenditure occurs which is termed the 'multiplier' effect (see Figure 8.6). The value of this multiplier is affected by 'leakages' as some of this initial increase in expenditure does not continue to be passed on. Some is saved and not passed on, some is paid in tax and is therefore not available to the consumer to spend and

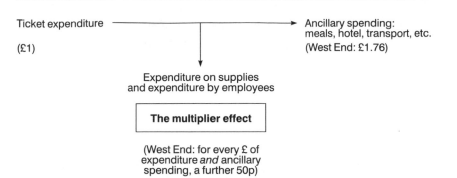

Figure 8.6 'Spill-over' effects of spending by arts-related tourists

some is spent on foreign goods and services and therefore does not generate further expenditure in this country. The value of the multiplier can be quite low in a country that is very dependent on imports.

There are a number of variations of the multiplier. A commonly used one in arts and tourism studies relates the original direct expenditure to final total expenditure (see Figure 8.7). In his Glasgow study, Myerscough (1991)

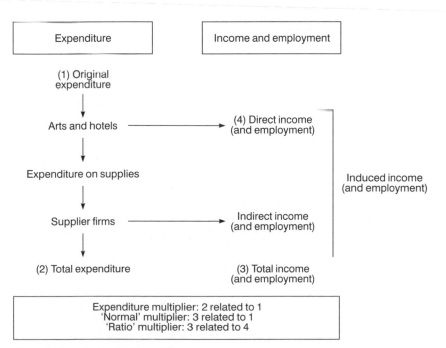

Figure 8.7 The multiplier effect

considered that the multiplier value would be 1.2. In the West End study it was stated that 'multipliers typically used in studies of this kind suggest the multiplier effect will be in the range 1.0 to 1.5' (Travers, 1998: 11). The implication of such figures is that an initial increase in expenditure of £1 or $1 will result in multiplied expenditure in these ranges of 1.0 to 1.5. Other estimates are higher as is shown below.

- **New York-New Jersey:** visitors who came primarily for the arts (or extended their stay because of the arts) were responsible for direct expenditure of $1300 million (26.3 per cent of total direct expenditure), which resulted in an overall impact of $2300 million (a multiplier of 1.76) (Port Authority of New York and New Jersey, 1993).
- **Broadway:** spending by visitors (additional to ticket sales) was $971 million with a total impact of $1719 million (multiplier of 1.77). This 'visitor ancillary spending component is the most significant contributing factor to Broadway's economic impact' (Hauser and Lanier, 1998: 7).
- **The Wyndham report on the West End** did not separately estimate visitors' impact but total expenditure by all audiences (and theatre companies) was £715 million. This resulted in an overall economic impact on the whole economy of £1075 million, a multiplier of 1.5 (Travers, 1998: 11). There was no attempt to determine how much of theatre-goers expenditure was directly due to the drawing-power of theatre.

A variation of the multiplier is to relate the direct expenditure not to the final amount of expenditure created but to the income created (the 'normal' multiplier) (see Figure 8.7). Expenditure will create income for the firms that receive the expenditure and for employees of those firms (direct income) and for suppliers (indirect income). Some of the income will be spent by employees on goods and services, as would any other consumer, and that creates further income (induced income). The value of this 'multiplier' is the total of this direct, indirect and induced income related to the original change in expenditure. A rise in consumer expenditure of £10 million may result in total income of £3 million – a multiplier of 0.3 – which may seem not to be a multiplied amount at all but in this case it is the income that is multiplied not the expenditure.

- The **Adelaide Festival** generated 'new' expenditure of A$13 million leading to (wage and salary) incomes of nearly A$8 million (multiplier of 0.6) (Market Equity and Economic Research Consultants, 1996).
- The **Edinburgh Festivals** generated £258 million of direct expenditure in the city and surrounding region and that, in turn, resulted in £63 million of local income (multiplier of 0.2) (Jones Economics, 1996).

The multiplier concept has many shortcomings, most of which are widely recognized, but it continues to be applied routinely and indiscriminately (Hughes, 1994b). Inadequate data and restrictive and unrealistic assumptions limit the value of the technique. Calculated multiplier values are widely mis-understood and mis-used and the apparent precision of the technique leads to undiscriminating interpretation of values. Significant effects are often claimed but:

1 It does require considerable resources to calculate accurately and, as a result, rough estimates are often made. In Myerscough (1991) and Travers (1998), multiplier values from other studies were transferred across to Glasgow and the West End. In the 1991 study of the Edinburgh Festivals it was stated that 'we use a multiplier of 0.2087 to convert direct expenditure to total local income; this figure is taken from Myerscough's study of economic importance of the arts in Glasgow' (Scotinform, 1991: 99). This suffers from two problems, namely that the figure relates to a different place and to a different time (at least three years earlier).

2 There are many different types of multiplier which are often confused (see Figure 8.7):
   ■ the expenditure multiplier that relates original expenditure to final expenditure;
   ■ the 'normal' multiplier that relates total income to original expenditure;
   ■ the 'ratio' multiplier that relates total income to direct income.
   It was seen above that the values of each can be quite different (e.g. 1.2 and 0.2) and sometimes the wrong value is applied to a particular situation, by claiming for instance that £1 of expenditure leads to £1.20 of income (i.e. applying an expenditure multiplier to a 'normal' multiplier situation).

3 There are problems in obtaining reliable data on numbers of tourists (which usually rely on site surveys) and on tourist expenditure.

4 Relationships between expenditure and income or between expenditure and jobs are estimates of the current situation and they would not necessarily hold in the future nor for any increases in expenditure (as they are average figures not marginal). It would be misleading to claim that a future increase in expenditure would generate expenditures and incomes of the same magnitude. This was emphasized in the Port Authority of New York-New Jersey study (1993).

5 Attribution: The authors of the New York-New Jersey study (1993) recognized that there could be reservations about the extent to which the expenditure was actually caused by the arts and how much would have occurred anyway.

In addition employment figures are conversions of unreliable expenditure figures. In the Wyndham report on the West End, it was estimated that between 55 and 75 per cent of expenditure went on labour costs (Travers, 1998). These costs would then be divided by an average wage to give an estimate of direct jobs. In the New York-New Jersey study it was estimated that over 40,000 direct jobs and over 60,000 other jobs were associated with the expenditure. In Edinburgh the number of jobs was estimated at 2500 full-time equivalents in 1996 and in Adelaide at 270 full-time equivalents. In reality, however, much of the effect of 'new' expenditure may be in terms of additional hours worked by existing employees rather than new jobs. Many new jobs may also be casual and have little long-term effect.

Many indirect jobs (and even some of the direct jobs) may exist anyway despite the audience spending. It may well be justifiable to attribute direct jobs to audience spending but it becomes rather more problematic to claim indirect jobs (i.e. jobs in suppliers) in the same way. 'About 41,000 UK jobs depend on West End theatre – 27,000 directly and 14,000 indirectly' (Travers, 1998: 18). The implication is that if it were not for the direct expenditure these indirect jobs would not exist and if the expenditure fell then the jobs would fall. Direct jobs in theatres and concert halls may not exist if it was not for audience expenditure but jobs in hotels and restaurants may exist anyway. The effects of arts audiences' spending may be marginal on any one business (though together may appear substantial). Some of the tourists would have come to the country anyway. Even if they had not come it may be that the effect on jobs would have been marginal because some employment will be indivisible and discontinuous and not possible to adjust finely. The effect on any one organization may be slight.

The same argument can be applied to expenditures and incomes apparently generated by tourists' spending. If jobs would have existed anyway it is possible that some proportion of the indirect and induced expenditures and incomes would similarly have occurred and have been earned anyway.

6 A final comment on the multiplier is that the technique distracts from other fundamental issues. As a mathematical concept, it is relatively easy to estimate and it may overshadow issues, such as the alternative use of resources, which cannot be expressed so easily in figures. The economic evaluation of effects usually ignores wider issues such as opportunity costs. In the case of prestige events or projects, in particular, resources may be diverted from other uses which might be considered more 'productive' or 'useful' activities but comparative multipliers are rarely estimated.

There is an obvious tendency to assess the worth of tourism in economic terms, often to justify public expenditure. Tourism, like many other forms of activity, is not often nor as easily evaluated in non-economic terms. It is evident that the determination of the economic effects of arts-related tourism is subject to considerable speculation and margins of error. Expenditure figures are estimates derived from surveys and employment figures are frequently conversions of those expenditure figures. The un-reliability is especially acute in the case of the effects beyond the direct (indirect and induced effects) which are estimated utilizing the multiplier technique.

Chapter summary

There is considerable enthusiasm for developing the relationship between the arts and tourism as they are seen as being mutually beneficial. Tourism can bring new audiences and sources of revenue for the arts and the arts provide an attraction within the tourism experience that the tourism industry can utilize. Much of the discussion is in terms of international tourism and does not differentiate between arts-core and arts-peripheral tourists. It is seen for instance as a new and growing market (with an implicit assumption that it is arts-core) when, in fact, entertainment, in particular, has long been something that tourists have seen and heard.

Regardless of this, there is an obvious benefit for the arts and entertainment from any additional source of income, whether it be from tourists or a more local audience. Employment is created or secured, local residents benefit from the existence of the arts and, in some cases, art forms continue that would otherwise disappear. There may be a particular advantage to be got in raising sponsorship and generating support, by pointing out that audiences are tourist.

From the tourism perspective, the existence of the arts and entertainment can influence the decision of tourists about visiting a town or country, without any direct connection between the arts and the tourism industry. Tourism benefits indirectly but will have an interest in the well-being of the arts and entertainment. Tourism focused on culture generally and on the arts in particular is regarded favourably as it is seen as a new and growing activity. A more direct connection occurs when the tourism industry itself (tour operators and hotels) uses the arts and entertainment in an inclusive tour or the hotel industry provides its own entertainment.

There are, however, a number of criticisms levelled at the relationship. In particular, the fact that reliance on tourism can make the arts exposed to fluctuations that are beyond their influence. In addition, by encouraging tourist audiences it is suggested that the arts have become little more than a tourist sight. To encourage such audiences, theatre productions are bland and unchallenging and are able to have long runs fed by a continual flow of new customers. This process however, like the increasing tendency to view the arts as an industry like any other, is not entirely attributable to tourism. There are significant pressures in society that have contributed to both. In addition, individuals and firms in the arts have themselves been eager to take up the opportunities provided by tourism.

The joint influence of the arts and tourism on urban regeneration is considered to be particularly important by governments and development agencies. The arts are believed to regenerate partly through their ability to attract tourists and tourism affects regeneration partly by promoting the arts (and also heritage) as an attraction. There is a consensus about these cultural and tourism strategies that includes influential local residents, business people and local government. This, in turn, has been subject to the criticism that it focuses on a set of narrow interests and does not give sufficient acknowledgement to the needs of many other residents of cities who are less articulate, organized or influential. Projects and events may have too much of a tourist inclination and not enough local relevance.

Arts-related tourism is often measured and justified by reference to its economic impact though not all tourist spending can be considered to be beneficial as some, for instance, may have occurred anyway. Its multiplier effects have been a particular focus of attention. Any tourist spending will have an expanded, or multiplier, effect as it is received and gets spent by suppliers and employees. Estimates of these effects are common but they do need to be treated with caution as the basis for the estimates can sometimes be weak. They are open to misinterpretation and they also reinforce the tendency to view the economic aspect of activities as being the most important.

9

Conclusions and implications

Introduction

From a tourism perspective, the focus of this book has been a particular form of tourism. From the arts perspective, the focus has been the members of an audience who are not local. Previous chapters have examined a number of issues including how the relationship between the arts and tourism has developed and discussion of the factors that have influenced it. Chapter 8 focused on the effects of the relationship. It was seen that the effects were complex and wide-ranging and say something about the way in which societies are developing. It is more than a simple business relationship with implications for marketing. There are wider ramifications of what is going on and it is symptomatic of much wider transformations in society. There are, of course, marketing implications and some of these will be discussed in this chapter along with other consequences of the relationship and its effects.

This chapter includes:

■ conclusions arising from the issues raised in previous chapters;
■ discussion of some of the implications and of some appropriate strategies for future development.

Conclusions

This book has concentrated on tourism and the performing arts rather than on the whole of cultural tourism. Existing studies of cultural tourism have often included activities which were so different that they should be studied in isolation (at least at first) (see Figure 9.1). There is also an omission in many studies: that of entertainment. In addition, the term cultural tourism has been frequently used to cover all visits to museums, historic houses or theatres regardless of whether or not those were the reason for being a tourist in the first place.

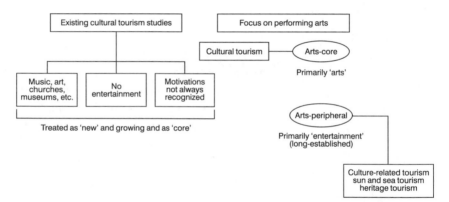

Figure 9.1   The performing arts and tourism and the relationship with cultural tourism

There are two perspectives on the relationship between arts and entertainment and tourism (see Figure 9.1). One is the arts-core situation in which a person travels with the sole or primary purpose of seeing a show or concert. The other is the arts-peripheral situation where the arts and entertainment are not the main reason for travel and something such as a business trip or a holiday for sun and sea or for heritage are the most important reasons. The visit to the theatre or concert hall in these situations occurs as something that is incidental to the main purpose or even is accidental in that it did not feature at all in the visit decision.

The existing discussions of cultural tourism tend to view the interest in culture as more core than peripheral and are also more focused on heritage than on the performing arts. The analyses are concerned with explaining its recent emergence and the justification for believing it to be a new form of tourism that will continue to grow. This approach is not wholly appropriate for the study of the performing arts in the tourism context where it is probable that there has long been participation by tourists and as a secondary activity (arts-peripheral) when on holiday.

Arts-core tourism may be considered to be part of 'cultural tourism' whereas the arts-peripheral may be best considered as a separate distinct activity. It is probable too that the former may be concerned with the arts (as traditionally defined) and the latter with entertainment though this distinction is by no means unequivocal.

Entertainment has certainly featured in all forms of tourism from the earliest times. The growth of seaside resorts and 'mass' tourism from the mid nineteenth century encouraged the development of a large tourist-related entertainment business. The places that holiday tourists now wish to visit have changed but there is still a demand for visits to theatres and concert halls whilst on holiday, whether domestic or international, city or coast. Surveys of audiences and tourists have deficiencies which mean it is difficult to obtain a clear picture of the arts–tourism relationship but it would appear that many tourists do not go to see the arts and entertainment. Nonetheless a good number do and, of these, many are there as a result of a decision to visit the place for some other reason; they are arts-peripheral. A similar view is emerging that 'increasing attendance at cultural heritage sites is primarily the result of a growing number of 'passer-bys' . . . Usually culture is not the prime motive for visiting a city or region' (de Haan, 1999: 124).

There are also, in some cases, large proportions of tourists in audiences who are arts-core for whom the arts or entertainment have been the only or the main reason for the visit. It is probable that the motivations and socio-demographic characteristics of such tourists will differ from those of arts-peripheral tourists. This remains unexplored.

Further development

The ways forward include:

- greater information about the arts–tourism relationship;
- practical operational strategies.

There is not a great deal of information available generally about the arts–tourism relationship. The reality is that 'little to nothing is known about (cultural) tourists' motivations' (de Leeuw, 1999: 10) and some of the requirements for a more complete picture are summarized in Figure 9.2. The number of surveys is limited and there are problems with individual surveys. The number needs to be expanded and refinements to surveys are required before the exact role of the performing arts can be established and the several types of arts-related tourist identified. For instance, the size of an arts-related tourism market, the intent of tourists and the drawing power of the arts are currently difficult to determine with certainty. Much of the encouragement from bodies in the arts and tourism is based on hunch and a few successful cases. It is not yet possible to see the complete picture.

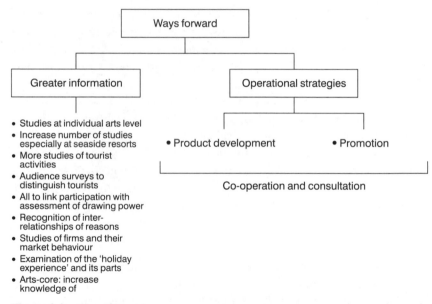

Figure 9.2 Ways forward

In part, this is because cultural tourism studies have analysed global concepts such as the arts or culture or heritage. This will be clarified ultimately only by further studies which analyse at the level of individual art forms – the performing arts, museums, art galleries, etc. – rather than at less focused levels. There is a need for more such focused studies and the places covered need to be extended. With respect to the UK, for instance, surveys are confined to London or to the country as a whole and a few major arts events.

The scope of studies requires widening to include more individual towns, cities and regions with perhaps a special need to analyse seaside resorts.

Where studies have been more focused, other issues arise. In constructing audience survey questionnaires, day-visitors and staying tourists, those on holiday, and domestic and overseas tourists are not always separately identified. In addition, it would assist strategic decision making if these categories were cross-referenced with questions relating to the reason for visit to the destination and the importance of the performance within that. Finally, when examining the influence of the performance in the decision to visit the destination, it is not sufficient to evaluate the importance of it in isolation. More meaningful responses would result from the requirement to evaluate in relation to other influencing factors.

Surveys conducted amongst the tourist population in general (and not just those in audiences) have greater potential for evaluating drawing power. Surveys do, however, need to be conducted with greater consistency in the coverage of influencing factors and the terms used in evaluating the factors. More significance will be attached to tourists' evaluation of factors where the range evaluated is wide though the factors included must be pertinent. The influences on destination choice are numerous and varied but the focus should be on the attributes of a destination. Some such attributes are 'determinant' in that they determine choice whereas others may be salient, i.e. significant and conspicuous features, but which do not necessarily influence choice. The identification of 'determinant' attributes requires analysis beyond the surveys that are current. Other apparently important factors in consumer choice (such as 'recommendation') are not destination attributes at all and cannot validly be combined in the same analytical process.

A further issue associated with tourist surveys is – given that the consumer choice decision is a complex one – that it is not sufficient to expect individual attributes to be determinant in isolation from each other. Attributes of the destination will be determinant in combination, and studies should acknowledge this. There is a need for studies that demonstrate the 'strength' of various combinations of attractions and activities in influencing a decision to visit a destination. (For relevant approaches such as multi-attribute models and conjoint measurement, see Ryan, 1995.)

Tourist surveys do not yet permit the assessment of arts-core and arts-peripheral. Most published material does not link arts participation with the significance of the arts in the visit decision.

Both audience and tourist surveys have been preoccupied with foreign tourists and data on domestic tourism, and the role of the arts within that is limited. Further information about this segment is required if more meaningful management strategies are to be developed. There has also been a neglect of entertainment. It is not, for instance, recognized in UK national tourist board data collection where the list of activities is limited. It needs to be recognized and monitored more closely, in resorts in particular both over time and across the whole country.

It is also apparent that there is limited knowledge currently not just about consumers but also about firms in the arts and tourism sectors. The dynamics and market behaviour of theatre firms, of arts and entertainment producers in cities and resorts, of the tour operators (especially in-coming) and of hotels and clubs in providing entertainment and of how the two sectors relate to each other are all poorly researched.

Particular areas for future research include, for instance, audiences and tourists at seaside resorts. The audience composition is not known from published material and it is not known what the drawing power is of the arts and entertainment in such holiday areas. Similarly, there is no distinction in such local tourist studies either of participation in arts and entertainment or of their drawing power. The arts-core, arts-peripheral breakdown is not known from either audience or tourist surveys.

The survey approach clearly has its limitations. The adoption of more qualitative approaches may add to knowledge about the arts–tourism relationship. These approaches could be used to explore the 'holiday experience' – whether at the coast or in the city – in order to determine what it is that people believe constitutes a holiday. Such studies would seek to discover what are the necessary ingredients, the extent to which certain activities and attractions are important singly or jointly and to determine the role of arts and entertainment in that holiday experience. It would indicate how far people feel that entertainment and the arts are a necessary or significant part of the whole holiday experience or whether it is regarded, for instance, as a secondary diversion.

There is little knowledge of the arts-core market in terms of its size, its growth and its product preferences. The potential for further growth and development is unexplored, as is whether or not the motivations and socio-demographics of the arts-core tourist differ from those of the arts-peripheral tourist.

Strategies for the individual theatre

Despite the limitations to current knowledge discussed above there is, as seen in Chapter 8, a firm belief amongst many that there is a significant arts–tourism relationship and this is basically beneficial and should be encouraged. What then are the options open to the individual theatre, concert hall, hotel or tour operator to pursue this relationship further? There is an abundance of relevant practical advice in publications such as *The Arts Tourism Marketing Handbook* published by the ETB in 1993 and *Tourism and the arts: advice pack* published by the BTA and Arts Council of England in 1997. There also practical recommendations in the studies of cultural tourism in Canada (Canadian Tourism Commission, 1997a, 1997b, 1998) and in South Australia (Leader-Elliott, 1996). Marketing of services, of not-for-profit services and specifically of the arts are also well covered in a number of books (such as Hill, O'Sullivan and O'Sullivan, 1995 and Getz, 1991). In the remaining part of this chapter the intent is to avoid unnecessary duplication with these and the discussion relates to the more specific issues that have arisen from the earlier chapters of this book. It does though also draw, where appropriate, on these and related publications and seminars and on strategies previously discussed in Chapter 6.

This discussion will, for the sake of clarity, be from the perspective of the individual arts organization: a theatre. From this it will become apparent what the implications are for the arts sector as a whole and for the tourism industry. The particular issues surrounding festivals are dealt with in detail in, for instance, Getz (1991).

It is clear from the earlier chapters of this book that a relationship between the performing arts and tourism does exist. In Chapter 4 it was suggested that tourists in an audience could be classified according to whether (i) arts-core or arts-peripheral and (ii) holiday or non-holiday. Strategies for attracting each may well differ.

A word of caution is appropriate however. The arts–tourism relationship is not of significance to all in the arts and tourism (despite the fact that this book has focused on the relationship). It is easy and tempting to over-exaggerate the relationship but there is not always a need nor the opportunity for a productive arts–tourism relationship.

- For some arts organizations a local audience may be sufficient to fill seats and there is no obvious need to attract an audience from further afield.
- In other cases there is little opportunity because not all towns and cities or arts products have significant potential for attracting long-distance audiences or for holiday tourism.
- There are those in the arts who would regard it as undesirable to target tourists for reasons that have been discussed in Chapter 8. There is a reluctance on the part of some to regard themselves as a tourist attraction.

- The effort involved in determining who is in the audience in such a way as to identify market segments and in targeting those segments may be beyond the capabilities of many individual arts organizations and the pay-off may not be worth the effort. This suggests a case for some form of joint activity with others in both the arts and tourism (see Chapter 6).
- Similarly, each tourist market segment may not be large enough nor readily identifiable nor reachable in a cost-effective way.

The arts–tourism connection needs to be kept in perspective as it is not applicable to all.

For any arts organization, tourism can however be seen in un-threatening terms as part of the normal process of attracting more customers. The prospect of widening the catchment area may be something a greater number of arts organizations might find worth considering, even if they do not pursue it. In some cases there is no point in developing the relationship. In others however there may be great potential but this is not yet recognized or acknowledged. In such cases there is a fairly fundamental hurdle to be crossed before action occurs but a first step is the determination and evaluation of the potential returns from any extra effort involved in attracting a non-local audience. Some of the problems faced in attracting non-local audiences were discussed in Chapter 6, along with a number of possible strategies.

Market research

The strategy that any one arts organization adopts will depend on many factors but a fundamental requirement is to be aware of the characteristics of the existing audiences through market research. Not all arts organizations have that information and many rely on their mailing lists as indicators of their audiences. This has a number of defects, in particular, the fact that mailing lists and audiences are not necessarily the same. People buy tickets without being on the mailing list and not all those on the mailing list buy tickets or are necessarily keener or more frequent attenders than those who are not.

Audience surveys assist in building up the picture of audiences but are time-consuming and costly. In addition, it has already been noted that audience surveys do not always contain information that bears directly on tourism. Once existing audiences are identified, arts organizations can move to the next step, that of identifying potentially productive markets to target. This may be evident from audience surveys which reveal tourists (if any) as coming from a particular geographical area or belonging to a particular socio-economic group and having a particular reason for travelling to the location and for being in the theatre or concert hall, i.e. where in the arts-core, arts-peripheral, holiday, non-holiday matrix they can be located.

If tourists are not present in audiences currently, arts managers can utilize secondary sources of information compiled and published by others to enable them to target non-local audiences if they so wish. These will include surveys and reviews of related tourism markets (such as published by tourist boards) and more general sources of consumer expenditure patterns such as ACORN data and the Target Group Index which indicate, amongst much other information, the characteristics and location of consumers of the arts and holidays.

Product development and promotion

Once convinced that there is potential then an individual arts organization may adopt one or both of two broad approaches: product development and/or promotion.

Product development

The modification of an existing arts product so that it is more likely to attract audiences from outside the locality. This is probably especially relevant for arts-core. It implies the production of something distinctive:

- **rarity:** performances of rarely produced pieces – music, plays, operas, etc. – that will be of interest to a large but perhaps scattered audience;
- **quality:** productions that are similar to those elsewhere but which are distinguished by high standards in production and/or performance;
- **star names:** in productions that can be seen elsewhere (without such a star) or as star concerts on a one-off basis or on tour.

If it was to appeal to a holiday audience (often arts-peripheral) then the product development may take a different form such as the production of plays, concerts, shows, etc. that are relatively light and diversionary. This will include some of the more popular shows, such as musicals, that are produced in non-holiday areas as well as up-dated variations of the traditional variety show.

In coastal resorts it may be necessary to accept the challenge of other places of entertainment (such as hotels and clubs) and create something different in style and presentation that others cannot offer. It may be appropriate too to develop an interchange of 'package' summer shows with other resorts so that costs are shared.

189

Product development may lead to the setting up of special events or festivals that have particular tourist dimensions. The initiative and development of these will extend beyond the resources of any single arts organization.

Promotion

The product may well have tourist appeal (whether holiday or non-holiday) and the appropriate strategy may lie more in the promotion of such an existing arts product that has unexploited tourism potential. Campaigns directed at the non-local target segments may take several forms; they were discussed in Chapter 6. Those approaches fell into three broad categories: (i) promotion outside the destination, (ii) inside the destination and (iii) promotion of the destination itself. These should be referred to during the following discussion.

The need for communication and consultation

Some of the strategies suggested go beyond the individual efforts of any theatre, concert hall or arena. Some require working with others in the arts and some require a relationship with sectors of the tourism industry. Much of the advice by bodies such as the BTA and ACE focuses on the benefits to be achieved through working with others (ETB, 1993) or, at the least, through the achievement of a greater understanding by each of the other's objectives and interests (Austwick, 1991). 'Success requires the development of a mutually reinforcing relationship between the cultural, heritage and tourism sectors' and of improved communication between them (Canadian Tourism Commission, 1997a: 1). Implicit throughout is the view that each sector can benefit from the other in the ways identified in Chapter 8. Much of the practical advice centres on how the two sectors may be enabled to reach a greater understanding and a greater degree of co-operation in order to facilitate a mutually beneficial development.

Limited contact between the two parties in the past has led to limited awareness and to misunderstanding and misrepresentation. There have been few formal joint communication mechanisms between arts and tourism. As each sector works independently of the other, at the least it seems desirable to have a means of communicating. Contact between the tourism and the arts has been intermittent and haphazard which, given the nature of the two, is not surprising. Tourism in particular is characterized by a large number of firms, especially hoteliers, and each sector has had quite different objectives, with commercial considerations being of more importance to tourism and artistic considerations to theatres. Differences in revenue sources have contributed to different approaches and philosophies with tourism relying more on earned revenue and the arts more on subsidy and sponsorship (see Chapters 2 and 3). In addition, each has not necessarily seen any need to talk to the other about the relationship.

The opportunities that arise from the relationship are, though, becoming more evident and the development of the relationship more necessary for many. In practical terms, there are already many close relationships between organizations in tourism and the arts, which have the effect of identifying opportunities and the means of profiting from those. Many arts organizations are becoming more commercially minded.

The communication and cooperation can be at many different levels, from the individual hotelier and theatre manager through local tourist and arts boards and trade associations to national government bodies and ministries. Local and regional bodies may need to take the initiative to bring individual arts and tourism companies and organizations together with a view to those individuals ultimately working together. There may be an unfortunate lack of co-ordination within each sector let alone between the sectors especially within the arts and cultural sector itself (Canadian Tourism Commission, 1997b). In Scotland, for instance, it has been considered that event organizers tend not to co-ordinate their activities and, as a result, dates conflict (Scottish Tourism Co-ordinating Group, 1993). The getting together of the two sectors could facilitate the sharing of information that each has, such as databases and market research. Theatres could be offered the opportunity to include questions on any local tourism surveys and surveys could be jointly commissioned by arts and tourism. The ETB itself offers to supply information from its own comprehensive databases that would be useful for targeting particular markets. Local, regional and national bodies (arts and tourism) may need to improve the nature and extent of information available about the arts-tourism market.

The development of umbrella bodies such as tourist boards (at national through to town and city level) and of arts boards permits an easier dialogue and means of co-operation between the two sectors. It may be partly an 'educational' function. Misunderstandings about each other may have limited the scope for co-operation (Leader-Elliott, 1996; Canadian Tourism Commission, 1997b). The tourism industry may underestimate the potential for arts-related tourism and lack understanding of the rationale for and methods of operation of the arts. Similarly people in the arts may be suspicious of tourism as being something that would compromise their standards and creativity and they may have limited appreciation of the way in which the tourism industry works. There is a view that within tourism, there is limited personal interest in the arts and a consequent under-estimation of the potential for related tourism. There is a need therefore to 'educate' the tourism industry about the arts (Leader-Elliott, 1996). Apart from tourist boards providing opportunity for dialogue and co-operation there is also opportunity for the arts to influence the promotional strategies of boards and ensure adequate significance is attached to this sector in the marketing of a destination.

Tourist boards and arts boards in Britain are, however, different types of body and a working relationship may be difficult to achieve. Tourist boards are open to commercial membership and their main function is marketing (usually promotion) whereas arts boards tend to be funding and development bodies that also have an interest in marketing. Appropriate action recommended often includes arts organizations joining tourist boards and for the tourist industry to be represented on arts boards. Any communication and co-operation may therefore need to occur by any of several means and not relying solely on tourist and arts boards, including through trade associations such as local chambers of commerce or hoteliers' associations.

The communication and consultation processes may also result in activities such as joint initiatives for marketing and promotion discussed in Chapter 6. It is a common view that the arts and cultural sectors lack marketing expertise and the resources to develop the product. There is opportunity for the tourism sector to assist here and for the two sectors to engage in joint activities (Leader-Elliott, 1996; Silberberg, 1995). Many arts organizations may need training and business development assistance including improvement of market knowledge and of marketing practices (Scottish Tourism Co-ordinating Group, 1993). Arts organizations may also have particularly limited knowledge of the tourism market and of trends in that market.

The tourism industry (including transport operators) can be encouraged to sponsor arts events that will in turn encourage people to travel. An arts board or equivalent may contribute to joint familiarization tours for the media. Each sector may advertise or seek to be featured in the publications of the other and arts organizations can participate in travel trade fairs to directly reach the tourist trade. London theatres have themselves (through SOLT) organized a similar trade fair where theatres and the travel trade have been brought together to discuss potential but more importantly to provide an opportunity to undertake business with each other. SOLT also produces a manual aimed at the travel trade.

At another level, co-operation may include the development of training programmes in areas such as customer care or languages. Such joint activity and sharing of resources may avoid duplication of effort and the achievement of economies of scale.

The development of long-term strategy statements that focus on joint needs, aspirations and activities is probably desirable as is the identification of the opportunities for each to contribute to the other. Tourism and cultural and arts strategies need to acknowledge, where appropriate, the possible contribution of the 'other' sector. The drafting of joint arts-tourism strategies would take this one step further and this may include statements of intent and of support from national bodies and relevant government ministries. The two industries might join together in any lobbying they undertake of government or funding bodies. In a review of cultural tourism in Canada, it was concluded that there was a lack of knowledge on the part of governments of the positive economic benefits of the arts and their contribution to the tourism sector (Canadian Tourism Commission, 1997b). At individual town and city level, tourism action plans may include and even be largely based on the arts.

Approaches for each segment

This discussion has been in general terms but it may be that different approaches may be applicable to each of the segments identified in Chapter 4. Undoubtedly some approaches are common to all and, as noted previously, if each segment is a small or not easily identifiable one then it would not be cost-effective to apply a different approach to each anyway. There are, nonetheless, certain strategies that do seem to be especially relevant to a particular segment in being able to 'capture' that segment (see Figure 9.3).

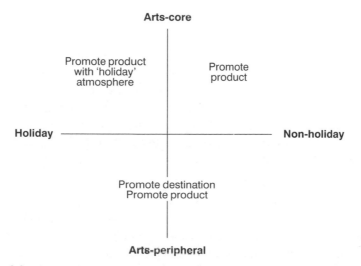

Figure 9.3   Approaches to the arts-related tourist

Arts-core, non-holiday

Such a trip is likely to be undertaken by someone with a keen interest in arts or entertainment. A product that is distinctive (in whatever sense) may be most successful in attracting such a segment. It may be particularly attractive if offered with other productions and if offered in a pleasant place. Making it easy to book tickets, accommodation and transport in one package will assist the process.

It is the product rather than the destination that has priority in the promotion process and the product will need to be publicized outside the destination in the ways discussed in Chapter 6.

Arts-core, holiday

This segment is also likely to be drawn by a distinctive product. The provision of packages, especially short duration, may be successful in making the trip more desirable especially if offered with other attractions and in a 'holiday' place. It may be that such products pick up a larger number of holidaymakers if offered out-of-season as main holidays are often sea and sun and additional holidays are more likely to be arts-based. Some however will want an arts-based main holiday.

Here too it is the product rather than the destination that has priority in the promotion process.

Arts-peripheral, holiday

For those on a 'fun' holiday (whether seaside or city), light and diversionary productions would seem appropriate. This, of course, is not necessarily so as some will come to see 'heavier' productions whilst on holiday. This may be because they are different from what they usually see or because they have a certain status-enhancing effect. An easy system for booking through informal channels would encourage holidaymakers to buy tickets and, for many, it may be necessary to remove the mystique surrounding theatre-going making it an informal, easy-going event.

Theatre would be promoted as part of the holiday experience. The destination promotion would be first, followed by promotion of the production. It is possible, though, that destination choice may be influenced by theatre and its productions in which case it is a parallel rather than two-step process.

Theatres therefore would need to help promote the destination, ensure 'entertainment' is emphasized in the destination promotion and promote to holiday-makers when in the destination.

Arts-peripheral, non-holiday

The product and approaches here will be similar to the equivalent holiday segment. For some in this segment, being away from home may be an opportunity to see 'heavier' productions that they were unable to see at home.

Much of the promotional activity will be centred on consumers when they are in the destination and could include targeting local hotels and also local firms who are known to have regular visitors and targeting local conference and exhibition venues. It would seem appropriate to help promote the destination as a business, conference and exhibition location and to target conference and exhibition organizers. In that promotion the arts and entertainment elements should be emphasized. It is also important to establish knowledge amongst local residents especially for cultivating the friends and relatives market.

Destination promotion would be first followed by promotion of the production. Here too, though, destination choice may be influenced by theatre and the process would be a parallel one rather than two-step.

Target segments for each product

When considering which segment to target particular arts products at, it may seem, at its simplest, that light entertainment at the seaside is most suitably marketed to the arts-peripheral holiday-maker. Similarly, opera in a city might be thought of as being suitable only for marketing to arts-core, non-holiday-makers (see Figure 9.4). It is obvious, however, from the previous discussions that virtually any arts product can be aimed at any of the target segments.

If a product at the seaside or in a city is 'distinctive' or not available elsewhere then it may draw a non-holiday market and it can be promoted directly outside the destination. It can, of course, be made more attractive by having a holiday context. For a product at the seaside or in a city which is not particularly distinctive or which is more widely available, the holiday context may be more important in order to draw non-local audiences. It may be more significant to promote the destination and promote the product to the target markets once they are there in the destination.

With regard to light entertainment, it might seem that is most appropriate for holiday-makers at the seaside or in the city especially those whose interest

195

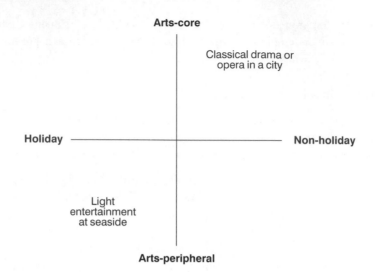

Figure 9.4   Productions and the arts-related tourist

is secondary to sea and beach, or heritage in a city (arts-peripheral, holiday). It may, though, also be successful in attracting holidaymakers whose visit is focused on seeing a particular production as a particular show or star can be the main reason for holidaying in a particular place (arts-core, holiday). Equally it can attract tourists who desire to see the production but whose visit and stay are not regarded as a holiday (arts-core, non-holiday) and those on a conference trip who seek a night out (arts-peripheral, non-holiday).

Similarly, opera in a city (or at the seaside) may seem most appropriate for the arts core, non-holiday segment. It can, though, also be targeted at the arts core holiday-maker as well as at holiday-makers and non-holiday-makers whose visits are secondary to other reasons for being in the city, such as heritage or business.

Strategies for tourism

For hotels, tour operators, travel agents, tourist boards and city marketing boards most of the approaches for developing arts-related tourism are evident from the previous discussion. For them it is largely a case of using the arts product for their own purposes. The need for improved communication and consultation therefore obviously applies here too. It seems obvious too that direct links for the opportunity to negotiate with the arts about use of mailing lists, packages and the selling of theatre tickets should be encouraged. It does also however make sense for tourism to develop indirect links through encouraging the development of the arts and entertainment by financial support and sponsorship or appropriate lobbying. It would appear relevant to encourage development that might be particularly successful in attracting non-local audiences. The tourism industry might advise on how such audiences could be targeted successfully. The relevant promotional bodies in tourism should also, where appropriate, recognize the role of arts and entertainment in destination choice and use this in promotion campaigns.

The industry should also be prepared to recognize why the relationship is not always welcomed. Arts-related tourism may not always be in the best interests of the arts, at least as perceived by those who work in the arts. There is some tension here. It may be naive to assume that commercial organizations will forgo revenue and profit in the cause of artistic integrity and creativity and of stimulating new, experimental and minority-appeal artistic creations but, at the least, the tourism industry should be aware of the tension and of the consequences of their activities. It is, of course, not only the tourism industry that exploits the arts as a tourist resource. Much of the change in the nature of productions put on in large cities is due to companies in the arts taking the initiative and taking advantage of the tourism potential. The issue reflects wide changes in society and it may be too much to expect either of the arts or tourism sectors individually to do anything about it. A way forward is for tourism and arts organizations, firms and public sector bodies to be altruistic and support some productions that are not aimed at the tourist market.

The cultural and tourism policies of cities were identified as a particularly contentious issue. The tourism industry and tourist boards should re-consider the arts and culture that are promoted as the attractions of cities, perhaps by drawing more on indigenous and local activity. The likely outcome would be a perspective that recognizes the multi-faceted nature of artistic activity in this country, which may lead to a more successful and sustainable tourism.

It is also necessary to see arts-related tourism in perspective in the economic sense. It is undoubtedly beneficial financially to many theatres and tourism companies but the impact on local economies is often exaggerated. It is difficult to isolate the influence of the arts on tourism and therefore it is a little imprudent to claim a certain value of expenditure, income and employment as being due to such tourism. There are many influences on a tourist's decision to visit a destination. It is also rather meaningless to identify the supposed economic impact of this form of tourism without comparing it with other forms of tourism or with other forms of economic activity. In addition the shortcomings of the widely used multiplier technique need to be more widely recognized and the temptation to utilize it at all times and in all circumstances should be avoided. Economic measurement may also be a distraction from other issues and there is a need to extend the criteria by which tourism and cultural policies are judged so that opportunity costs and the distribution of income, for instance, are recognized. Strategies, projects and events should be subject to evaluation by the fullest criteria including social and environmental concerns. This is not to suggest that economic evaluation should not be undertaken nor that it is without merit but rather that it should be but one of many approaches to assessment.

Strategies for local government

The role of local government has been critical in the past and is likely to remain so. It has given financial support to theatres, concert halls, arenas and arts centres and, in seaside resorts in particular, has had a leading role in the financing of summer seasons. Its role has been changing and will continue to do so. There is a greater involvement of the private commercial sector, often in partnership with local government. Many 'tourist' local authorities see a need for arts and entertainment in their towns and cities as attractions for tourists and despite financial and political pressures, they endeavour to continue the support. The input of the private sector may be considered appropriate as the operation of theatres, concert halls and arenas requires considerable flair and entrepreneurial skill, which may not be so readily found in local government. The private sector may be reluctant to be involved in the arts in holiday areas because of the short season and, in some cases, low visitor numbers. Involvement is most likely where theatres are relatively large, where capacity audiences are foreseen and year-round audiences can be attracted, leaving smaller resorts facing a dilemma. Local government involvement in the arts (more particularly entertainment) at seaside resorts has always been justified in economic terms, as an investment in order to encourage tourism. Local government involvement elsewhere has been seen more as 'social welfare', as provision of services for local residents. In this sense, resort local authorities have been ahead of city governments who have only recently turned towards the economic potential of tourism as was seen in the discussion of urban regeneration in Chapter 8.

Overall conclusions

This book started from the point that existing cultural tourism studies were too broad and that only by examining each component could the culture–tourism relationship be clarified. The focus was therefore solely the performing arts and tourism. From the discussion, however, the relationship, even at this level of analysis, is not clear-cut and there are a number of unanswered questions and outstanding issues. There is further research to be undertaken.

The same sort of focused study can also be undertaken for each of museums, art galleries, historic houses, castles and cathedrals separately rather than under the broad heading of culture or heritage. There will then be a build-up of material relating to the component parts of cultural tourism. It may be that they have much in common and that there are considerable similarities and connections, but for the moment it is not known one way or the other.

This book has focused on one part of the culture–tourism relationship, that relating to the performing arts. For this one sector it is suggested that there are several segments that can be distinguished, classified by arts-core or arts-peripheral and by holiday or non-holiday. It is likely that many tourists, and much tourism, discussed within the category of 'cultural tourism' are holiday-makers who, as part of that holiday experience, require entertainment in the evening almost as an add-on to the main daily activities of heritage or beach. It might be difficult to justify classifying these 'theatre' tourists as cultural tourists and the performing arts and tourism relationship may need to treated separately. This may not, of course, be so true in the case of visitors to museums or historic houses though even here there is a recognition that culture is increasingly an additional rather than a central element of the holiday (Richards, 1999).

It should be recognized too that many of those who go to the theatre as part of a holiday are often not included in the discussion of cultural tourism at all. This relates especially to holiday-makers who go to see a show at seaside resorts. Data is frequently collected through audience and site visitor surveys, usually at theatres in cities and at museums, art galleries and historic sites, rather than through general tourist surveys. The tourist who visits the theatre when on holiday at a coastal destination does not often feature in the data-collection but arts and entertainment in these other places and other forms is a significant part of the holiday experience.

In addition, however, there are tourists in audiences who are drawn entirely by the arts with no concept, for them, of holiday (or tourism) surrounding the visit (arts-core, non-holiday). Although technically tourists, they are not in the same category as the arts-core holiday-maker in whom the tourist industry appears to be more interested if only because of the likelihood of greater expenditure.

These distinctions are not evident when cultural tourism is regarded as an entity. There is justification therefore for examining the components of culture separately. This does not, however, detract from the idea that the influence of any one cultural component may be joint with the others and with non-cultural resources of a destination. The initial suggestion was that the components of culture should be separated out for analysis. In the case of the performing arts this has identified a rather more complex situation than was evident when it was subsumed under the category of cultural tourism. It is likely, for instance, that much of the discussion explaining cultural tourism or special interest tourism, in terms of 'learning' in particular, does not readily explain tourists' interest in the performing arts. It is doubtful whether the continuance in the West End of 'The Mousetrap' since 1952, 'Cats' since 1981 and 'Les Miserables' since 1985 can be explained by anything other than a desire for 'a good night out'.

Some illustrative cases

New York: Broadway

The term Broadway is applied to about 38 theatres in Manhattan, New York, which are either on the street Broadway itself or in the surrounding streets. Broadway refers more to commercial orientation and to the size of theatre than to location. Broadway theatres usually have over 1000 seats and operate for profit. Most Broadway theatres are not on the street but in the Times Square area. The Broadway area including Times Square has had a reputation in the past as being rather seedy though Mayor Giuliani's clean-up campaigns have changed that. Broadway is commercial, for-profit, theatre whereas the not-for-profit theatre is off-Broadway. There is commercial theatre off-Broadway but it is small compared with either Broadway itself or the not-for-profit sector. There is a particular concentration of off-Broadway theatres in the Greenwich Village area. Off-Broadway theatres are associated with newer, avant-garde productions and new American productions are more likely to be found here than on Broadway. Some productions do though move from off-Broadway to Broadway.

New York's dominance of theatre in the USA has reduced as regional theatre, especially in Chicago and Los Angeles, has become more important in the development of new productions. Many of these then go on to Broadway.

Attendances at Broadway theatres were nearly 12 million in 1998–99 compared with 7 million in 1984–85 but this has not been an uninterrupted growth. There was, for instance, a decline in numbers for most of the 1980s. Playing weeks have risen from 1078 in 1984–85 to 1441 in 1998–99 with a low of 905 in 1991–92. The composition of Broadway audiences is similar to that in many other places. Two-thirds are aged 35 or older, three-quarters are Caucasian and over half (compared with 14 per cent of the US population) have an annual income of $75,000 or more. There has, however, been a doubling, between 1991 and 1997, of the number of Broadway theatre-goers under the age of 18 partly due to the number of 'youth-friendly' productions. Whilst personal recommendation is the single most important reason for choosing to see a show, one in five of audiences indicated that newspaper reviews were important.

As in London's West End, new openings and existing playing weeks on Broadway have been dominated by musicals. Broadway is associated with large musical and drama productions. The name Broadway has become closely associated with a particular type of production such as the older musicals 'A Chorus Line' and '42nd Street', which ran for many years. As with many theatrical districts, there is a view that the nature of productions has changed compared with the early part of the twentieth century. Whereas New York was regarded as a place where many new productions occurred each year, Broadway theatres now concentrate on long-running plays and musicals in particular. Other productions do not get the opportunity to be seen; this criticism is levelled at London's West End also. By producing classic plays and musicals, risk is reduced especially as it is believed that many people desire the technological spectacle and diversion of musicals in particular. Broadway has become increasingly a place for 'a special event' complete with merchandising. Often productions rely on famous name film or television stars to increase ticket sales. The name Broadway has been used as a term of abuse by critics. A review, in the British *Sunday Times* (April 2000), of the London West End production of 'The Graduate' included the comment 'the show is like the worst of Broadway, shallow and celebrity-driven, with ghastly merchandise being sold in the foyer'.

New York is a major tourist destination including some of the most famous landmarks in the world such as the Empire State Building and the Statue of Liberty. In 1999, there were over 34 million visitors to New York city and, of these, nearly 6 million were international, mostly from Canada (0.9 million) and the UK (0.8 million). Broadway is regarded as a tourist attraction of the city and the name has become universally recognized as being 'theatre in New York'. It was seen in Chapters 6 and 7 just how significant theatre is in drawing visitors to the city. To facilitate booking, there is a charge-free information and booking 'hot-line' and the Broadway Ticket Center located in the busy visitor area of Times Square.

Despite this, as seen in Chapter 6, the proportion of audiences who are visitors from the rest of the USA continues to fall though there has been a slight increase in the proportion of international visitors (to one in ten of audiences). An increasing proportion of audiences are resident in New York city or the surrounding suburbs. The suburban element has shown the greatest growth. About 17% of 'locals' go to a Broadway show at least once a year and there is a core of regular theatregoers (6%) who account for over 30% of all tickets sold.

There are shows such as 'Cats' (running since 1982 making it the longest running musical in Broadway history), 'Les Miserables', 'Chicago', 'Phantom of the Opera' and 'Fosse' which are being performed in New York and London (and other cities) at the same time. In recent years there has been a large number of 'imports' of productions from abroad especially from Britain. These have included a new production of 'Cabaret' (1998) by Sam Mendes, later the Oscar-winning director of the film 'American Beauty' as well as, in 1999, plays such as Eugene O'Neill's 'The Iceman Cometh' and David Hare's 'Via Dolorosa'. This is partly a matter of economics, being cheaper to bring in an established play or musical instead of starting the production process from the beginning. Some originated in the more heavily subsidized theatre of Europe and, in a sense, the USA is capitalizing on that investment of public funds. The risk of new and 'straight' plays is reduced by buying-in from elsewhere. There is an argument too that American 'classics' are limited in number compared with those from Europe. There is however, also a reverse transfer with productions such as 'Chicago' and 'Rent' originating in the USA and then being produced in London.

The economic impact of Broadway on New York city was estimated at $2724 million in 1996–97 and, as seen in Chapter 8, $1719 million of this was due to visitor spending. The total impact was calculated by adding the initial visitor spending other than on tickets to the set-up and operating costs of Broadway companies and the spending on capital improvements to theatres. This was subject to a multiplier effect. Compared with 1991–92, there was a 37 per cent increase in impact (after allowing for inflation). The spending of locals was not included as such. In the case of visitors from outside the city, the only spending that was included was that of people who indicated that Broadway was the main reason for the visit. In addition, a part of the spending of visitors who extended their visit in order to go to Broadway theatre was included. The proportions of visitors for whom Broadway was the main reason, or was a reason for extending the visit, were not estimated at the same time as the audience surveys were undertaken (1996–97) but from the earlier Port Authority surveys in 1992.

These Port Authority surveys also estimated economic impact and included commercial off-Broadway theatre and also 'Road productions'. These are

Broadway shows that are performed elsewhere but which have an economic impact in New York in the form, for instance, of royalty payments. This impact has been declining partly because of local financing, because of touring productions originating elsewhere including the rest of the USA and the influx of productions from the UK.

Sources: the League of American Theatres and Producers; Port Authority of New York and New Jersey; *Sunday Times* 'Culture' 9 April 2000; *the Guardian* 10 April 1999; *the Observer* 15 November 1998; New York Convention and Visitor's Bureau

London: West End

London, apart from being the centre of government in the UK and a major international commercial and financial centre, is also the most important tourist destination in the country. Total tourist visits to London are over 20 million and over half of these are international. The attractions of London are mostly 'heritage' though 'pop' culture, clubs, fashion, restaurants and lifestyle are claimed to be of increasing importance. London also has a large number of theatres which act as a tourist attraction. Over a quarter of all professional theatres in the UK are in London and there is a particular concentration within London's West End. Many of the more significant theatres in London are members of the Society of London Theatre (SOLT) known, until 1994, as the Society of West End Theatre (SWET). SOLT is a trade association with a membership of about 50 of London's theatres most of which are 'West End' theatres. They are located in central London with several distinct, but close, theatre clusters contributing to the leisure zone of the city. The concentration is itself considered to have a positive influence on attracting visitors to the city. SOLT theatres range in size from the relatively small at 250 capacity through to a few larger theatres at over 2000 seats. Most are operated as commercial concerns and few are subsidized. Attendances at SOLT theatres during 1997 were about 11.5 million compared with 10.5 million on Broadway the previous year though Broadway does include fewer theatres.

It was seen in Chapter 6 how important the West End is in attracting tourists to London and how the proportion of tourists in audiences has fluctuated. The share of international tourists in audiences is currently much less than it has been during the 1980s.

One of the most noticeable recent features of the West End is the increased importance of musicals and the reduced importance of plays and this has been linked with the tourist market (domestic and international). Nearly two-thirds of all attendances in West End theatres in 1997 were at 'modern musicals'. This is markedly different from the situation outside London. It was seen in Chapter 6 that tourists are a higher proportion of musical audiences than they are for other productions. For many observers, the tourist audiences are believed not to be particularly discerning and want little more than a 'glitzy night out'. One theatre critic was disappointed, in 1997, that the stage version of Disney's 'Beauty and the Beast' at the Dominion theatre was welcomed as favourable for West End jobs and tourism, and not seen as a threat to national heritage. Another critic condemned as undesirable and a sell-out to 'West End' values, the programming (in 1998) of the musical 'Oklahoma!' at the National Theatre. This had been created as 'a radical alternative to a complacent commercial theatre'.

Not only are musicals denigrated but also their impact on the rest of theatre is considered undesirable. Musicals and other 'tourist' productions have long-runs ('the Mousetrap' since 1952, 'Cats' since 1981 and 'Les Miserables' since 1985) and, as discussed in Chapter 8, so-called serious plays are squeezed out and the turnover of new plays is restricted. It is not just musicals that are seen as the problem but also revivals of popular plays and associated long-runs of many of these. Access to theatres and to finance and artistic talent is restricted for the non-musical and the new play. There are several reported instances of productions, such as the award-winning 'the Late Middle Classes', being unable to find a West End venue because of the desire to produce musicals, in that case a musical about a boy band which closed after a few weeks (1999). The actor and playwright Steven Berkoff complained, after his controversial new play 'Messiah' was turned down by the National Theatre in 2000, that theatres were too safe and were unwilling to take risks. It is obviously less risky for large commercial theatres to produce blockbuster musicals or plays than it is to put on experimental, innovative or controversial productions that may not sell on a large scale. The tourist market is one that is large and continually turning over and renewing itself every few days or weeks, an ideal scenario for investment in large-scale spectaculars. Corporations are able to absorb early losses and to subsidize the early days of one production from the revenue of another until the break-even point is reached.

There are, however, some West End theatres, usually subsidized, which are some of the most adventurous and prestigious theatres in the country; the Donmar Warehouse, the Royal Court, the Royal National Theatre and the Barbican until recently a London base for the Royal Shakespeare Company. There have been a number of successful transfers, such as 'Les

Miserables' and 'the Herbal Bed', from the subsidized sector to the commercial sector. In addition to these theatres many of the more innovative and limited interest productions take place off-West End in smaller theatres or in regional theatre. It is claimed that a 'significant proportion' of West End productions have originated in regional or non-SOLT theatre before transfer.

West End productions also transfer to regional theatres often as a national tour and also to other countries. In 1997, 'Phantom of the Opera' was performed in Australia, New Zealand and 17 cities in the USA and 'Buddy' in Japan, Germany, Canada, South Africa and USA. Earnings from international performances such as these were estimated at between £40 to £60 million in 1997.

The concentration of theatre ownership and of influence over productions is likely to have had a direct impact on the pattern of programming. Ownership of the commercial theatres is diverse but certain organizations and individuals appear dominant. By early 2000, there were two large corporations dominating ownership of London theatres. The Ambassador Theatre Group, which is part owned by the US corporation SFX, owned eleven after purchasing nine smaller theatres in February and the Really Useful Group owned thirteen having purchased ten from Stoll Moss the previous month. As seen in Chapter 2, SFX had already purchased the large national Apollo group in 1999, four of whose theatres are in London. The Really Useful Group is owned by the composer Andrew Lloyd Webber (Cats, Starlight Express, Phantom of the Opera and many others). The producer Cameron Mackintosh bought two theatres in 1999 to join the three that his company currently co-owned. The impresario Bill Kenwright has also been responsible for a large number of West End productions in recent years. Theatre ownership is therefore being combined in the same organization with composition, production, play and concert promotion. There is, in addition, a concentration of influence into fewer hands including, for instance, through joint Mackintosh-Webber productions. All of this could lead to significant control and influence over the programming of theatres in the West End. For the firms concerned, such integration yields economies and spreads risks.

Sources: Casey *et al.*, 1996; Lipman, 1996; Gardiner and Dickety, 1996; Billington, 1998; *the Guardian* 6 December 1999; *the Observer* 13 February 2000; *the Guardian* 10 February 2000; MORI 1998; Travers 1998; *Sunday Times* 'Culture' 9 April 2000

Las Vegas

Las Vegas (Nevada, USA) is perhaps the best-known instance of a tourist centre with an 'entertainment-core'. The main attraction of Las Vegas is gaming and until recently Nevada was the only state to legalize casino gaming in the USA (legalized 1931). Las Vegas receives over 30 million visitors a year (1998) of whom 70 per cent were there for vacation, pleasure or gambling. It is also a major centre for conventions. It claims to have more hotel and motel rooms (at 109,000) than any other resort destination in the world and 19 of the 20 largest hotels in the world. The MGM Grand, for instance, has over 5000 rooms. At Atlantic City most gamblers are day-trippers but Las Vegas is more a destination for the staying tourist. Most visitors do not have children with them and the average age is late forties. A high proportion (three-quarters) are repeat visitors and nearly all gamble during their stay. The average stay is short at just over three nights but nearly a third of visitors are from neighbouring California, half from the Western states and one in ten is international. The city has its own international airport with direct flights from countries such as the UK and Japan.

The key attraction of Vegas has been gambling but it has always been associated with live entertainment. Casinos are usually based in hotels that also provide a variety of live entertainment in order to attract and retain gaming customers. Most Las Vegas entertainment is associated with hotels rather than with separate theatres or concert halls. The musical 'Starlight Express' was, for instance, staged at the Las Vegas Hilton. The entertainment ranges from musicians in bar and lounge settings through circus and illusionists to national and international stars in large purpose built theatres and concert arenas. Some of these operations are so huge that effectively they operate as separate enterprises. Caesar's Palace (1500 rooms) has a 4500 seat indoor theatre and a 15,300 seat outdoor events stadium and MGM Grand has a similar size events centre as well as its own 33 acre theme park. At Circus Circus there is free circus in addition to a 5 acre indoor theme park.

There is a style of show, the glitzy spectacular floor-show with dancers and singers, that is referred to universally as a 'Las Vegas-type show'. The 'Official Visitors Guide' to Las Vegas refers to 'other parts of the casinos (where) entertainers adorned in glittering costumes join forces in lavish stage spectaculars ... Extravaganzas costing millions to produce surround visitors in a fantasy of shapely dancers, intricate choreography and special effects'. Las Vegas is also a centre for many associated spectacular events including boxing.

Just under half of Las Vegas visitors attend a show during their visit though spending on shows only accounts for about 8% of expenditure per visitor compared, for instance, with 38% on food and drink and 22% on shopping. Entertainment has been regarded as an incidental attraction and has been justified by its ability to attract people to gamble. It was initially regarded as a loss-leader in order to attract high-spending gamblers. There is now, however, more emphasis on entertainment as a profit centre. This, in conjunction with rising costs, has resulted in a shift from the star-centred shows towards smaller-scale variety (or revue) shows and musicals.

The city has long had a reputation for being an adult destination with gaming associated not only with adult entertainment but also organized crime and prostitution. It has in recent years sought to re-position itself as a tourist destination. Casino gaming is now legal in more places in the USA, including Atlantic City and many Native American reservations, and Las Vegas can no longer rely on its virtual monopoly to attract visitors. It is therefore developing as a family holiday destination. In order to do this, more family-oriented entertainment has been offered in the form of virtual reality experiences, theme parks and free open-air events such as an erupting volcano outside the Mirage hotel and a pirate battle performed outside the Treasure Island hotel. The emphasis on Las Vegas as a gaming centre has been reduced but it is still the hotels that maintain a connection with entertainment, albeit in a different form.

These developments have had mixed fortunes and, whilst such entertainment has undoubtedly broadened the appeal of Las Vegas, some gaming operators have found that certain forms of entertainment compete with, rather than complement, gaming. There are several other concerns associated with this re-positioning, such as the increased number of 'non-gamblers' and 'low-roller' gamblers in the city and the loss of its distinctive character. In addition some casino executives are not skilled in providing these types of experience and there have been some noticeable failures. There has been a concern that the city has gone too far along the route of a family-friendly destination and some business people have been anxious to maintain the reputation as an adult destination. This is partly due to the lower gaming spend of tourists with children. Nonetheless some of the more recent developments, such as the New York, New York with its own rollercoaster and the Venetian Casino Resort complete with upscale shopping mall and Grand Canal, have continued the wider appeal.

Las Vegas is very much a one-industry city with just over half of the labour force in southern Nevada being employed in the city's tourist and gaming sector. It has been pointed out that this means low-skill, low-wage and un-unionized employment for many and also an excessive influence of the gaming and hotel corporations on the political and development process. Since the 1950s there are now fewer individuals and more corporations owning and operating casinos in the city. The needs of the industry may have been prioritized over the social community and welfare needs of the local population and the sustainability of the local natural environment. There would appear to be a coalition of interests between local hotel-casino operators, other business people, development agencies, the visitor bureau, airlines and local government that exerts a powerful influence in encouraging free-enterprise and growth.

Sources: Las Vegas Convention and Visitors Authority; Christiansen and Brinkerhoff-Jacobs, 1995; Thompson, Pinney and Scibrowsky, 1996; Parker, 1999

British seaside resorts: early developments

There are features of the seaside resort in Britain in the past that have been unique features of the entertainment industry. The significance of this lies in the fact that their influence lingers on to the present-day. As seaside resorts became more popular during the latter part of the nineteenth century there was considerable investment in theatres, pavilions, concert halls and 'pleasure palaces'. Some of these, such as the Winter Gardens in Blackpool (1878), initially represented a more serious purpose by including gardens and library. The Winter Gardens in Rhyl (North Wales) built in 1876 included a zoo, theatre, seal pond and skating rink. At this time music hall was flourishing and halls were built in resorts, firmly establishing the tradition of the variety show at the seaside.

As the seaside began to attract the working classes there was a need to change what was on offer and from the end of the nineteenth century investment in entertainment rose dramatically. Theatres and halls existed in many resorts offering variety, melodrama and farce and more 'serious' plays, drama and musicals during the season to a predominantly middle class audience alongside a more informal, often out-door and beach entertainment. These included circuses, fairgrounds, 'black-face' minstrels, Pierrots and Punch and Judy shows geared to a more working class audience. The Punch and Judy Show has been synonymous with the seaside though it had originated at inland fairs. The 'black-face' minstrels were a prominent feature of English seaside resorts, dominating popular entertainment until the 'more refined' Pierrots, originating in France, appeared. Entertainment became increasingly commercial.

Some of the attractions became more bizarre and included waxworks and freak shows as well as an assortment of fortune-tellers and healers and talks, lectures and lantern slides by dubious 'experts'. A major attraction in several resorts during the 1930s was the 'Rector of Stiffkey' who had been dismissed from the church for sexual misconduct. He earned a living in a sideshow in Blackpool which included him living in a barrel and also being 'devoured by the flames of hell'. He later appeared in a show in Skegness only to be killed by one of the lions in 1938.

Piers were also particularly associated with entertainment. Although most were originally intended for the arrival and departure of ships, they soon became geared towards entertainment. Holiday-makers were able to extend their walking and display from the promenade itself to a promenade over the sea. Piers often included money-generating facilities such as pavilions and concert halls, refreshment rooms, machines and mechanical devices, booths and kiosks. There was often an 'end-of-the-pier show' performed by concert parties of small groups of artists all of whom sang, danced, told jokes and performed short sketches. They were particularly popular from the 1920s through to the late 1930s.

Military and brass bands also played in open-air bandstands and in pier pavilions. Most resorts also had an orchestra, however small, which invariably played in pavilions on piers. Most resorts had an orchestra at some time during the late nineteenth and early twentieth centuries and the continuing existence of orchestras owes a great deal to the holiday-maker. The conductors, musicians and singers were among the most able and famous of the day. They included (Sir) Malcolm Sargent at the seaside town of Llandudno (Wales) who was later conductor of many famous orchestras and chief conductor of the annual BBC Proms festival 1948–66 and Granville Bantock (at New Brighton, a resort near Liverpool) who was later Professor of Music at Birmingham University. As employment in such orchestras was usually seasonal, musicians from non-tourist area orchestras were able to find year-round employment. In the early part of the twentieth century the Pier Orchestra at Llandudno was made up largely of members of the Halle Orchestra (Manchester), which is Britain's longest established professional symphony orchestra (founded 1858). The seaside resort of Bournemouth, on the south coast of England, had the distinction of having the first year-round permanent orchestra in England (1893) and it has since become an important touring symphony orchestra. Musical programmes were usually short and light for background or promenading, but most orchestras endeavoured to provide symphony concerts in addition and to work the 'more serious' works into their programmes.

The 'holiday camp' is also of particular significance in the history of holidays and entertainment. All-inclusive centres for a holiday had existed for some time. Some originated in the early twentieth century as a form of self-help, self-improvement movement where a sense of community in a healthy environment could be fostered. These holidays, often in tents, included organized games and entertainments that were often self-entertainment. Commercial camps emerged during the 1930s and of particular significance were the holiday camps established by Billy Butlin (initially in Skegness in 1937 for 1000 campers and in Clacton in 1939). Holiday-makers did not need to leave the holiday camps during their stay as, apart from the chalet-type accommodation, there were catering halls, swimming pools, games and sports areas, theatres and dance halls. Access to all of these was without further charge. In the seaside tradition, entertainment followed the variety revue pattern and also dance bands and children's entertainers. There was also an emphasis on holiday-makers making their own entertainment. Organizers variously known as Red Coats (Butlins) or Blue Coats (Pontins) organized games and competitions for campers and entertainment by campers as well putting on shows themselves. The holiday camp was particularly popular during the 1950s. They were major providers of seaside entertainment and were a significant 'breeding-ground' for new performing talent.

Sources: Ward and Hardy, 1986; Walton, 1983a; Walvin, 1978; Bainbridge, 1986; Young, 1968

Blackpool

Blackpool is the largest seaside resort in the UK and Blackpool's Pleasure Beach (an amusement park complex) is currently the most popular of all English visitor attractions. The holiday season that is usual in UK seaside towns is longer in Blackpool because of the 'Illuminations'. These are illuminated tableaux (usually from late August through to early November) that stretch the length of the seafront. Blackpool is a resort that has an image of liveliness and vitality and has been described as working class and vulgar. Its reputation has always been slightly down-market with entertainment that often verged on the 'bizarre'. Blackpool is not typical of the UK seaside resort but it has a long tradition of live shows and end-of-pier entertainment and there is currently a large entertainment industry in the resort. There are also numerous bars and clubs where some form of entertainment is offered as well as considerable in-hotel provision. Much of the entertainment industry in Blackpool is in the hands of commercial providers and local government has had little role in the provision of entertainment.

Venues include two large 'conventional' theatres, the Grand Theatre (1200 seats) and the Opera House (2980 seats). The former was built in 1894 and is now owned by a non-profit-making trust the Grand Theatre Trust Ltd. Until relatively recently most of the older venues were owned by 'local' companies. The Opera House is part of a larger leisure, conference and exhibition complex (the Winter Gardens) and was, until 1998, owned by the public company First Leisure. This company also owned the three piers each with their own theatres (North, Central and South which have theatres between 300 and 1500 seats) and the Blackpool Tower complex. This contains a number of 'family activities' including play centres, aquarium, a circus (1800 seats) and ballroom. These were all disposed of in 1998 to a private purchaser, Trevor Hemmings. The remaining major entertainment facility is at the Pleasure Beach (the amusement park complex) owned by a private, family company. There are several venues, between 450 and 2300 seats, here including the Arena.

All summer show productions run for a season from either late May or early July through to early November. Many can be categorized as 'traditional variety', a succession of light entertainment acts with headline minor star(s) who have usually had some television exposure. There is an emphasis on the family audience, though some of the shows do have slightly different formats and content in the later performances. (There are often two performances of some shows: afternoon and evening or early and mid evening performances.) In part, this strategy is designed to catch the day-tripper market. Performances are usually either Monday through Saturday or Tuesday through Sunday so there are no 'dead' nights in the town during the week. There are also separate Sunday shows at some of the theatres.

The nature of the Blackpool variety shows has changed and there is a consensus that they are not as lavish or glamorous as they were, for instance, in the 1950s and 1960s. The Pleasure Beach however continues to offer lavish shows with special effects and lighting. The Ice Show, a spectacular, Las Vegas-style, variety show, maintains elements of old style glamour especially in the glitzy costumes. It is one element of the live entertainment product in Blackpool that has remained since its establishment in 1937. The company deems these aspects important enough to invest heavily in and employs in-house designers, pattern cutters and beaders. These shows started as a peripheral activity but are now important profit generators. The strategy had been designed to attract visitors, particularly day-trippers, to stay later. The Pleasure Beach is the only major 'producing' venue in Blackpool as the others contract out to producers. It has become an established production company operating under the name 'Stageworks Worldwide Productions' and shows are sold to venues in Europe and Asia. During 1997, nearly 700,000 tickets were sold for shows in the Pleasure Beach's five venues.

New products are evident however. The Opera House has had a recent policy of offering a different type of entertainment and has hosted established and popular musicals such as 'Joseph and the Amazing Technicolor Dreamcoat' or 'Cats' for the season. These are not the usual seaside fare and are also presented at theatres across the country especially in urban centres. The Grand Theatre is a 'local' theatre. It was threatened with demolition in the 1970s but rescued by the action of a local pressure group. Its policy is to offer a year-round programme that includes ballet, opera, plays and classical and jazz concerts. Its survival though is very much dependent on the summer show. Some of the big shows at other theatres are pointedly aimed at a 'non-family' audience such as an 'adult' stand-up comedian targeted at a weekend and day-visitor market of young single males.

Sources: Hughes and Benn, 1998; Blackpool Borough Tourism Services

Atlantic City

Atlantic City, New Jersey, is one the earliest seaside holiday destinations in the USA. It was developed as a purpose built resort in the mid-nineteenth century with the building of the railway. It has an eight mile beach and the earliest boardwalk. It became a popular destination for holiday-makers from the heavily populated north-east of the USA, especially Philadelphia (60 miles away) and New York (100 miles). It has had several piers including the Steel Pier (1898), which offered 16 hours of entertainment for one admission. It included famous name bands, vaudeville and television stars.

Atlantic City's popularity waned however during the mid twentieth century as alternative destinations became available and air travel made it possible for people to travel quickly and cheaply to Florida and the west coast for their holidays. By 1975 it had lost a quarter of its population and was the poorest city in the state.

Its renewed prosperity is based on casinos which include names familiar from Las Vegas such as Hilton and Caesars, Harrahs and Sands and also several Trump casinos. New Jersey was the second state (after Nevada) to legalize casino gambling, which was introduced from 1976 onwards. By 1994, the industry provided over 60 per cent of all jobs in the city and average income per head had risen from being below the national average to considerably above. There has been rather closer regulation of gaming than has been the case in several other places and all licensed establishments have had to provide a full range of services including hotel services, restaurants, bars and entertainment. As in Vegas, each of the 12 casinos has considerable and lavish entertainment provision. They usually include international singing and cabaret stars as headliners as well casino revue shows. There are far fewer casinos in Atlantic City than in Las Vegas and casino hotels are generally smaller with the largest being Bally's at 1265 rooms and Trump Taj Mahal at 1250 and most of the others between 500 and 800 rooms. Theatres vary in size from 5500 seats at the Trump Taj Mahal to under 500 seats at Bally's, Showboat and Trump Castle.

Most visitors to Atlantic City continue to be from the region and the near-by markets of New Jersey, New York, Pennsylvania and Maryland. A significant factor in the early growth was the 'bus program', which offered transport to day-trippers from the region. Most of the participants were middle aged or retired and were offered a free buffet and show as part of the program. Atlantic City is currently the most popular resort destination in the USA, ahead of Las Vegas and Orlando, with over 34 million visitors a year. It has a high number of day visitors but the casinos are the major attraction of Atlantic City for the vast majority of both staying and day visitors. The night-life, including entertainment, is an important factor in the popularity for staying visitors.

Sources: Atlantic City Convention and Visitors Authority; Braunlich, 1996; Schrank, 1987

Coney Island

Coney Island is in the south part of the borough of Brooklyn (New York) and is a one-hour subway ride from midtown Manhattan. It is a pleasure ground of sideshows, fun fairs and theme parks. It was connected to the mainland by road in 1823 and, by the late nineteenth century, was attracting long-stay visitors. The proximity to New York along with the completion of the subway in the 1920s were sufficient to increase its popularity rapidly and it experienced an influx of cheaper boarding houses, vaudeville theatres, brothels and gambling houses.

It is currently a day-tripper destination rather than a long-stay tourist town but it retains the flavour of its origins as one of the earliest 'mass' tourist destinations in the USA. Its main market has been, and remains, the lower income New Yorker. It is a relatively poor area itself and has a rather run-down air with derelict buildings and attractions remaining. The first roller-coaster in the country was built here in 1884 and it retains the world's oldest working Ferris wheel (1918). The two large amusement parks have about 30 rides each including the Wonder Wheel and the Cyclone roller-coaster (1927), both of which are designated as national landmarks. The rides in all of the several funfairs tend to be traditional and there is little of a high-tech nature even now. One of its most well-known and oldest attractions (dating from 1902–03) is Luna Park. This was an 'electric city by the sea' with a number of themed areas including parts purporting to represent Venice and Japan. In addition there was live entertainment that included re-enactments of disasters arising from floods, volcano eruptions and fires.

Coney Island is also characterized by its wooden boardwalk, which extends along the seafront with a range of stalls selling such items as hot dogs, pizzas, ice cream, candy and beer.

Despite its decline as a 'staying' tourist destination, its live entertainment is reminiscent of the older, down-market, seaside destination. Its claim to fame is 'Sideshows by the Seaside' promoted as 'the last place in the USA where you can experience the thrill of a traditional ten-in-one circus sideshow' (entry $5). The emphasis is on the bizarre and what are termed 'freaks' including a 'killer clown', a 'bearded woman', a fire-eater, sword-swallower, an 'elastic lady' and a 'snake enchantress'. The same organization promotes the annual Mermaid Parade of mermaids and neptunes to celebrate the beginning of the summer.

Sources: Daily Telegraph 29 May 1999; *the Observer* 12 March 2000; Brooklyn Tourism Council

Cromer and Bexhill

Cromer, on the north Norfolk coast, is a small, relatively quiet, seaside resort (population 5000) that has attracted a different type of holidaymaker from those who go to Blackpool. The building of railway links in the late nineteenth century led to its popularity with the upper and middle classes. King Edward VII was a frequent visitor before and after becoming king in 1901 and there was a determination on the part of the local council to keep the town as a resort for the well-to-do. Its pier was opened in 1901, complete with bandstand, which was later transformed into the Pavilion Theatre. Military bands and concert parties performed here in the early years of the twentieth century. The concert parties were revived in the 1970s so that Cromer now claims to hold the only remaining authentic end-of-pier show. It has attracted a cult following as well as being popular with elderly day-trippers. The small theatre has 440 seats and an average cast size of 15, each of whom performs any of comedy, dance, singing and playing music.

Bexhill-on-Sea is a similar small, quiet seaside resort on the coast of Sussex, about 70 miles from London. Its De La Warr pavilion was opened in 1935 as an entertainments pavilion, or 'people's palace', on the seafront. The building was the outcome of an international design competition won by a German architect, Erich Mendelsohn. The architectural significance of the building is recognized by its protection as a Grade 1 listed building. It is owned by the local council but has been run by the Pavilion Trust since 1989 and has been subject, in recent years, to renovation and restoration in an endeavour to capture its original glory. It is being developed as an arts and social centre with an art gallery, bars, restaurant, cafe and meeting rooms. The art gallery shows exhibitions of twentieth century art, architecture and design. A summer entertainments season is held in the original 1000-seat theatre. The programme is a mixed one of music, plays, dance and comedy, which are usually one-nighters. It does also however present children's shows. There is also a first-floor sun terrace leading off the restaurant where there are jazz and brass band concerts and children's entertainment during the summer. In 2000, the local council is considering the sale of the pavilion to a national chain of public houses largely because of the difficulty of finding funds to finance the high costs of restoration, maintenance and operation. This chain is well-known for its sympathetic re-use of older buildings, though what its policy would be with regard to the wider use of the pavilion remains to be seen.

Sources: Rother District Council (East Sussex); *the Guardian* 7 August 1999; *the Guardian* 27 March 2000

Adelaide Festival

The Adelaide Festival is a three-week festival established in 1960 which is held every two years, during March. Adelaide itself has a population of about one million and is capital of the state of South Australia. As a tourist destination, its heritage, the arts and beaches are promoted. Attractions include a zoo, art galleries and museums including the 'Bradman Collection' relating to the famous Australian cricketer. The casino, which opened in 1985, attracted over two million visitors in 1998–99 of whom 42,000 were international. The beach areas are extensive and include provision for sailing, diving and fishing as well as the usual sunbathing.

In the surrounding parts of South Australia, attractions include the McLaren Vale and the Barossa wine-making districts. One of the most significant attractions close to Adelaide is Kangaroo Island which includes Flinders Chase National Park, well-known for its natural wildlife especially penguins and sealions.

Tourist attractions include a number of events such as regattas and horse-racing as well as arts festivals and, for ten years until the mid 1990s, the Formula One Grand Prix. The Glenelg Jazz Festival (October) had attendances of 11,600 in 1998, of whom 3% were international and 5% out of state. WOMAD (World of Music and Dance) was first held in Australia in 1992 and in 1999 had attendances of 65,000. There are also a number of successful festivals associated with the Barossa Valley including annual gourmet festivals and vintage festivals. There is also an International Barossa Music Festival (since 1991) with international performers giving concerts in wineries and churches. Attendances in 1997 were 20,000 of whom 12 per cent were out of state.

In 1998 there were 300,000 international visitors to South Australia, compared with 2.2 million to New South Wales (Sydney). Two-thirds were holiday visits and over a third had visited the Adelaide beaches and surrounding countryside including the Barossa Valley. Under 20 per cent had visited Kangaroo Island. The single most important international tourist-generating country was the UK. There were also 1 million interstate visitors in 1997, most of whom came from the neighbouring state of Victoria. Just under a third were there for holiday purposes and the most popular destination was Adelaide itself.

The South Australian Tourism Commission recognizes the significance of festivals and events as tourist generators though the primary tourist attractions of the state are its beaches, scenery, wineries and wildlife. The state government itself established a short-lived organization, Australian Major Events, to provide financial assistance for the development and marketing of festivals and events that have economic significance. Its merger into the Tourism Commission indicated the interest in the tourism dimension of events. The Adelaide Festival is considered to be Australia's major cultural event and includes music, drama, ballet, opera, dance, art exhibition and light entertainment. There is a particular emphasis on innovation, experiment and outreach. The opening night has usually seen the performance of new productions of twentieth century operas. In 1998 this was a State Opera production of 'Flamma Flamma' by Lens and in 2000 was a Netherlands Opera production of 'Writing to Vermeer' by Andriessen. An 8-hour epic, 'The Ecstatic Bible' by Howard Barker was a highlight of the 2000 Festival. Dance performances are usually contemporary dance though the music programme does include the 'classics' and performances by, for instance, the Adelaide Symphony Orchestra and the Brodsky Quartet. Typically performers are drawn from many countries and in the 1996 Festival over 30 countries were represented. A Fringe runs alongside the Festival and attendances at this were 857,000 in 1998.

The Adelaide Festival Centre was opened in 1973 and is home to the Festival. It is managed by a trust on behalf of the South Australian government. The Centre has four performance venues including the 2000 capacity Festival Theatre, a 600 seat Playhouse, a flexible performance space and an outdoor amphitheatre.

The Festival was the subject of an extensive impact study in 1990 and 1996. In 1990 over 9000 out-of-state visitors attended the Festival and Fringe of whom 6000 were specifically attracted by the Festival or Fringe. The 1996 study focused on the Festival only and there were separate surveys of attenders, performers, sponsors, the media and organizers and volunteers. The 1996 Festival incurred operating expenditure of nearly A$12 million of which A$2.4 million was covered by box office income, A$3.5 million from the South Australian government and A$0.4 million from Adelaide City Council.

It is estimated that 42,000 individuals attended Festival events in 1996, of whom most were Adelaide residents, 2% from the rest of South Australia and 18% out-of-state. International visitors were 13% of all visitors and of these the single most important places of origin were UK, USA, New Zealand and Germany. The average stay in South Australia was 7 nights for interstate visitors and 18 nights for international visitors.

Attenders were classified into residents, visitors and 'Festival Visitors'. The latter were visitors who had visited Adelaide specifically to attend the Festival and were identified as people who had said they would not have come to Adelaide if the Festival had not been held or whose visit was an additional visit especially for the Festival. As seen in Chapters 6 and 8, the Festival was responsible for a significant number of visitors coming to Adelaide and of residents staying rather than going somewhere else. The festival had a greater pull for 'local' Australian visitors than it did for international visitors who were more likely to be in Adelaide for other reasons.

Visitors attended an average of four Festival performances whereas Festival Visitors attended an average of just over four and residents attended three. Apart from a general awareness of the Festival's existence, the next most important source of information about the Festival for visitors was 'word of mouth'. Nearly half of visitors had attended a previous Adelaide Festival and almost two-thirds intended to return for the next one. It is noticeable that visitors and Festival Visitors in particular were more regular theatre goers than were residents.

The economic impact of the Festival was estimated by adding Festival-generated expenditure of visitors, residents, performers, sponsors, the media and organizers and volunteers and other Festival income from outside the state. All of the expenditure of 'Festival Visitors' was included whereas in the case of other visitors only the part incurred in the extended part of the stay was included. Only the expenditure of residents who had chosen to stay at home rather than go away was included. Their spending per person was double that of other residents in large part because of greater spending on tickets. Sponsorship received could have been spent elsewhere in South Australia and it was important to exclude this money and, similarly, money which could have been spent outside the state but which was spent in South Australia should be included.

In total the Festival was estimated to have generated extra expenditure of A$13 million in the state of South Australia.

Sources: South Australian Tourism Commission; the Telstra Adelaide Festival; Market Equity and Economic Research Consultants; *the Guardian* 8 March 2000

Buxton Festival

Buxton has a population of about 19,000 and lies in the southern Pennines, an upland area approximately midway between the major cities of Manchester and Sheffield in the UK. It is surrounded by the Peak District National Park and the town is in a basin ringed by hills and mountains. There is not a great deal of industrial or commercial development in Buxton but it has had a long history as a tourist destination. Its present day distinctive buildings and layout are a consequence of its development as a tourist destination and are the focus of current tourist re-development. As a spa centre, Buxton was probably one of the earliest tourist areas in Britain. In the twentieth century there was a decline of spas in Britain and spa towns have sought other tourist attractions or roles. There are few major attractions in Buxton itself and its attraction probably is its location as a centre for Peak District touring and in its own right as a 'pleasant town' in a rural setting. It has an unspoilt and un-commercialized nature, a quiet 'refined' ethos and pleasant buildings and layout.

The town has a compact tourist area with a distinct cluster of facilities on one level. The most dominant feature is the Crescent (1780–84). A number of nineteenth century spa buildings are part of the tourist infrastructure. The Natural Baths are part of the Crescent complex and are used for the Tourist Information Centre and capping of the spring water. The Thermal Baths have been redeveloped as specialist and tourist shops. The Pump Room in the Crescent was originally a venue for drinking the waters and socializing. The Pavilion Gardens is a major park area at the western end of the Crescent. At one end of the Gardens is the Opera House (1903) restored in 1979 to its use as a 'receiving theatre' after use as a cinema and subsequent neglect. Accommodation in Buxton comprises about 16 hotels and over twice as many guest houses. The largest of the hotels is the Palace (1868) with 122 bedrooms.

The annual festival of the arts held in Buxton since 1979 is a festival with an opera core. The Festival was originally held over two or three weeks in July and August and offered two operas every year. The operas were initially produced by the company itself and are operas that have rarely, if ever, been professionally staged before in Britain. The Festival opened, and has continued, as an arts festival with operas forming the basis for a number of other linked events such as concerts, recitals, drama and revue. The intention had been to present thematic festivals though this approach has not always been maintained. The core of the themed festival would be the professionally staged operas.

The founders were initially moved to establish the Festival out of a desire to save and restore the Opera House, which then provided the opportunity to present rare operas. The rationale for producing rare opera lay partly in the belief that most opera-goers are reasonably well served by existing professional provision of the main repertoire. Given this existing provision in the region and the relatively small size of the opera market, a policy of producing non-standard pieces on a professional basis seemed appropriate. Additionally, in view of the limited resources at its disposal, the company would probably not have been able to mount productions of standard works that competed effectively with those of the 'national' companies. The artistic standards achieved in the opera production, at least in the past, have been generally recognized to be high.

The rarity of the operas combined with the theme approach, the setting in the Peak District and the Opera House itself (1000 seats, built in 1903 and restored in 1979) were believed to constitute a unique product. The Festival company also considered that having its own opera production company was an important distinguishing feature of its activity as is the fact that productions are fully professional. The company had to abandon its 'own-production' policy in 1993 but it has been revived on a more limited scale recently so that there is a mix of own-productions with those by other small companies.

In targeting local, regional, national or international audiences, the Festival would face little difficulty as few other companies provide the same product. The potential market is therefore geographically very large. From the outset the company talked in terms of 'aiming at both a local and visiting audience' and of the Festival being 'publicized internationally' It is likely that people will travel in order to see a rare piece but also the size of the local population is such that it could not generate large enough audiences locally for such productions. The location of the Festival may have been fortuitous in this respect, in that Buxton has been and remains a tourist destination. The operas (and Festival as a whole) have not however been regarded by the Company primarily as tourist attractions. They were seen originally and primarily as artistic events, the audience for which is widely dispersed.

Audience surveys have been carried out during several of the Festivals. They have confirmed that just over half of opera audiences were tourists and nearly half of these classified their visit and stay as 'non-holiday'. The length of stay was not long but a third stayed three nights or more. For over 80% of tourists in opera audiences, the Festival was the main or only reason for the visit to and stay in Buxton and without the Festival those visits would not have occurred. Within the Festival it was the operas themselves that had drawn the tourists though nearly all attended other Festival events. The location in Buxton and the Opera House itself contributed greatly to the decision to attend the Festivals. Nearly all were 'opera-enthusiasts'.

Source: Buxton Arts Festival

Glastonbury Festival

There is a large number of pop, rock, dance and folk festivals in the UK including the Reading Festival and WOMAD and dance festivals such as Tribal Gathering and Homelands. Phoenix Festival, staged since the early

1990s near Stratford-upon-Avon, failed in 1998 and led to concern about over-supply. Most festivals are supported by large corporate sponsors including Virgin, Sony and Diesel. They are eager to relate to this youth market but the festivals themselves have run the risk of being perceived of as being commercial and moving away from their origins which often lay in some form of anti-establishment, rebellious youth culture. The dance festival, Tribal Gathering (Oxford) has tried to avoid such commercial connections and is re-emphasizing its origins as an underground dance festival.

Homelands, held near Winchester, is an outdoor celebration of club culture and is sponsored by Ericsson, the mobile phone company. In 1999 it had 100 acts and attendances of 35,000. It is promoted by the Mean Fiddler organization, as was Tribal Gathering until it decided to return to its roots. Mean Fiddler is one the country's major concert promoters and runs the Reading, Leeds and Creamfields festivals as well as a number of bars and clubs in London. The Phoenix festival was also a Mean Fiddler promotion.

Glastonbury Festival is unusual in being organized by what almost amounts to a one-man organization centred on a local dairy farmer Michael Eavis. It does not, either, have the high-profile sponsorship associated with other festivals. The festival takes place over three days in Pilton, Somerset and is claimed to be the largest rock festival in Europe. It started in 1970 as Pilton Pop Festival and has been held nearly every year since. Eavis decided to run his own festival after visiting Bath Blues Festival. It is held on Eavis' own farmland on Worthy Farm. Initially it coincided with the harvest festival, it featured Marc Bolan and Tyrannosaurus Rex and attracted an audience of 1500. In the following year it was shifted to midsummer as a 'hippy-type' Glastonbury Fayre. David Bowie and Joan Baez were amongst the performers and it attracted 12,000 people. Various informal festivals continued to be held after that until a formal relaunch in 1979 and in 1981, a decision to raise money for the local branch of the Campaign for Nuclear Disarmament (CND).

The festival takes place on 800 acres of farmland, only half of which is owned by Eavis. The rest is leased from neighbouring farmers. There are no permanent facilities and every festival involves erection of stages, perimeter fences, turnstiles, stalls, portable toilets, and the hiring of drainage equipment when necessary. Festival-goers often stay in tents on the festival site giving the festival a particularly informal and easy-living atmosphere.

It is claimed to be the least commercial festival in the world. It is only recently that headliner performers have been announced in advance and there is little indication of when bands will actually perform during the three days.

The justification has been that the festival is not just who is appearing but 'an experience'. It has a reputation for attracting people with alternative lifestyles and also 'conventional' people who will happily experience that for the duration. Glastonbury has long been associated with myths and legends especially relating to King Arthur, the Knights of the Round Table and the Holy Grail. The area has always had an appeal to those of a mystical nature. For most of its early years it was a free festival that attracted the free-loving, environmentally-friendly individualist and New Age travellers. Its links with CND and, more recently, with Greenpeace, the environment pressure group, have appealed to a particular non-conforming type of person. Festival-goers are drawn from all over the country and even from other countries.

The festival is not easily categorized musically and covers a wide range of popular musical tastes. It includes a jazz and world music stage and a dance stage. Performers in 1999 included Beautiful South, Billy Bragg, Barenaked Ladies, the Corrs, Lenny Kravitz, REM and Texas. In the previous year there had been appearances by Tony Bennett and Bob Dylan.

About 90,000 tickets were sold for the 1997 festival. It is estimated that 80,000 people attended in 1999, which, with performers, crew, staff, media and guests, meant that over 100,000 people had been on site during the three-day festival. The festival is largely an open-air one and, as a consequence, can be affected considerably by bad weather. There are market stalls, refreshment tents and marquees, a cinema marquee, poetry readings, craft demonstrations, a circus, and a stage for theatre, cabaret and comedy. The performances are broadcast on national radio and television and the festival is sponsored by a major national 'serious' newspaper.

The festival's popularity has led to a change of emphasis. Entry, for instance, is controlled by charging for entry (£83 per head for three days in 1999), by erecting temporary fencing and 'watch-towers', by banning certain people and a more careful vetting of who is allowed in. Some more permanent facilities including water mains and toilet blocks have also been introduced though tents remain the main form of accommodation. There are even cash machines on site for the duration of the festival.

Despite the size of the festival it continues to be run by Eavis who combines it with being a full-time farmer. He is very much hands-on with respect to the festival and personally chooses bands and performers. The festival is, though, big business with a turnover of more than £5 million (1997) and £6.5 million in 1999. In 1997, £1.5 million was spent on performers, which is probably less than the 'market rate' as many are prepared to play Glastonbury at low fees. A further £760,00 was spent on administration and over £1 million on fencing, security and policing. Local farmers whose land is rented, received £170,000. Bad weather can raise costs significantly. There was particularly heavy rain during the 1997 and 1998 festivals. During 1997, groups' tour buses were unable to approach the stage areas, one stage are was closed by the local council as being unsafe and another was eventually opened after the laying of 3500 tons of gravel. Inevitably some bands were cancelled and others re-scheduled. In other parts of the festival ground, straw, wood and stones laid on the muddy ground necessitated extra expenditure of £250,000.

The festival made a profit for the first time in 1981 and has a had a policy of making contributions to charities including Greenpeace, Oxfam, WaterAid and CND and also to over 50 local organizations including schools. Over £700,000 was distributed in 1998, though it is claimed by some to be a sop to reduce local complaints about the disruption brought by the festival.

There has always been a problem of relationships with the local community. The type of festival-goer, especially in the early days, did arouse great feelings of hostility amongst the rather more staid and conservative local population. There continue to be problems of noise and the pressure of such a large number of people on a small agricultural community. Many of the festival-goers have unorthodox lifestyles and little regard for conventional lifestyles. On site there have been problems associated with drugs and violence. Increased security has reduced some of the more serious problems that seemed to have been associated with a heavy presence of drug dealers. The festival has also experienced some conflict between different festival-goers. One group of festival-goers refused to leave the site for two months in 1987 and another looted the site in 1990 causing £50,000 of damage. There is a continuing problem with thieves stealing from tents whilst their owners are at the performance areas. A police presence was introduced in 1989 and the Festival's security has been increased greatly since 1990. Security and policing on site cost £1 million in 1997.

Sources: the Glastonbury Performing Arts Festival; *the Observer* 2 May 1999; *the Guardian* 4 June 1999; *the Guardian* 20 June 1999; *the Observer* 29 June 1999; *the Guardian* 21 June 1997

Mardi Gras

Mardi Gras is a period of festivity that takes place annually in a number of places worldwide, in the days before Lent. This 40-day Lent period is one of abstinence, which, in its early Christian observance days, usually meant the giving up of meat. The origins of the pre-Lent carnival are obscure but it can traced back to pre-Christian times and celebrations of the new year, fertility and rebirth of nature. Although the timings of carnival differ, many now are timed so as to finish on Shrove Tuesday (February or March). The name Mardi Gras for these carnivals is believed to derive from the custom of using up all fats before Lent.

These events are associated with parades and festivities rather than with arts or entertainment as such. They, and especially parades, may nonetheless be considered 'live performances before an audience' in as much as parade participants wear costume, dance and sing and play music as part of the celebrations. Although these carnivals have a long history as local celebrations they have become tourist attractions which feature, for instance, in tour operators' brochures, in tourist board and tourist bureau promotional campaigns and literature and in travel articles and supplements in newspapers and magazines. Many of the more famous are heavily promoted to tourists but are not organized by tourist-oriented bodies and they still maintain a strong local significance and involvement in balls and parades, for instance.

In Europe, perhaps the most well known Carnival is that in Venice (Italy) for about ten days prior to Shrove Tuesday. Venice is itself a major tourist heritage city famous for its canals and historic churches and other buildings. Tourist numbers to this relatively small city of 80,000 inhabitants, are about 1.5 million staying visitors and 7 million day visitors per year with the height of the tourist season during the summer. The Venetian Carnival dates from the eighteenth century but was revived in 1980. It includes a masked procession and a masked ball. Masks are traditional and have their origin in the desire to remain anonymous and avoid the strict social codes and social barriers of the city. Anonymity could confer social equality. Masks are now a significant tourist souvenir of Venice and there is a local craft industry creating masks both for carnival itself and for the tourist trade.

Probably the most famous of all is Carnival in Rio de Janeiro (Brazil). The 4-day period is characterized by parties and parades with samba having particular prominence. Samba groups compete with different themes and style of costume.

Mardi Gras in Sydney (Australia) has become an event with a particular gay and lesbian emphasis. It has its origins in a gay rights march held in 1978 as part of a commemoration of the 1969 'Stonewall riots' in New York. In 1981 it was shifted to the pre-Lent period and two years later an accompanying arts programme was introduced. By 1991 the parade was the largest in Australia's history and the arts programme had been extended in 1992 to four weeks.

225

Currently there is a three- to four-week-long arts festival and sporting events culminating in the parade and post-parade party. Despite being labelled Mardi Gras, it clearly has its roots elsewhere than in the traditional pre-Lenten carnival. The parade in 1982 was watched by 10,000 and by 1996 by 650,000. It was shown on the national television network in 1994 and on a commercial channel the following year, gaining record ratings on each occasion. The 1998 Festival had an estimated A$99 million economic impact on the city which is claimed to be greater than any other cultural or sporting event in Australia. It is sponsored by Qantas and by the national telecom corporation, Telstra, and receives funding from South Sydney Council. The festival is regularly advertised by specialist gay and lesbian tour operators in North America and Europe.

In the USA, the principal carnival celebration is in New Orleans (Louisiana, USA) where the season starts in January through to Shrove Tuesday. The city of New Orleans has about 1.3 million inhabitants and is located close to the mouth of the Mississippi river on the Gulf of Mexico. It has a particular image associated with music. It is credited as the birthplace of jazz in particular and is famous for its association with musicians such as Jelly Roll Morton, Louis Armstrong and Mahalia Jackson. Its nickname of 'the Big Easy' is derived from an early dance hall. The city also claims to have had an important influence on the development of rock-and-roll, rhythm-and-blues, gospel and Cajun music. The annual 10-day Jazz and Heritage Festival features over 4000 musicians, cooks and crafts people in a celebration of local culture and crafts. There are many outdoor events throughout the city and, in 1999 the Festival attracted attendances of 450,000 at the Festival grounds alone.

It was originally a French settlement and the 'French Quarter', dating from the eighteenth century, is today one of the major tourist sights. Bourbon Street in the French Quarter is particularly well-known in jazz circles as a 'party' place and is also a definite tourist sight. As well as the French influence there has also been a strong African and Caribbean influence seen in the Cajun and Creole cuisine and, most dramatically, in the references to voodoo as a tourist attraction. It rapidly established itself as major religion in the city and, in the nineteenth century, public out-door ceremonies drew crowds of tourists as well as of adherents. The city has a 'Historic Voodoo Museum'.

Mardi Gras in New Orleans originated with the pre-Lenten balls started in the eighteenth century when New Orleans was under French rule but which were banned under Spanish rule. They were revived in 1827 after Louisiana had been purchased by America. In 1857 the first 'Krewe' was founded, one of the 'secret' organizations dedicated to organizing Mardi Gras. It presented a themed parade with floats and costumed riders and a tableau ball. It is billed currently as a period of parties, parades, balls and celebrations starting in early January. Currently nearly 70 parades are held during the 12-day period prior to Shrove Tuesday. There are few seats along the routes and spectators therefore stand and walk. Each individual parade is organized by its own krewe and has its own theme. Each usually has its own king and queen who are honoured at a formal ball which is by invitation only. There is a tradition of participants distributing 'throws' to spectators. Parades in the French Quarter are generally considered to be a little more 'wild' than are the family-friendly parades elsewhere in the city. The season culminates in Carnival Day celebrations led by 'Rex'. During 1998, there were an estimated 3.7 million spectators at New Orleans Mardi Gras and of these, 1.4 million were day trippers or were staying with friends and just under a million were tourists staying in hotels.

Sources: the Guardian 8 January 2000; *the Observer* 23 January 2000; New Orleans Metropolitan Convention and Visitor Bureau

Oberammergau

Oberammergau is a village in the southern part of Bavaria (Germany) about an hour's drive time from Munich. It is located in a valley in the Alps and has a population of about 5000. Every ten years a Passion Play, which has its origins in the seventeenth century, is performed in the village. The Black Death had been sweeping Europe and the villagers of Oberammergau promised to present a passion play depicting the live and death of Christ if no further deaths from the plague occurred. The first play was held in 1634 and has been performed every decade since. It is still performed by the villagers, about half of whom (2200) are involved at one time or another as actors, singers, in the orchestra or backstage. There is double-casting of main roles in order to share the work. The current version of the play dates from the nineteenth century though music and words are continually updated. The re-working for 2000 is the most substantial yet and removes a great deal of material that has led to criticisms that the play is anti-Semitic.

Performances last the whole day and are held on five days of every week from May through to October. They are now held in a purpose-built theatre with a seating capacity of 4700. Although these seats are covered the performances are in the open-air, which adds to the atmosphere and authenticity. About 500,000 visitors were expected for the performances in 2000. It is promoted by the local and Bavarian tourist offices and features as part of the programme of specialist tour operators.

The subject of the play will obviously have considerable appeal to Christians throughout Europe and North America in particular but it also has a novelty value in its local participation by most of the inhabitants and its rarity. The village itself is picturesque and there has been a local tradition of painting on the outside walls of houses. These usually depict biblical scenes and some date back to the eighteenth century. These too are promoted as tourist attractions. The area has also been a centre for wood-carving for over 800 years and 'good quality' carvings, mostly religious, feature strongly for sale to tourists.

The location in the Bavarian Alps adds to the appeal of the event. Apart from the Alpine scenery there are a number of well-known historical sights including castles such as Neuschwanstein built by Ludwig II a nineteenth century king of Bavaria. Ludwig was a patron of the opera composer Richard Wagner but he also supported the Oberammergau play and donated a marble crucifixion scene to the village in gratitude for having seen a performance in 1871. This and the closest of his castles at Linderhof (about seven miles away) also feature in tourism promotion. The village is also just over an hour's drive from Innsbruck, an attractive city in Austria. A visit to Oberammergau can therefore be combined with a touring holiday and a great deal of sight-seeing or mountain climbing or walking.

Sources: the Independent 22 May 1999; Tourist Office of the community of Oberammergau

References

Alzua, A., J. O'Leary and A. Morrison (1998) Cultural and heritage tourism: identifying niches for international travellers. *Journal of Tourism Studies*, **9** (2), 2–13.

American Council for the Arts (1981) *The arts and tourism: a profitable partnership*. Papers of a conference in Toronto October 1980. New York: American Council for the Arts.

Arts Council of England (1999) *Facts and Figures About the Arts*. London: Arts Council of England.

Arts Council of Great Britain (1985) *A Great British Success Story*. London: Arts Council of Great Britain.

Ashworth, G. (1993) Culture and tourism: conflict or symbiosis in Europe? In *Tourism in Europe: Structures and Developments* (W. Pompl and P. Lavery, eds) pp. 13–35. Oxford: CAB International.

Ashworth, G. and J. Tunbridge (1990) *The Tourist Historic City*. London: Belhaven.

Audit Commission (1991) *Local Authorities, Entertainment and the Arts*. London: HMSO.

Austwick, D. (1991) Summary and conclusions. In *Today's arts, tomorrow's tourists: report on a seminar on the arts and tourism* (Arts Council of Great Britain). London: Arts Council of Great Britain with the Museums and Galleries Commission.

Australian Bureau of Statistics (1999a) Attendances at selected cultural venues 1999, No 4114.0. Canberra: Australian Bureau of Statistics.

Australian Bureau of Statistics (1999b) *Australia now: a statistical profile: Tourism*. Canberra: Australian Bureau of Statistics.

Bainbridge, C. (1986) *Pavilions on the Sea: A History of the Seaside Pleasure Pier*. London: Robert Hale.

Baudrillard, J. (1983) *Simulations*. New York: Semiotext.

Bianchini, F. (1993a) Remaking European cities: the role of cultural policies. In *Cultural Policy and Urban Regeneration: The West European Experience* (F. Bianchini and M. Parkinson, eds) pp. 1–20. Manchester: Manchester University Press.

Bianchini, F. (1993b) Culture, conflict and cities: issues and prospects for the 1990s. In *Cultural Policy and Urban Regeneration: The West European Experience* (F. Bianchini and M. Parkinson, eds) pp. 199–213. Manchester: Manchester University Press.

Bianchini, F. (1999) The relationship between cultural resources and tourism policies for cities and regions. In *Planning Cultural Tourism in Europe: A Presentation of Theories and Cases* (D. Dodd and A. van Hemel, eds) pp. 78–90. Amsterdam: Boekman Foundation and Ministry of Education, Culture and Science.

Bianchini, F. and M. Parkinson (eds) (1993) *Cultural Policy and Urban Regeneration: The West European Experience*. Manchester: Manchester University Press.

Billington, M. (1998) Oh no. Not Oklahoma! *Guardian*, 12 August.

Bourdieu, P. (1984) *Distinction: A Social Critique of the Judgement of Taste*. London: Routledge and Kegan Paul.

Braunlich, C. (1996) Lessons from the Atlantic City casino experience. *Journal of Travel Research* (Winter), 46–56.

British Tourist Authority (1983) *The Arts as an Attraction for Overseas Visitors to Britain*. London: British Tourist Authority.

British Tourist Authority (1992) *Digest of Tourist Statistics. No 16*. London: British Tourist Authority and English Tourist Board.

British Tourist Authority (1999a) *Tourism Facts and Figures*. London: British Tourist Authority.

British Tourist Authority (1999b) *Digest of Tourist Statistics. No 22*. London: British Tourist Authority.

British Tourist Authority and English Tourist Board (1985) *Overseas Visitor Survey 1984*. London: British Tourist Authority and English Tourist Board.

British Tourist Authority and English Tourist Board (1996) *Overseas Visitor Survey 1995*. London: British Tourist Authority and English Tourist Board.

Britton, S. (1991) Tourism, capital and place: towards a critical geography of tourism. *Environment and Planning D: Society and Space*, **9**, 461–478.

Brown, G. (1996) 'Bright lights, big pity' Night and Day, *Mail on Sunday*, 8 December.

Bruce, G. (1975) *Festival in the North: The Story of the Edinburgh Festival*. London: Robert Hale.

Bywater, M. (1993) The market for cultural tourism in Europe. *Travel and Tourism Analyst*, No 6, 30–46.

Canadian Tourism Commission (1997a) *Fulfilling the promise of cultural and heritage tourism in Canada: a discussion paper*. Ottawa: Canadian Tourism Commission.

Canadian Tourism Commission (1997b) *Fulfilling the promise: a report on six regional round tables on cultural and heritage tourism*. Ottawa: Canadian Tourism Commission.

Canadian Tourism Commission (1998) *Minutes of the National Roundtable on cultural and heritage tourism*. Ottawa: Canadian Tourism Commission.

Casey, B., R. Dunlop and S. Selwood (1996) *Culture as a Commodity? The Economics of the Arts and Built Heritage in the UK*. London: Policy Studies Institute.

Casson, L. (1974) *Travel in the Ancient World*. London: George Allen and Unwin.

Central Statistical Office (1995) *Social Trends 1995 edition*. No 25. London: HMSO.

Christiansen, E. and J. Brinkerhoff-Jacobs (1995) Gaming and entertainment: an imperfect union? *Cornell Hotel and Restaurant Administration Quarterly*, **36** (2), 79–94.

Cohen, E. (1974) Who is a tourist? A conceptual clarification. *Sociological Review*, **22** (4), 527–555.

Cohen, S. (1997) More than the Beatles: popular music, tourism and urban regeneration. In *Tourists and Tourism: Identifying with People and Places* (S. Abram, J. Waldren and D. Macleod, eds) pp. 71–90. Oxford: Berg.

Cooper, P. and R. Tower (1992) Inside the consumer mind: consumer attitudes to the arts. *Journal of the Market Research Society*, **34** (4), 299–311.

Craik, J. (1997) The culture of tourism. In *Touring Cultures: Transformations of Travel and Theory* (C. Rojek and J. Urry, eds) pp. 113–136. London: Routledge.

Crompton, J. (1979) Motivations for pleasure vacation. *Annals of Tourism Research*, **6** (4), 408–424.

Cultural Assistance Center and the Port Authority of New York and New Jersey (1983) *The Arts as an Industry: Their Economic Importance to the New York and New Jersey Metropolitan Region*. New York: Cultural Assistance Center.

de Haan, J. (1999) Planning of cultural tourism: opportunities and constraints. In *Planning Cultural Tourism in Europe: A Presentation of Theories and Cases* (D. Dodd and A. van Hemel, eds) pp. 122–138. Amsterdam: Boekman Foundation and Ministry of Education, Culture and Science.

de Leeuw, R. (1999) Foreword. In *Planning Cultural Tourism in Europe: A Presentation of Theories and Cases* (D. Dodd and A. van Hemel, eds) pp. 9–15. Amsterdam: Boekman Foundation and Ministry of Education, Culture and Science.

Department of the Environment (1990) *Tourism and the Inner City.* London: HMSO.

Department for Culture, Media and Sport (1999) *Tomorrow's Tourism: A Growth Industry for the New Millennium.* London: Department for Culture, Media and Sport.

Dimaggio, P. and M. Useem (1978) Social class and arts consumption. *Theory and Society,* **5** (March), 141–161.

Dodd, D. (1999) Barcelona, the making of a cultural city. In *Planning Cultural Tourism in Europe: A Presentation of Theories and Cases* (D. Dodd and A. van Hemel, eds) pp. 53–64. Amsterdam: Boekman Foundation and Ministry of Education, Culture and Science.

Dodd, D. and A. van Hemel (eds) (1999) *Planning Cultural Tourism in Europe: A Presentation of Theories and Cases.* Amsterdam: Boekman Foundation and Ministry of Education, Culture and Science.

Dunlop, R. and J. Eckstein (1995) The performed arts in London and regional theatres. *Cultural Trends,* **22,** 1–27.

English Tourist Board (1980) *Tourism and the Inner City: A Planning Advisory Note.* London: English Tourist Board.

English Tourist Board (1981) *Tourism and Urban Regeneration: Some Lessons from American Cities.* London: English Tourist Board.

English Tourist Board (1982) *Provincial Theatre and Tourism in England: An Analysis of Trends Between 1975 and 1981–82.* London: English Tourist Board.

English Tourist Board (1984) *Curtain up on the Resorts: A Report by the ETB's Entertainment Working Party.* London: English Tourist Board.

English Tourist Board (1993) *The Arts Tourism Marketing Handbook.* London: English Tourist Board.

English Tourist Board, Northern Ireland Tourist Board, Scottish Tourist Board, Wales Tourist Board (1998) *The UK Tourist: Statistics 1997.* English Tourist Board, Northern Ireland Tourist Board, Scottish Tourist Board, Wales Tourist Board.

Evans, G. (1993) *An Urban Renaissance? The role of the arts in urban regeneration.* London: University of North London Press.

Eyre, R. (1998) The Eyre Review: the future of lyric theatre in London. London: the Stationery Office.

Falk, N. (1986) Baltimore and Lowell: two American approaches. *Built Environment,* **12** (3), 145–152.

Featherstone, M. (1991) *Consumer Culture and Postmodernism*. London: Sage.

Feifer, M. (1985) *Going Places: The Ways of the Tourist from Imperial Rome to the Present Day*. London: Macmillan.

Feist, A. (1998) Comparing the performing arts in Britain, the US and Germany. *Cultural Trends*, **31**, 29–47.

Fiske, J. (1989) *Understanding Popular Culture*. London: Unwin Hyman.

Foo, L. and A. Rossetto (1998) *Cultural Tourism in Australia: Characteristics and Motivations*. Bureau of Tourism Research occasional paper no 27. Canberra: Bureau of Tourism Research.

Foster, N. (1999) Foreword. In *Modern Britain 1929–1939* (J. Peto and D. Loveday, eds). London: Design Museum.

Gallup, S. (1987) *A History of the Salzburg Festival*. London: Weidenfeld and Nicolson.

Gardiner, C. (1982) Audiences for London's West End theatres. London: Society of West End Theatre (Unpublished).

Gardiner, C. (1986) The West End theatre audience 1985–86. London: Society of West End Theatre (Unpublished).

Gardiner, C. (1991) The West End theatre audience 1990–91. London: Department of Arts Policy and Management, City University (Unpublished).

Gardiner, C. and J. Dickety (1996) *The Society of London Theatre Box Office Data Report 1995*. London: Society of London Theatre.

Getz, D. (1991) *Festivals, Special Events and Tourism*. New York: Van Nostrand Reinhold.

Gilbert, D. and M. Lizotte (1998) Tourism and the performing arts. *Travel and Tourism Analyst*, **1**, 82–96.

Gratton, C. (ed.) (1996) *Work, Leisure and the Quality of Life: A Global Perspective*. Sheffield: Leisure Industries Research Centre, Sheffield Hallam University.

Gratton, C. and P. Taylor (1992) Cultural tourism in European cities: a case study of Edinburgh. *Vrijetijd en Samenleving*, **10** (2/3), 29–43.

Griffiths, R. (1993) The politics of cultural policy in urban regeneration strategies. *Policy and Politics*, **21** (1), 39–46.

Hall, C.M. (1992) *Hallmark Tourist Events: Impacts, Management and Planning*. London: Belhaven.

Hall, C.M. and B. Weiler (1992) What's special about special interest tourism? In *Special Interest Tourism* (Weiler, B. and C. Hall, eds) pp. 1–14. London: Belhaven.

Hannigan J. (1998) *Fantasy City: Pleasure and Profit in the Postmodern Metropolis*. London: Routledge.

Harland, J., K. Kinder, K. Hartley and A. Wilkin (1996) *Attitudes to Participation in the Arts, Heritage, Broadcasting and Sport: A Review of Recent Research: A Report for the Department of National Heritage*. London: National Foundation for Educational Research.

Harvey, D. (1990) *The Condition of Postmodernity*. Blackwell.

Hauser, K. and C. Lanier (1998) *The Broadway Industry: Its Economic Impact on New York City 1997*. New York: the League of American Theaters and Producers Inc.

Hauser, K. and S. Roth (1998) *Who Goes to Broadway? A Demographic Study of the Broadway Audience 1997*. New York: the League of American Theaters and Producers Inc.

Heilbrun, J. and C. Gray (1993) *The Economics of Art and Culture: An American Perspective*. Cambridge: Cambridge University Press.

Hewison, R. (1987) *The Heritage Industry: Britain in a Climate of Decline*. London: Methuen.

Hill, E., C. O'Sullivan and T. O'Sullivan (1995) *Creative Arts Marketing*. Oxford: Butterworth-Heinemann.

Hodson, D. (1986) *Arts, Local Authorities and the Future*. Birmingham: Institute of Local Government Studies, University of Birmingham.

Holcomb, B. (1999) Marketing cities for tourism. In *The Tourist City* (D. Judd and S. Fainstein, eds) pp. 54–70. New Haven: Yale University Press.

Howes, F. (1965) *The Cheltenham Festival*. London: Oxford University Press.

Hudson, J. (1992) *Wakes Weeks: Memories of Mill Town Holidays*. Stroud: Alan Sutton.

Hughes, G. and M. Boyle (1992) Place boosterism: political contention, leisure and culture in Glasgow. In *Leisure in the 1990s* (J. Sugden and C. Nash, eds). Eastbourne: Leisure Studies Association.

Hughes, H. (1991) Holidays and the economically disadvantaged. *Tourism Management*, **12** (3), 193–196.

Hughes, H. (1994a) Tourism and government: a subset of leisure policy? In *Tourism: The State of the Art* (A. Seaton *et al.* eds). Wiley.

Hughes, H. (1994b) Tourism multiplier studies: a more judicious approach. *Tourism Management*, **15** (6), 403–406.

Hughes, H. (1997) Holidays and homosexual identity. *Tourism Management*, **18** (1), 3–7.

Hughes, H. (1998a) Sexuality, tourism and space: the case of gay visitors to Amsterdam. In *Managing Tourism in Cities* (Tyler, D., Y. Guerrier and M. Robertson, eds) pp. 163–178. London: Wiley.

Hughes, H. (1998b) Theatre in London and the inter-relationship with tourism. *Tourism Management*, **19** (5), 445–452.

Hughes, H. (1999) Hotels and entertainment. In *Accommodation Management: Perspectives for the International Hotel Industry* (C. Verginis and R. Wood, eds). London: International Thomson Business Press.

Hughes, H. and D. Benn (1997a) Tourism and cultural policy: the case of seaside entertainment in Britain. *European Journal of Cultural Policy*, **3** (2), 235–255.

Hughes, H. and D. Benn (1997b) Entertainment in tourism: a study of visitors to Blackpool. *Managing Leisure: An International Journal*, **2** (2), 110–126.

Hughes, H. and D. Benn (1998) Holiday entertainment in a British seaside resort town. *Journal of Arts Management, Law and Society*, **27** (4), 295–307.

Hunter, C. and H. Green (1995) *Tourism and the Environment: A Sustainable Relationship?* Routledge.

Jansen–Verbeke, M. (1986) Inner city tourism: resources, tourists and promoters. *Annals of Tourism Research*, **13** (1), 79–100.

Jansen–Verbeke, M. (1996) Cultural tourism in the twenty-first century. *World Leisure and Recreation*, **31** (1), 6–11.

Jones Economics (1996) *Edinburgh Festivals Economic Impact Study.* Edinburgh: Jones Economics.

Kneafsey, M. (1994) The cultural tourist: patron saint of Ireland? In *Culture, Tourism and Development: The Case of Ireland* (U. Kockel, ed.) pp. 103–116. Liverpool: Liverpool University Press.

Laws, E. (1997) *Managing Packaged Tourism.* London: International Thomson Business Press.

Leader-Elliott, L. (1996) *Cultural Tourism Opportunities for South Australia.* Adelaide: South Australian Tourism Commission and the Department for the Arts and Cultural Development.

Levin, B. (1981) *Conducted Tour.* London: Jonathan Cape.

Lewis, J. (1990) *Art Culture and Enterprise: The Politics of Art and the Cultural Industries.* London: Routledge.

Light, D. and R. Prentice (1994) Who consumes the heritage product? In *Building a New Heritage: Tourism, Culture and Identity in the New Europe* (G. Ashworth and P. Larkham, eds) pp. 90–116. London: Routledge.

Lipman, C. (1996) Walt Disney waltzes into the West End. *The Independent*, 20 October.

Loftman, P. and B. Nevin (1992) *Urban Regeneration and Social Equity: A Case Study of Birmingham 1986–92.* Research Paper no 8. Birmingham: Built Environment Development Centre, University of Central England in Birmingham.

London Tourist Board and Convention Bureau (1995) *Survey Among*

Overseas Visitors to London: Summer 1995. London Tourist Board and Convention Bureau.

Market Equity and Economic Research Consultants (1996) *1996 Adelaide Festival: An Economic Impact Study* (prepared for the South Australian Tourism Commission, Department for the Arts and Cultural Development and the Australia Council). Market Equity SA Pty Ltd and Economic Research Consultants.

Martin, A. (1998) West End theatre impact. *Insights* (September), A31–A34.

Martin, B. and S. Mason (1993) Special interests and activities: the tourism of the future. *Insights* (November), A49–A55.

Mass Observation and Greater London Arts (1990) *Arts in London: A Survey of Attitudes of Users and Non-Users; February 1990*. London: Mass Observation Ltd.

Mathieson, A. and G. Wall (1982) *Tourism: Economic, Physical and Social Impacts*. Longman.

McDougall, L. (1998) A close-up of culture/heritage travel in Canada. *Focus on Culture* (Summer), 5–7. Ottawa: Statistics Canada.

MEW Research (1994) Short break destination choice. *Insights* (January), A77–A94.

Moore, J. (1998) Poverty and access to the arts: inequalities in arts attendance. *Cultural Trends*, **31**, 53–73.

MORI (1998) *The West End Theatre Audience: A Research Study Conducted for the Society of London Theatre 1996–97*. London: Society of London Theatre.

Myerscough, J. (1988) *The Economic Importance of the Arts in Britain*. London: Policy Studies Institute.

Myerscough, J. (1991) Monitoring Glasgow 1990. Glasgow: Glasgow City Council (Unpublished report).

Myerscough, J. (1996) *The Arts and the Northern Ireland Economy*. Belfast: Northern Ireland Economic Council.

National Endowment for the Arts (1998a) *1997 Survey of Public Participation in the Arts*. Research Division Note #70. Washington DC: National Endowment for the Arts.

National Endowment for the Arts (1998b) *Count of Performing Arts Organisations up by Over 30%, 1987–92*. Research Division Note #62. Washington DC: National Endowment for the Arts.

National Endowment for the Arts (1998c) *Theaters Report 22% Growth in Economic Census 1987–92*. Research Division Note #66. Washington DC: National Endowment for the Arts.

National Endowment for the Arts (1999a) *Demographic Characteristics of*

Arts Attendance. Research Division Note #71. Washington DC: National Endowment for the Arts.

National Endowment for the Arts (1999b) *Basic Facts About the NEA*. Washington DC: National Endowment for the Arts.

O'Connor, J. and D. Wynne (1996) *From the Margins to the Centre: Cultural Production and Consumption in the Post-Industrial City.* Aldershot: Arena.

Page, S. (1999) *Transport and Tourism*. London: Longman.

Parker, R. (1999) Las Vegas: casino gambling and local culture. In *The Tourist City* (D. Judd and S. Fainstein, eds), pp. 107–23. New Haven: Yale University Press.

Pearce, D. (1992) *Tourist Organisations*. Harlow: Longman.

Pimlott, J. (1947) *The Englishman's Holiday: A Social History* (reprinted 1976). Hassocks: Harvesters Press.

Port Authority of New York and New Jersey (1993) The arts as an industry: their economic importance to the New York–New Jersey metropolitan region. Part I of *Tourism and arts in the New York and New Jersey region.* The Port Authority of New York and New Jersey; Alliance for the Arts; New York City Partnership; Partnership for New Jersey.

Port Authority of New York and New Jersey (1994) Destination New York–New Jersey: tourism and travel to the metropolitan region. Part II of *Tourism and arts in the New York and New Jersey region.* The Port Authority of New York and New Jersey; Alliance for the Arts; New York City Partnership; Partnership for New Jersey.

Prentice, R. (1993) *Tourism and Heritage Attractions*. London: Routledge.

Prohaska, S. (1995) Trends in cultural heritage tourism. In *Island Tourism: Management Principles and Practice* (M. Conlin and T. Baum, eds) pp. 33–51. Wiley.

Quinn, B. (1996) The sounds of tourism: exploring music as a tourist resource with particular reference to music festivals. In *Culture as the Tourist Product* (Robinson, M., N. Evans and P. Callaghan, eds) pp. 383–396. Newcastle: the Centre for Travel and Tourism, University of Northumbria with Business Education Publishers.

Redden, N. (1989) Summary of remarks. Chapter 6, in *Arts and the Changing City: An Agenda for Urban Regeneration* (British American Arts Association) pp. 39–41. London: BAAA.

Research Surveys of Great Britain (1985) *Holiday Entertainment Survey: A Report on Live Entertainment in Summer 1985*. London: RSGB for the English Tourist Board (Unpublished).

Richards, G. (1993) Cultural tourism in Europe. In *Progress in Tourism,*

Recreation and Hospitality Management (C. Cooper and A. Lockwood, eds), vol. 5, 99–115.

Richards, G. (1995) Politics of national tourism policy in Britain. *Leisure Studies*, **14** (3), 153–173.

Richards, G. (ed.) (1996) *Cultural Tourism in Europe*. Wallingford. CAB International.

Richards, G. (1999) European cultural tourism: patterns and prospects. In *Planning Cultural Tourism in Europe: A Presentation of Theories and Cases* (D. Dodd and A. van Hemel, eds) pp. 16–32. Amsterdam: Boekman Foundation and Ministry of Education, Culture and Science.

Ritzer, G. and A. Liska (1997) McDisneyization and post-tourism: complementary perspectives on contemporary tourism. In *Touring Cultures: Transformations of Travel and Theory* (C. Rojek and J. Urry, eds) pp. 96–109. London: Routledge.

Roberts, K. (1981) *Leisure*. London: Longman.

Roberts, R. (1983) The Corporation as impresario: the municipal provision of entertainment in Victorian and Edwardian Bournemouth. In *Leisure in Britain 1780–1939* (Walton, J. and J. Walvin, eds) pp. 137–157. Manchester: Manchester University Press.

Robinson, M., N. Evans and P. Callaghan (eds) (1996) *Tourism and Culture*, conference proceedings (4 volumes). Newcastle: the Centre for Travel and Tourism, University of Northumbria with Business Education Publishers.

Roche, M. (1994) Mega-events and urban policy. *Annals of Tourism Research*, **21** (1), 1–19.

Rolfe, H. (1992) *Arts Festivals in the UK*. London: Policy Studies Institute.

Ryan, C. (1995) *Researching Tourist Satisfaction: Issues, Concepts, Problems*. London: Routledge.

Schrank F. (1986–87) The evolution of the casino hotel: Atlantic City. *HSMAI Marketing Review*, **5** (2), 17–22.

Schuster J. (1989) Summary of remarks. Chapter 1 in *Arts and the Changing City: An Agenda for Urban Regeneration* (British American Arts Association) pp. 13–16. London: BAAA.

Scotinform (1991) *Edinburgh Festivals Study 1990–91. Visitor Survey and Economic Impact Assessment. Final report*. Edinburgh: Scottish Tourist Board.

Scottish Tourism Co-ordinating Group (1993) *Tourism and The Arts in Scotland: A Development Strategy*. Edinburgh: Scottish Tourist Board.

Shaw, G. and A. Williams (1997) (eds) *The Rise and Fall of British Coastal Resorts: Cultural and Economic Perspectives*. London: Mansell.

Shaw, K. (1993) The development of a new urban corporatism: the politics of urban regeneration in the north east of England. *Regional Studies*, **27** (3), 251–259.

Sheldon, P. (1990) A review of tourism expenditure research. In *Progress in Tourism, Recreation and Hospitality Management* (C. Cooper, ed.), vol. 2. London: Belhaven.

Silberberg, T. (1995) Cultural tourism and business: opportunities for museums and heritage sites. *Tourism Management*, **16** (5), 361–365.

Smith, C. (1998) *Creative Britain*. London: Faber and Faber.

Smith, C. and P. Jenner (1998) The impact of festivals and special events on tourism. *Travel and Tourism Analyst*, **4**, 73–91.

Smith, R. (1996) The UK short holiday market. In *Marketing Tourism Products* (A. Seaton and M. Bennett, eds) pp. 291–317. London: International Thomson Business Press.

Smith, V. (ed) (1989) *Hosts and Guests: The Anthropology of Tourism*. Oxford: Blackwell.

Smith, V. and W. Eadington (eds) (1995) *Tourism Alternatives*. Wiley.

Smith, V. and H. Hughes (1999) Disadvantaged families and the meaning of the holiday. *International Journal of Tourism Research*, **1** (1), 123–133.

Society of West End Theatre (1981) *The West End theatre audience*. London: Society of West End Theatre.

Society of West End Theatre (1982) *Britain at its Best: Overseas Tourism and the West End Theatre*. London: Society of West End Theatre.

South Australian Tourism Commission (1998) *A Summary of Wagner's Ring Cycle, Adelaide 1998: A Study of the Economic Impact of the Event and Associated Issues*. Adelaide: South Australian Tourism Commission.

Spring, J. (1991) *Culture on Holiday: A Survey of Australian Domestic Tourists' Cultural Participation 1990–91*. Sydney: Australia Council.

Spring, J. (1995) *Arts and Cultural Attendance by International Visitors 1993 and 1994: With Comparisons 1986 to 1992*. Research Paper no 15. Sydney: Australia Council.

Statistics Canada (1997) *Canadian Travel Survey: review of the 1996 results*. Ottawa: Statistics Canada.

Storey, J. (1993) *An Introductory Guide to Cultural Theory and Popular Culture*. London: Harvester Wheatsheaf.

Thompson, W., J. Pinney and J. Scibrowsky (1996) The family that gambles together: business and social concerns. *Journal of Travel Research*, **XXXIV** (3), 70–74

Tighe, A. (1985) Cultural tourism in the USA. *Tourism Management*, **6** (4), 234–237.

Towner, J. (1996) *An Historical Geography of Recreation and Leisure in the Western world 1540–1940*. Chichester: Wiley.

Travel Industry Association of America (1999) *Research and Statistics: Fast Facts*. Washington DC: TIA.

Travers, T. (1998) *The Wyndham Report: The Economic Impact of London's West End Theatre*. Society of West End Theatre.

Tusa, J. (1999) *Art Matters: Reflecting on Culture*. London: Methuen.

Urry, J. (1990) *The Tourist Gaze: Leisure and Travel in Contemporary Societies*. London: Sage.

Varlow, S. (1995) Tourism and the arts: the relationship matures. *Insights* (January), A93–98.

Voase, R. (1997) The role of flagship cultural projects in urban regeneration: a case study and commentary. *Managing Leisure*, **2** (4), 230–241.

Walle, A. (1998) *Cultural Tourism: A Strategic Focus*. Boulder: Westview Press.

Walton, J. (1983a) *The English Seaside Resort: A Social History 1759–1914*. Leicester: Leicester University Press.

Walton, J. (1983b) Municipal government and the holiday industry in Blackpool 1876–1914. In *Leisure in Britain 1780–1939* (Walton, J. and J. Walvin, eds) pp. 159–185. Manchester: Manchester University Press.

Walvin, J. (1978) *Beside the Seaside*. London: Allen Lane.

Ward, C. and D. Hardy (1986) *Goodnight Campers! The History of the British Holiday Camp*. London: Mansell.

Waters, S. (1998) *Travel Industry World Yearbook: The Big Picture 1997–98*. New York: Child and Waters.

Wheat, S. (1999) All that jazz. *Leisure Management*, **19** (10), 14–16.

Wiener, L. (1980) Cultural resources: an old asset – a new market for tourism. *Journal of Cultural Economics*, **4** (1), 1–7.

Williams, R. (1988) *Keywords: A Vocabulary of Culture and Society*. London: Fontana.

Withey, L. (1998) *Grand Tours and Cook's Tours: A History of Leisure Travel 1750 to 1915*. London: Aurum Press.

Young, K. (1968) *Music's Great Days at the Spas and Watering Places*. London: Macmillan.

Zeppel, H. and C.M. Hall (1992) Arts and heritage tourism. In *Special Interest Tourism* (Weiler, B. and C.M. Hall, eds) pp. 47–68. London: Belhaven.

Index

Notes:

Terms such as 'arts', 'entertainment', 'tourism', 'theatre' and 'heritage' occur continually throughout the book. Most individual festivals, musicals, hotel companies, tourist boards, tour operators and travel agents are not listed separately but can be found under these general headings as are individual performers at festivals.